SALT AND LIGHT

BERNADETTE CHOVELON

SALT AND LIGHT

The Spiritual Journey of Élisabeth and Félix Leseur

Translated by Mary Dudro

IGNATIUS PRESS   SAN FRANCISCO

Original French edition:
Élisabeth et Félix Leseur
Itinéraire spirituel d'un couple
© 2015, Groupe Artège
Éditions Artège
10, rue Mercoeur – 75011 Paris
9, espace Méditerranée – 66000 Perpignan
www.editionsartege.fr

Cover by Riz Boncan Marsella

Adapted from the original cover by
Éditions Artège

Contents

Preface

When it was suggested to me that I write a biography of Élisabeth and Félix Leseur, I was disconcerted at first because I was not familiar with the incredible journey of this ordinary twentieth-century Parisian couple. I was told that their influence stretched far beyond the borders of France and extended to England and the United States.

However, the psychological and spiritual path of a couple at once so close and so disparate, so loving and so different, a twentieth-century couple, attracted me right away. The thought of diving into new research, a lot of reading, an in-depth study of the history of the beginning of the twentieth century, crossed by so many different spiritual and atheistic movements, so many discoveries and changes, excited me.

I am very fond of Élisabeth and Félix. With them, I was able to live their everyday lives marked by significant hardships: the major health issues from the first months of their marriage, the loss of close relatives, profound differences about faith, the daily encounter of two worlds in their relationship, that of atheism and that of faith. Their human love was profound and fruitful beyond all hope.

However, their life was not extraordinary; they lived as many other people live nowadays, with the same plans, the same joys, the same suffering.

They were very much in love right to the end. They loved comfort, travel, evenings with friends. They lived through the advancements of their century with enthusiasm. They were a happy couple in a world where progress was advancing by leaps and bounds. They knew how to sample and fully benefit from the comfort that stemmed from new technologies.

7

They suffered from radical differences of faith like many couples who daily meet with hostility or indifference from their spouses.

Élisabeth's long illness was a major trial in their life as it is for many homes that walk a similar way of the cross.

They lived an ostensibly ordinary life.

From Élisabeth's writings, always filled with a very strong admiration and love for her husband, I could see how well she had known how to sow the seeds of faith, silently and gently, in his heart. Until the end, she had the courage to believe that their profound human love could have no other source but God, who is love, and that it would be powerful beyond her expectations. "The kingdom of God is as if a man should scatter seed upon the ground, and should sleep and rise night and day, and the seed should sprout and grow, he knows not how" (Mk 4:26–28).

This image from the parable perfectly expresses what happened in the Leseur couple. The seeds sown by Élisabeth were long in germinating, but, by the strength of her faith, she knew that they would sprout one day. In her lifetime, she did not see them bloom, but other people, unknown to them, have gathered the fruit.

If certain pages of Élisabeth's writings sometimes seem marked by the religious expression of the last century, their content, clearly inspired by the action of the Holy Spirit, remains profoundly alive and moving.

From the beginning of her marriage, Élisabeth wanted, and was convinced, that the militant atheism of her husband would fall down upon him as a shower of graces on a day appointed by the Lord. She was very strong in persevering in her faith despite all the obstacles placed in her path. She always believed, as Saint Paul says, that love "believes all things, hopes all things, endures all things" and that love and respect would be her only weapons for preserving their relationship and making her husband grow in faith.

Félix, in turn, after the death of Élisabeth, at last understood that the great love his wife had for him could only have come from God. This discovery allowed him to have the humility, courage, and love necessary to make a radical change in his life.

This couple was "the salt of the earth", the salt that gives good taste to everything. They were that first of all for each other, but they were also that for those around them: their families, their Christian and atheist friends, and their believing and unbelieving correspondents.

Their relationship was also "the light of the world" for all those whom their message touched, through Élisabeth's actions, before her death, as well as afterward through the mission to which Félix devoted himself in publishing her writings.

"Nor do men light a lamp and put it under a bushel, but on a stand, and it gives light to all in the house" (Mt 5:15). My work consisted simply in putting their light, the light that their relationship radiated, "on a stand" so that it might "shine before men".

—Bernadette Chovelon

A Big Wedding in Saint-Germain-des-Prés

On Wednesday July 31, 1889, on a particularly glorious morning, a young couple solemnly advanced down the long nave of the old abbey of Saint-Germain-des-Prés. Surrounded by a large crowd of relatives and friends, certain of the happiness that awaited these two very similar people, they slowly crossed the abbey between its multicolored pillars. Before God and before men, they were going to consecrate their great love by giving each other the sacrament of marriage.

Élisabeth Arrighi, the young bride, so beautiful and elegant in her white gown, glowed with happiness. She was twenty-three years old. She was marrying a man she admired and loved, with whom she shared a fondness for literature, art, and, above all, music. She was happy to build a home with him and dream of the many children that their love would raise.

They had known each other only a few months: visiting mutual friends, they had met by chance while on vacation in Passy, where the two families usually spent the summer. The houses were sufficiently close to allow the young people to visit each other easily, thanks to the complicity of the groom's uncle.

Félix Leseur, a medical student, was very quickly charmed by Élisabeth's culture, by her grace, beauty, lively intelligence, and erudition; he deeply admired her capacity for kindness toward others and her love for those she met. He appreciated her gaiety, her spontaneous and interesting conversation. The harmony between them was so obvious that their mutual friends understood right away that wedding plans for them would become increasingly natural. During the winter that followed their first meeting, Félix accompanied Élisabeth to many parties where they frequently danced together and talked at length with lively, mutual pleasure. Very soon Félix's parents, seeing him so in love with a young woman whose choice could only fill them with joy, asked Élisabeth's parents for her hand, according to the custom at that time.

The official engagement took place the following May 23, in the intimacy of the family.

The Nuptial Blessing was given to them by a priest friend: Father Bordes, of the Oratory, a teacher whom Félix had esteemed at the high school in Juilly, where he had pursued his secondary education, and for whom he had a trusting affection.

However, there were a few shadows over their happiness: the groom's father was absent, detained at Reims by a serious health issue. Élisabeth was also thinking about her young sister Marie, who had died, in a saintly way, two years before, carried off in a few days by a violent typhoid fever. She had been the youngest of the family, cherished and admired. She was barely twelve years old. It was a loss from which her family, her parents, her brother, and her two sisters, could not recover.

There was also another shadow for Élisabeth: she, so deeply Christian, had only just learned, on the eve of her wedding, that she was marrying a deliberately agnostic man, who had renounced the faith that his parents and the priests at his high school had given to him. The engaged couple had, no doubt, spoken little of this complete rejection before planning their wedding. Since the two families were Christian, it was taken for granted by everyone that the future bride and groom had adopted the beliefs of their parents.

During the ceremony, Élisabeth might have wondered: What do these signs of marriage, however rich in meaning, and these eagerly awaited blessings mean to him now? Does he hear them without agreeing with them? Are they merely gestures of worldliness or social convention for him? She knew, however, that the "yes" that this man spoke to unite his life with her own was worthy of the greatest trust.

At the same moment, he strongly felt a completely opposite inner conviction: this young woman, so naïve about life, must become a truly liberated woman, thanks to him. One day, he would make her understand that her faith was nothing but a refuge for the weak; he would bring her back to the path of common sense and would turn her away from her religion. He was sure of it. For now, he loved her too much and admired the sincerity of her faith too much to confront her directly and shock her in her deepest beliefs. But with time, things would be done insidiously without her noticing it. He would have discussions with her; he would reason with her for as long as it took; he would introduce her to intelligent, atheist friends who would expose her to the works of Enlightenment authors, of the most famous rationalists who had the audacity to deny everything. Without a doubt, he would not lack the arguments to convince her. He knew that this path to his truth would certainly take some time, that the roots of her family faith would take a long time to pull out, but no matter! The whole future was before them on this day when they joined their lives, and this was probably not the essential problem! Out of gentleness of heart and love for her, he had promised to accompany her to Mass when she asked him, to allow her the complete freedom to practice her faith; he had committed himself to respecting her beliefs . . . at least for a certain, yet to be determined, period of time.

On this day of celebration, all these plans remained in the silence of their hearts; the newlyweds, surrounded by their families and friends, sipped champagne, celebrating their brand-new love during a warm and joyful banquet.

As was customary at that time, the very afternoon of the wedding, the young couple left for Fontainebleau for a few days of rest, with a desire to enjoy the freshness and calm of the forests after those tiring days. They also needed to savor their love in solitude, just the two of them.

Élisabeth had left her family nest and, especially, her parents, not without a certain amount of heartache. In her thoughtfulness, the very morning of her wedding, before putting on her wedding gown, she wrote them a letter.

When leaving with her new husband, she entrusted her envelope to the servant, asking her to give it to them as soon as possible after her departure. This longstanding servant, already elderly, having seen the children grow up, was so much a part of the Arrighi family that everyone called her "Granny".

July 30, 1889

Dear parents,

I entrust this little note to Granny, so that it will come to surprise you when you wake and will be for you like the daily kiss of your child.

My heart is full right now; full of memories of my childhood and my youth that reappear with incredible force; full of confidence for the future that you have prepared me for and that God will bless, I hope; but above all, full of tenderness for you, for all of you, more ardent and deep than I have ever felt? I also feel the need to express it to you better than I have perhaps done until now, and it is from the bottom of my heart that I thank you for the good that you have done me, for the joy that you have given me and that made my youth such a happy time and a blessed memory; thank you for the affection with which you have surrounded me; thank you for everything, because everything I have and everything I am, I owe to you.

And allow me to tell you how much I have enjoyed this happiness, how much I have appreciated this affection; my own, far from diminishing, becomes deeper still, and more than ever I feel full of gratitude and love for you and for those much beloved sisters and brother who have made my life what it has been so far: happy and blessed. For them also, my marriage will change nothing of our tenderness for each other; I have a large enough heart for a new affection to do no harm to the old, and when we have loved each other as we have, for so many years, we can be sure of loving each other forever. . . .

Let us enjoy the happiness God gives us and if that of your children might do you a little good, tell yourselves that, despite the great emotion that I feel in changing my life, I am deeply happy and grateful to God because I have found in Félix everything I desired and I have the utmost confidence in our future.

And now, dear, beloved parents, your child gives you a kiss in which she places all her affection and that you will pass on to my beloved brother and sisters. One last time, thank you. I still sign: Élisabeth Arrighi.[1]

---

[1] R. P. Marie-Albert Leseur, *Vie d'Élisabeth Leseur* (Paris: Éd. J. de Gigord, 1931), 92.

Back in Paris, the young couple, not yet having an apartment, went to stay at Élisabeth's parents' house while they were on vacation at Champrosay near Corbeil, on the banks of the Seine. They took advantage of this Parisian stop to visit the World's Fair on the Champ de Mars, where the highlight was an extremely tall tower, 1063 feet high, built by Gustave Eiffel, to the consternation of many Parisians.

Both of them especially enjoyed the bustling life of Paris; even more, they admired the technical and industrial innovations displayed in the capital at this end of the nineteenth century.

They then departed on a real honeymoon to Luxembourg and Germany: the banks of the Rhine, Trier, Cologne, and Spa. Félix had studied German. The exploration of Germany was fashionable in France at that time, as the humiliation of the 1870 defeat receded into the past.

Élisabeth wrote to her parents: "All of this has delighted me; we have been full of a gaiety, or rather, an unimaginable madness the whole time, and if there have ever been two happy people on earth, I believe it is certainly us."

2

She and He

She: Élisabeth Arrighi

Élisabeth Arrighi's childhood took place in a family environment where affection and love were closely connected to intellectual, artistic, and spiritual aspirations.

As her birth certificate, preserved at the city hall of the first arrondissement, attests, Pauline Élisabeth was born October 16, 1866, in Paris, at 3 rue Baillif. This street, which ran alongside the Palais Royal, no longer exists; it was demolished to make room for the expansions to the Banque de France's facilities.

The parish registry of the church of Saint-Roch states that she was baptized the following November 27 by Father Gallet, the vicar of the parish.

Élisabeth's parents were young when she was born. Her father, Antoine Arrighi, came from an excellent family from Corte. He went to Grenoble to prepare his doctorate in law, then he settled in Paris, where he carried out several legal functions. At the time of the birth of his first daughter, he was a lawyer at the Imperial Court. He was thirty years old.

Madame Arrighi, born Marie-Laure Picard, was twenty-three years old when Élisabeth was born. Three daughters and a son followed this first child: Amélie, September 4, 1868, Pierre, August 13, 1870, Juliette, September 5, 1872, and Marie, March 18, 1875.

This family, united around children so close in age, formed a particularly loving little community. The father was a man of great kindness who listened attentively to his children. The mother combined the qualities of the heart with those of intelligence so well that, for a woman of her time, she had a wide knowledge that she would make it her duty to pass on to her children.

As the family grew, the young household was forced to move. They settled at 45 rue de Rennes on the third floor of a family apartment building, where their best friends, Baron and Baroness Le Gros, already lived on the fifth floor.

Madame Arrighi's oldest sister, Madame Villetard de Prunières, her husband, and her son, Maurice, for their part, had their apartment on the fourth floor. The two sisters were extremely close. From floor to floor, they were all close neighbors in the most complete simplicity and privacy. Sundays alternately gathered the inhabitants of the house, who were also neighbors during the summer at Passy and Auteuil, for a traditional lunch.

At that time, those two little towns, surrounded by parks, gardens, and large trees, were not yet integrated neighborhoods in the Parisian urban area; they were in the countryside. Most bourgeois families, from the beginning of the hot weather onward, settled there in private houses, small mansions amid the greenery of beautiful gardens. The husbands, who left in the morning for their business affairs, could easily come back to sleep there every evening. The children, who were raised together, thought of each other as brothers and sisters, and the wives met in the afternoon under the trees to continue the intimate life they had at the rue de Rennes during the winter. A strong intellectual life united the members of these families who were always surrounded by numerous, highly intellectual friends.

Madame Arrighi had a strong sense of her responsibilities concerning the education of her children. Like many educated mothers, she taught them to read and write, to know the history of France and the masterpieces of great French authors, in a time when children were not sent to school before the age of ten.

As soon as they could talk, she taught them to make the sign of the cross, to pray, to recite the Commandments of God and the Church, and, above all, to discover the love of God and its place in their lives.

Later, when they were preparing for their First Communion, she would regularly accompany them to catechism and would take notes herself in a notebook, and she would have them write down the contents of the lessons in a personal notebook. Back at the house, she would have them study and repeat the lessons of the day written in their notebooks. This content would be verified by the priests of Saint-Germain-des-Prés. Élisabeth's catechism work would obtain "the great seal", that is, the highest award, because her analyses would be considered astute and profound for a child her age.

The rigorous Christian education of that time aimed, first and foremost, at perfecting character toward a holiness more grounded in the observance of the commandments than in the freedom and openness of the Gospels.

During her childhood, Élisabeth recorded the small events of her life every day.

Later, Félix would publish these two notebooks under the title *Journal d'enfant* (A child's diary).

Through this writing, already at a high level for a little girl ten to eleven years old, we can trace a bit of the Arrighis' life when the five children were at home. We read about their fraternal teasing, reprimanded by the firm but affectionate interventions of their papa, of family outings to Saint-Cloud Park in the summers and to the theater in Paris during the school year, of their joy at going to see, among other plays, *Scapin the Schemer*, *The Heir Apparent*, and *Monsieur de Pourceaugnac* at the Odéon.

We share with happiness and compassion the daily life of a very close family, full of love, tenderness, and care for each other. We see all the children cry on the station platform when their mother has to go away for a few weeks to take "the waters" and their unhappiness at everything, when, after having accompanied her, they return to the apartment without her; on her return, the children and their father arrive on the platform well in advance to welcome her; for several pages, Élisabeth describes her joy at finding her mother's presence once again in the house and the love that all seek to show her.

Concerning Christian life, Élisabeth's *Journal d'enfant* recounts the years that preceded her First Communion, her fervent anticipation of this moment for months, then the precise content of all the talks she went to during a three-day retreat, and finally an account of the "great day".

December 6, 1877

I have done everything, except for my stylistics homework that mother has not yet corrected. I have prayed a lot to the good God to help me work well; first to please the good God, to prepare myself well for my First Communion, and then to please my dear father and my good, beloved little mother.

December 16

I only write a word because we are going to dinner at Aunt's.[1]

I had a great deprivation today, I could not go to Mass, but I read my Mass, and I tried to sanctify the day of Sunday; but I have to go upstairs. Mother is calling me.[2]

Notice the generosity of spirit and the understanding of "religious obligations" in this little girl of eleven. So many people, especially at that time, were going to Mass out of habit or social convention and were completely forgetting the profound meaning of Sunday. Little Élisabeth had understood one of the meanings of Sunday; if she was forced to be absent from Mass, she did her best to sanctify that day on her own and read, in her missal, in union with the whole Church, the texts of the Epistle and the Gospel, at that time presented in two columns, one in Latin, the other in French.

June 15, 1877

Today while reading I thought of the happiness of the child who is going to receive Communion, and I could not convince myself that the next First Communion we will make at Saint-Germain-des-Prés, I will be there, and I will receive the good God in my heart. But am I worthy of it? Alas! no; but I will really try to make myself worthy of it.[3]

Élisabeth shows herself to be humble and perceptive. In many pages, she examines her behavior vis-à-vis her family; she seeks to

---

[1] The aunt was living on the floor upstairs on the rue de Rennes.
[2] Élisabeth Leseur, *Journal d'enfant* (Paris: Éd. du Cerf), 21.
[3] Ibid., 39.

identify the words or actions that might hurt her brother and sisters in order to correct herself and show them more love.

February 14

My chief fault is my contradictory spirit; when someone says something, I say the opposite, especially with Pierre; I want to make every effort to correct myself, and I will ask the good God for the grace to do it; I will pray to the Blessed Virgin especially when the temptation occurs.

February 15

Me, when someone asks me for something, I always refuse, to tease them, it's very naughty, and I want to try to correct myself; I implore the good God to give me the grace necessary to correct myself, and when someone asks me to do something, I will do it right away because I must prepare for my First Communion. Today, in three months, I will make it, in three months, it is very close, I have very little time, and I have not yet done anything.[4]

Concerning one of the retreat talks:

This morning, the preacher spoke to us about the mission of young girls and Christian women. He told us that our mission was divine, that we could, while on earth, do a lot of good or a lot of harm. I hope while on this earth to do a lot of good. My God, give me the means. My heart is yours. Bless all those I love, and may we all be happy one day with you in heaven.

Father Doyotte also told us that we must fear the selfishness that thinks only of one's self, that we must forget ourselves a little in order to think of others. He compared a woman to the heart, which exists only to spread blood and life into all the extremities of the body; in the same way, a woman must live for others, and give herself to those around her.[5]

At last the day of her First Communion arrived:

We entered the church in procession: the organ, the crowd, everything was waiting for me; I was telling myself: "Jesus is going to

---

[4] Ibid., 61.
[5] Ibid., 117.

come into my heart", and I was thanking him. It was especially when
we were in our places that I prayed to God . . . At last the first row
of girls rose, and, trembling, I steered myself toward the holy Table; I was saying in my heart: "My God, I am not worthy that you
should enter under my roof." I arrived near the holy Table, I fell to
my knees, I adored God in my heart, He who was going to descend
into my soul; at last the priest came toward me, and, placing on my
lips the body of Our Lord, he said: "May the body of Our Lord
guard your soul for everlasting life."

Oh, how to express the happiness that we taste in this moment! I
possessed Our Lord, he was mine, I was no longer alone. Oh! What
moments, and how I would like to be there again.[6]

During her school years, after one year of lessons at home, Élisabeth went every day to the home of two young ladies who had
founded a little school on the rue du Mail: Louise and Amélie de
Mas. They were two sisters from an elevated social background who
belonged to a family of intellectuals. With their father having had
a reversal of fortune, they, valiantly, had had to go to work, which
could have been a decline for women of their social class. The only
honorable professional activity that women of learning could undertake in that century was the opening of a private school in which
they themselves would do most of the teaching. They were courageous, dynamic, warm, and, after a few trial lessons in the homes
of their students, they had founded this school of which they were
the headmistresses. A good number of these small schools existed
at that time in Paris. They were mainly attended by the young girls
of the wealthy classes, who received there a quite remarkable intellectual and spiritual education.

The young de Mas ladies had been trained in teaching by the famous Mademoiselle Désir, the founder of the Normal school and
the principal of the celebrated private school on the rue de Rennes,
its close neighbor. The young de Mas ladies, with an excellent sense
of pedagogy, educated their little students with love and enthusiasm
and grew very attached to them. These young girls repaid them in
kind.

Despite her young age, Élisabeth knew how to appreciate their

---

[6] Ibid., 94–95.

freshness of heart and their great literary, musical, and artistic knowledge, so much so that she became, without great effort, a studious
and educated schoolgirl of whom her teachers were proud.

The young de Mas ladies recruited their students from a refined
social milieu. Most of them established deep friendships, and their
parents knew, liked, and socialized with each other. Respect and
politeness were not things to be learned. They went without saying.

In *Journal d'enfant*, Élisabeth repeatedly expressed her affection for
the young ladies who gave her lessons. They made affectionate visits to each other well outside school hours, as the "young ladies"
did not hesitate to go up to the Arrighi home to pay a friendly visit
when they had a moment.

Later on, Élisabeth's two younger sisters were in their turn enrolled in the de Mas School. The bonds of affection were such
between the dear ladies and their former students that many years
later, in 1911, Élisabeth, already married for many years, returned
to her old school, as if she were returning to her own family, to
attend a midnight Mass.

The de Mas ladies had great faith. They knew how to give their
students a solid Christian formation that was added to that received in the family and the courses of religious instruction at Saint-
Germain-des-Prés.

School and family combined to provide the young girls with mod-
els of "female sanctity". From the day of their birth to the day they
left the altar on the arms of their new husbands, these young girls
had to live in an atmosphere of purity from which any thought of
sexuality was banished. These young girls were happy; they laughed,
they sang, they danced, they played the piano, they read extensively
to educate themselves, they learned foreign languages, they put on
plays, they learned to become good housewives, and, from the age of
eighteen, they waited impatiently for the "prince charming" whom
they would marry and whose name they would take.

It was in this spirit that the young Élisabeth was going to make
her entrance into life, surrounded by a highly intellectual, gentle,
sensitive family full of affection and love for others.

He: Félix Leseur

Félix was born in Reims on March 22, 1861, into a close-knit, happy, lively, intelligent family, similar to Élisabeth's. A short time after Félix's birth, his father, first acknowledged in one of the early studies of the city, registered with the bar to become a prominent lawyer in Reims.

Very cultured, Monsieur Leseur senior was sharp-minded, a brilliant and charming conversationalist always liked in the salons. Steeped in Greek and Latin humanities, the foundations of his secondary education, he read authors in their original languages and, even at an advanced age, could recite by heart the monologues of Virgil or other Latin poets.

Passionate about history in general, and about the history of his city in particular, he had enough influence in the local government of Reims to have sculpted and erected in front of the cathedral a statue of Joan of Arc, of which he was especially proud.

Félix's parents, both of them very Christian, devoted part of their time to charitable organizations, among others, to the Society of Saint Vincent de Paul.

Reims, during that brilliant period of the Second Empire, was a prosperous city: the production of Champagne wines was not the only industry that built the fortune of early industrialists; the economic boom also extended to sheets, canvas, and biscuits. The city's motto was "Dieu en soit garde" (May God protect it). The Leseur family made it their own motto.

In that wealthy city, educational establishments, attended by the children of cultured families, flourished. Félix was placed in the primary school of the Brothers of Reims-Momignies, the most fashionable school in the city.

He was nine years old when the war of 1870 broke out. Despite his young age and the lack of news in the provinces at that time, he had no difficulty understanding France's defeat in Sedan and the distress of his parents at the sight of Prussian uniforms in the streets of Reims. He heard adult conversations and learned that civilians had been shot and that some friends of his parents had been taken as prisoners in Germany. It was a hard time of austerity and sadness that did not, however, hinder him from being a good student.

He pursued his secondary studies with interest, then prepared for his two baccalaureate exams in Seine-et-Marne at the high school of Juilly, run by the priests of the Oratory. As in all the Christian schools at that time, the instruction was stern and often strict, the discipline was harsh, and religion was a subject traditionally taught in the same way as mathematics or geography. The only difference was the addition of moral duties and obligations, non-observance of which was regarded as "sin" and, ultimately, the prospect of hell. With such an education, it is clear that no student could imagine that the faith might one day be a life for him, still less a joy!

A passionate and curious student, the young Félix quickly felt much more attractive aspirations rising in him: he secretly devoured works by authors of which his teachers pretended to be unaware, particularly the libertine writers of the eighteenth century, who fascinated him. He would later say: "All this was bubbling in my head and contributed to making very superficial a religious sentimentality whose roots all those books were little by little drying out."[7]

The descriptions of far-off lands, very fashionable at the end of the nineteenth century, when travel diaries abounded and stimulated the imaginations of their readers, quickly gave him a strong desire to see one day, when he had finished his studies, those unknown and alluring worlds. He dreamed only of travels to the other end of the world, of countries inhabited by indigenous peoples with customs to be discovered, of populations to be educated, of travel accounts that he would bring back to France to a public eager to know of his discoveries.

After his baccalaureate exam, he announced to his parents his desire to begin medical studies. Not in order to practice one day in a medical office or to become a professor of medicine, but simply because, for him, medicine would be but a springboard to the colonial career he ardently desired.

Since the age of ten, he had been drawn to geography, to the accounts of explorers, and, indeed, to colonial questions. It was the era of the great French overseas policy, of African and Asian explorations, the era of the Brazza, Ballay, and Marchand expeditions in Africa. It was also the era of Dupuis, Mouhot, Garnier,

---

[7] R. P. Marie-Albert Leseur, *Vie d'Élisabeth Leseur* (Paris: Éd. J. de Gigord, 1931), 105.

and Doudart de Lagrée in Laos, China, and Cambodia, of Pavie in Asia. Their accounts were published in different periodicals, like *Le Tour du Monde* (World travel), which Félix devoured. He had only one thought then: to participate, in turn, in a similar expedition.

He believed that, to achieve his goals, it was essential that he be a doctor, for himself and for those around him. Not only to accompany expeditions, but also to care for entire populations subject to destructive endemic diseases and bring them the benefits and advancements of French medicine.

More precisely, a goal for his future took shape in his mind: first, to get attached to a distant mission in Africa or Asia; then, once there, to exercise an influence over the natives that would be beneficial for his observations on the regions through which he had passed. No doubt, in his dreams, it was as a traveling researcher, an observer, a discoverer that he achieved his desire for colonialism more than as a philanthropist.

He confided in his spiritual director, Father Bordes: knowing Félix's generosity, as well as his weaknesses, he did not approve at all of this initial direction toward medicine. What would become of him in a milieu of those reputed to be the most immoral students? And, more importantly, how would his faith resist the confident and militant materialism of those medical professors, brilliant but also known for their atheistic proselytizing?

The source of this materialism was not only the professors! Since the eighteenth century, called "The Age of Enlightenment", a sly and recurrent movement had been attacking the world of Christianity. The writings of Voltaire had ravaged religion in France under the pretext of driving out "obscurantism", "superstition", and "fanaticism". The majority of the French intellectual and political class at that end of the century were more or less secretly affiliated with Freemasonry. For some years now, a muffled but rather merciless struggle had already begun to do away with the convents, the priests, and everything that concerned the outward manifestations of religion, especially the houses of religious education.

Father Bordes well knew that his order would, one day, have to suffer a fate that was becoming clearer every day, as France made increasingly anticlerical political speeches.

Students, especially in Paris, owing to their youth and their ardor, would be easy prey to convince and turn away from their religion. They might even become the fierce enemies of their parents' beliefs.

Father Bordes knew Félix well; he knew him to be weak, already very influenced by his eighteenth-century anticlerical and libertine readings; he also knew him to be very eager to detach himself from his family environment. Father Bordes warned his parents of these fears, which, to him, seemed justified.

Despite the warnings and legitimate hesitation of his family, Félix enrolled in the medical preparatory school of Reims, where he would remain for three years during which he would be "protected", since he would continue to live with his family. In spite of these precautions, Father Bordes' fears were soon realized: at the end of a few months, Félix, who already had strong doubts, virulently and proudly rejected the last surviving remnants of his family faith.

However, so as not to shock or hurt his family, he said nothing about it to anyone and continued, out of custom or submission, to accompany his parents to Mass or to their regular Christian gatherings.

After one year of military service in Lille, he continued to pursue his medical studies. But the preparatory school in Reims only provided its instruction for the first three years; the students then had to choose another city.

Consequently, Paris asserted itself to him, but not at all to his parents; they were reticent and very worried to see him leave for the capital without family protection. For them, it was an anxiety and a wrenching parting.

They made inquiries about the classes at the Paris Faculty of Medicine. Félix would have leading medical luminaries of the highest level for his professors, but for the most part they were founders of the society of free thinkers, known for their materialism. This prospect made his parents very anxious because they could easily imagine the influence these men would have on their son.

Monsieur Leseur confided his fears to one of his very dear friends, Maxime Gavignot, with whom he had gone to school in Reims. He, a lawyer in the court of appeals in Paris, reassured him and promised to watch over his son. From the moment the young student arrived in Paris, he immediately welcomed and opened his arms to him. Three times a week in a joyful and fraternal atmosphere, Félix dined around the family table where two daughters and a son, about his age, surrounded him and introduced him to Parisian life. The Gavignots quickly became a new family for him.

As for his lodgings, he shared a student room near the Luxembourg Gardens with a very trusted friend, Henri Cuvillier, whom he had met during his military service in Lille. He was far from feeling isolated during that first year in the capital.

At the Faculty of Medicine, he took courses daily from professors Landouzy and Pozzi, for whom, following exams, he became an extern; at the hospital, the day-to-day interactions with them, in situations that were often dramatic, facing life and death, facing discussions about religion, morality, and the power of money, offered many lessons; they inevitably exercised a great influence on the young Félix.

Doctor Landouzy, a renowned neurologist, was also from Reims, where he had studied the same curriculum as Félix during his first three years of medical studies. A professor of neurology in an age when Broca, a few years earlier, had discovered cerebral localization, Doctor Landouzy inspired his students with his knowledge and his experiences in these new sciences. A brilliant conversationalist and very distinguished, he had a reputation as a great socialite: the sumptuous receptions that he gave at his private mansion, Aligre, in the Faubourg Saint-Germain neighborhood, where the celebrities of the medical, literary, and musical worlds hastened to gather, were reported in the society gazettes that circulated from hand to hand among the students. All were very admiring.

Professor Pozzi, a renowned surgeon and gynecologist, was also an eminent figure in the Parisian world. Especially brilliant in his classes, he fascinated his students. How could Félix not have madly admired this teacher whose full-length portrait by John Singer Sargent, exhibited for a time in Paris, was to immortalize that slender silhouette? The painter depicted him in an elegant dressing gown in red, as appropriate for a surgeon. His students were especially proud of their professor's prestige.

Erudite, brilliant, well-read, familiar with the great Parisian families in the world of finance and the world of letters, with the

Rothschilds, with Anatole France, with Doctor Proust, and with that whole milieu that would be subtly analyzed a few years later by Marcel Proust, Doctor Pozzi was also a passionate collector of Greek statues, Tanagra figurines, and coins. When his students heard him speak about his research and discoveries, they experienced, in their turn, the desire to know everything, to understand everything.

His reputation as a ladies' man was so legendary that the witty Sarah Bernhardt, whom all of Paris rushed to see on stage, one of his most famous patients, had nicknamed him the "Love God", while, among themselves, women called him the "Love Doctor" after the name of a play by Molière. The students laughed and made fun of it, all the while admiring him.

Professor Pozzi, of Protestant origin, was openly an atheist and proud of it. He did not hide it from his students. However, after his dramatic death (he was assassinated by one of his patients in his office), his family requested a religious funeral for him that took place in the church of his hometown of Bergerac. His students had difficulty understanding. Nevertheless, faced with the admiration that he felt for this notoriously anticlerical figure, the young student of the Oratorians of Reims laughed more every day at the religious beliefs of his childhood.

It goes without saying that Félix was fascinated by these strong personalities, so different from all those whom had he met up until now in his family or among his educators. He wanted to adopt their way of living and their ideas, to resemble them one day. Seduced by the culture of his professors, he devoted all his free time to reading in order to educate himself in his turn. With his fine intelligence, he wanted to discover everything and understand everything.

He was more passionate than ever about all the geography books that were being published or that he could consult in the National Library. He had a special interest in those that mentioned French colonial policy.

He soon enrolled in the Geographical Society of Paris, which organized classes and conferences and published journals. He easily established friendly and close relationships with the most zealous supporters of the French colonial policy whom he met at these gatherings, where he was noticed and very popular, being the youngest.

But there was not only the Geographical Society! During his

first years in the capital, he wanted to discover everything: theaters, cabarets, concerts. Paris affected him like a stimulant. And he was insatiable. The desire to know everything in all the fields of art and science quickly captured him, like a fever. At that time, Paris was living through a festive age. The disasters of the war of 1870 had to be forgotten. Everyone celebrated everywhere; they sang; they danced. The French Cancan and the cabarets on Montmartre enchanted a young, more precisely, student audience. Offenbach triumphed on the Parisian stage. On street corners, they hummed his most famous tunes. Everything was good for having fun; it was "la Belle Époque". Félix was easily caught up in this whirlwind of pleasures, so different from the education he had received in Reims. He wanted to see everything, he wanted to know everything, to forget the austerity of his early years in the provinces.

It was in this atmosphere that, shortly after his arrival in Paris, he heard talk of student meetings that were held twice a week in the Latin Quarter. He learned that there they talked about literature, music, and philosophy under the chairmanship of a poet. This group was open to everyone, especially to those who aspired to the bohemian life-style that had become so fashionable Puccini would write an opera about it a few years later. It was exactly what Félix longed for!

For a student who had spent his childhood in a somewhat austere, middle-class milieu, this ideal of life, with its scruffy clothes, its poets, its great discourses that were reshaping the world, its intellectuals living in the misery of heartbreaking love, created an attraction into which Félix longed to immerse himself.

He plunged into it. He discovered a new universe: that of freedom and nonconformism. It was a world without constraint, thanks to which society was at last going to break free from conventions and make changes; it was the world of young artists, at least, of those who called themselves artists, with a glorious future and who held the keys to a future happy society!

The founder of these evenings in the Latin Quarter was Émile Goudeau, of whom Félix had never heard; when he was introduced to him, Félix admired him right away. He was a modest employee of the Ministry of Finance, who went to the office every day dressed in a black suit with his little binder in hand. But because of his charisma and his genuine talent as a poet, he had gathered around him a good number of young students eager to change everything in society. All were enamored with the bohemian life-style, with poetry, art, and freedom, in reaction to the bourgeois mentality of their parents. It was exactly what Félix wanted.

These young people, students for the most part, but also poets, painters, or musicians, were all part of the Hydropathes Club, an informal circle with a provocative title that was difficult to explain. There was only one rule: the principal drink of its members was absinthe, and the organizers were paid in drinks. As to the rest, it was up to everyone's fancy. During these boisterous evenings, it was enough to climb onto the stage and recite your poems or sing your songs in order to be applauded by shouting or the stamping of feet in a joyous and deafening din. Naturally, a road to literary or musical success was promised to each poet and each musician. Everyone believed it! For Félix, accustomed to a completely different way of life, what a new, audacious, and seductive world!

Located for a few months on the Left Bank, the Hydropathes Club moved, shortly after Félix's arrival, to the foot of the hill of Montmartre to the cabaret Le Chat Noir (The black cat). It was the golden age of Montmartre, the era when artists established their studios and their bohemian life-style there. Le Chat Noir soon became the fashionable cabaret where artists and students mixed with a freedom that excited Félix and helped him to discover a new world; Le Chat Noir would very quickly achieve a fame that still endures today.

Why did its sign display a common name that was nothing like that of the Hydropathes Club but that attracted Félix? Simply because Rodolphe Salis, the new owner, a friend of Émile Goudeau, had taken in a black cat wandering in the middle of the rubble. This black cat immediately became the poster image for the establishment, and, more importantly, it allowed Salis to open his doors to a wider public, one that was above all much wealthier than that of student poets. Now the well-to-do and snobbish classes hurried to Le Chat Noir every evening. We would now call this public the Bobos (bourgeois Bohemians).

Félix, very at ease in this atmosphere, regularly frequented this cabaret because he had a lot of fun there and encountered a circle of artists, of bourgeois who had broken with their traditional society, young intellectuals who wanted to have fun.

Every evening, at the entrance of Le Chat Noir, there was a Swiss Guard all dressed in gold and red velvet. He was in charge of bringing in painters and poets free of charge and throwing out "the military and infamous priests", a phrase that greatly amused him, but embarrassed him all the same because of his education.

He liked to sing popular refrains at the top of his voice with his new friends, among whom were Jean Richepin, Alphonse Allais, and many others who were already famous or who would not be long in becoming so. For several months, he regularly frequented this circle, while not neglecting his primary areas of interest.

Thanks to his connections in the Geographical Society of Paris, he had already published articles in the Parisian press to which he did not yet dare sign his name but that were already esteemed for their accuracy and perspicacity. He was commissioned several times to write editorials or news stories on geopolitical subjects, a science that was not yet named thus but that addressed the subjects that interested him.

In 1884, he had already published a study on China in *Le Nouvelliste du Nord et du Pas de Calais* (The north and Pas-de-Calais reporter); in 1886, he became a contributor to *l'Encyclopédie Universelle* (The universal encyclopedia), in which he published two long studies on Bolivia and Brazil. In 1888, he became a correspondent for the *Journal d'Indre et Loire* (The Indre Loire newspaper) on colonial questions. He was beginning to be known in newspaper editorial offices and in the political world.

While still a medical student, Félix was already a fervent supporter of French colonial policy. For him, it was first and foremost the immersion of a curious mind into an exciting new world to be discovered; it was a way to achieve the colonial career to which he aspired. He had decided not to accept, at any price, a position in his own country, much less in Paris, because he had decided to travel his whole life in countries that were expecting a lot of help from France.

So many fascinating countries were in need of young people capable of bringing to them the science and culture that would illuminate them with the French spirit! It was with this perspective that he devoured all the journals and books that addressed those topics and opened up unknown and fascinating horizons.

During his holidays, when Félix returned to his family in Reims, he was proud to talk to them about his progress on the path of knowledge about colonialism. But he was especially happy to rediscover the warm and soothing world that, despite the hectic Parisian life that was his own, he needed. His family opened their arms to him. He rediscovered the simple and affectionate life in which he had been raised.

He wrote: "It is sweet to escape for a few moments from the noise of the big city, the reading of the newspapers, all the active occupations, to savor the rest of the countryside in a charming corner of the Champagne vineyards."[8]

He welcomed the joy of living again, for a few days, with his parents, his brother Paul, who was finishing his law studies, and his young twenty-three-year-old sister, Claire. She was a very cultured young lady, very cheerful and good, involved with her mother in various charitable organizations. He greatly admired her and shared much in common with her.

No one around her could have imagined that Claire's life would be cut short. She would die very quickly a few months later during one of Félix's visits to his family; for the young man, this was the first time he was confronted with the death of someone so close. It would take him a long time to recover from it.

When he returned to Paris, the journal *La Marine Française* offered him a regular collaboration. The same offer was made to him by the weekly review *En Plein Air*. Still focused on his medical studies, he had not thought until then about becoming a journalist, but, for him, these opportunities, which he seized all at once, represented the first steps toward accessing the faraway missions of which he increasingly dreamed.

A member of other geographical and colonial societies, which earned him a certain notoriety for the quality of his articles, it was not long before he was solicited for conferences, papers, and publications. He no longer had the time to be interested in his medical studies. He had become, little by little, without really being aware

---

[8] Marie-Louise Herking, *Le Père Leseur* (Paris: Éd. J. de Gigord, 1952), 10.

of it, a much-sought-after journalist who specialized in colonial topics. His medical studies were over.

It was at this turning point in his life that he was going to meet Élisabeth and his life would change. He was twenty-seven years old, and his professional destiny seemed mapped out in the direction he had wanted for years. He was earning an honest living.

Since his arrival in Paris, despite the Hydropathes and Le Chat Noir, he had continued to go to the Gavignots' every week to dine with those who had welcomed him like a son; he did not yet suspect that it would be there, in that wise family, at a time when he had so little wisdom, that he would meet his future wife, Élisabeth Arrighi, a good friend of their eldest daughter.

The Arrighi and Gavignot families were close; they had lived for several years in the same building on the rue de Richelieu, which had created real bonds of friendship between their children, who were around the same age. In her *Journal d'enfant*, Élisabeth noted repeatedly that they had spent an evening at the Gavignots' or that the Gavignots had come to their home.

Élisabeth was twenty-one years old. She was fresh, simple, and pretty. Her conversation was lively, spontaneous, not banal; she was fundamentally happy and full of laughter. She was a young woman on whom he could count: she would be a good wife, a strong yet tender mother that he would want for his future children.

Félix, amazed by her knowledge of literature, music, and art, enjoyed sharing so many interests with her. They had the same intellectual curiosity, the same reactions to events. She played the piano with intelligent feeling. One day, he heard Élisabeth's younger sister, Amélie, say teasingly: "Élisabeth and M. Leseur are boring, they talk about Wagner all the time!"

Their eyes met more and more often at family dinners; a ray of silent tenderness that did not escape the more perceptive glimmered in the eyes of the two young people; Félix soon seemed very much in love. So did she.

The Gavignots watched this love grow before their eyes, week after week. They informed Élisabeth's parents, who were not unhappy about it.

A few weeks later, the Arrighis had Félix invited to a private ball that they were also attending; they watched the two young people dance together almost the whole time. They seemed well suited. No doubt they would make "a good match".

Amélie, Élisabeth's younger sister, wrote in her diary: "The evening went well. Élisabeth and Félix Leseur danced and talked a lot."

A few days later, Félix's parents, still mourning their daughter Claire, instructed the Gavignots to ask Élisabeth's parents, on their behalf, for her hand.

On Thursday May 23, 1889, the two young people were officially engaged. Much later Félix would write: "Without my knowing it, Providence came to guide me in its mysterious ways and to grant me, in its paternal and infinite solicitude, a grace whose importance and extent I would not, alas, fully appreciate until many years later."[9]

They would be married the following July.

---

[9] M. A. Leseur, *Vie d'Élisabeth Leseur*, 89.

3

The First Years as Newlyweds

On August 27, a month after their wedding, Félix, as an auxiliary doctor of the Reserves, had to go to Reims for a twenty-eight-day period of military instruction. His regiment, the 132nd Infantry, was in garrison there.

Naturally, Élisabeth accompanied him: she stayed with her parents-in-law, who were very happy to welcome their new daughter-in-law for a few days and to dine with their son every evening.

Shortly after their arrival, Élisabeth gradually felt an intense fatigue; at first, she said nothing about it to anyone: "No doubt these were the normal first symptoms, two months after her marriage, of a desired pregnancy." But the fatigue intensified; after a few days, she no longer even had the strength to get out of bed. They began to think it was a serious illness.

The doctors in Reims were perplexed by such severe symptoms, capable of so overpowering a young woman. The means of investigation at that time were still very elementary; they first diagnosed an abdominal abscess in the intestine; they were not unaware that this condition could, at any moment, cause peritonitis, which was usually fatal in that century when antibiotics did not exist.

Her mother-in-law cared for her with the gentleness, affection, and attentions of a mother, while waiting for the arrival of Madame Arrighi, who, distraught, hastened to her daughter's bedside.

The professors of medicine who had been consulted next quickly dismissed the possibility of an operation and agreed in forbidding the young woman to consider returning to Paris before an indeterminate period of time. Above all, no travel! Two long months in bed at Reims would be necessary before the young couple could return to their brand-new apartment in Paris on the rue de l'Université. And even then! The trip could only be made on a stretcher and would still be followed by several months in bed. It was an equally great trial for them both: for Élisabeth, a honeymoon bound in bed, and for Félix, a twenty-three-year-old wife who was seriously ill after two months of marriage!

Back in Paris, Félix asked his professors, who had become his friends, for a consultation. He had complete confidence in the reliability of their diagnosis. Doctors Pozzi and Landouzy were guarded. They also dismissed the idea of an immediate operation, but they did not conceal from Félix the seriousness of the illness. His wife would have it for the rest of her life, no doubt with periods of remission, but this illness would never be completely cured, and the young couple would have to plan their life accordingly. It was a big shock.

Both of them valiantly accepted this diagnosis.

In Paris, Félix continued his life as nurse and personal doctor with love and devotion; every day he had to give precise care to his patient, to remain by her bedside, to help her in the simplest tasks of everyday life.

Neither one of them had expected that their married life would be spent around the bed of a seriously ill patient. But their love, with all the gentleness of their hearts, strengthened them from day to day, and, above all, despite the prognoses, the secret hope that medical progress would one day come to defeat this disease gave them the courage to consider their shared future.

However, Félix began to sense that, if a medical career was already no longer an option for him, perhaps he would also be led to give up the colonial career of which he had dreamed since his childhood. He did not speak of it, but he did not yet dare to anticipate from the outset such a disappointment in the plans for the future that were so close to his heart.

Élisabeth, very aware of the almost certain collapse of her husband's dreams and of the sad newlywed life that her condition had imposed on him, bore this heavy ordeal with courage and resignation, helped by her faith and her trust in God. As for Félix, he completely rejected this consolation. But his parents had taught him that in hardship there was no other way than to live one day at a time and to accomplish every day, with complete love, the tasks that were incumbent on him. So, he devoted himself to it by devising potential travel plans to live fully the periods of remission that had been predicted by the doctors.

It was an equally heavy and unexpected suffering for them both. Their strengthened love had inevitably increased because both had realized how indispensable each was to the other. Since withdrawing inward would lead nowhere, each of them thought only of finding ways to ease the sorrow or sufferings of the other.

Élisabeth's parents often went to see their daughter and sit by her bedside to distract her and surround her.

A few days after Christmas, at the time of the famous, very deadly influenza epidemic of 1889, Madame Arrighi, to her daughter's surprise, came alone. Her husband had been stricken by the terrible virus and had to keep to his bed. She was worried. Without the proper medicine, he had rapidly fallen into a hopeless state. In learning of the seriousness of her father's illness, Élisabeth suffered a shock that was all the more profound since she was not able to go to his bedside. She had seen him full of life and affection for her the day before. It was impossible to imagine.

He died in forty-eight hours on December 29, 1889.

Due to her weakened condition, Élisabeth could not consider leaving her chaise longue, even for a few hours, to attend her father's funeral. She viewed it as an unbearable suffering, an additional trial to accept.

Félix, always so sensitively attentive to his young wife, understood her sorrow. He did not hesitate to undertake special steps with the funeral directors to get the funeral procession to adjust its route between Saint-Germain-des-Prés and the Montmartre cemetery.

Lying on her chaise longue, Élisabeth could then see her father's funeral procession pass beneath her windows on the rue de Rennes and, despite her immobility, could accompany it with her tears and her prayers.

But the young couple were not at the end of their trials: the following year, on April 22, Félix's father died in his turn at barely sixty-three years of age.

Little by little, with time, Élisabeth's health improved. She had a strong will and above all a great desire to make her husband happy. Not for anything in the world would she have wanted her illness to be an inconvenience or a handicap for him.

So, as soon as she was able to resume one almost normal activity, she no longer gave up anything. With her doctor husband near her, she could and she wanted to undertake everything.

Over the course of several years, Félix had done his best to rent pleasant and restful houses for the summer. In Marly-le-Roy, he found a charming one close to very dear friends, the Hennequins. At their home, in the countryside, Élisabeth would be able to rest.

Maurice Hennequin was a playwright whom Félix had known at Le Chat Noir when they were students, a friend from his youth. That bohemian time, when he had recited his poems, had passed. Now Maurice was experiencing his hour of glory. His name flourished on many posters. His comedies and his vaudevilles made all of Paris laugh and enlivened the salons. Full of humor and steeped in literary culture, he greatly amused his entourage with his jokes and his conversations, which Élisabeth greatly enjoyed.

Aimée, his wife, had an openness, an uprightness, a constant concern for others that instantly allowed her to form a profound friendship with Élisabeth.

Both Hennequins were deeply atheistic and anticlerical, which did not displease Félix and even determined the choice of their friendship. No doubt, with time, they would succeed better than he had in turning his young wife away from the faith. He counted greatly on their friendship and their influence. Élisabeth was completely unaware of the secret intention of her husband.

Over the course of long and warm conversations, the Hennequins were particularly respectful of the beliefs that the young woman did not hide from them. They were cheerful and happy so that, being in contact with them, she recovered her cheerful and crystalline laughter. The two couples thereafter met almost every day in Paris during the winter. They would remain close friends of the Leseurs until the end.

For several years, vacations were spent calmly and agreeably at Marly, at Vaucresson, and then at Bièvres, where the two couples rented a house together every year in the peace, tranquility, and greenery.

In 1891, Élisabeth was doing much better. On vacation at La Baule, where Félix had rented a villa, Élisabeth invited her mother and her sister Amélie to spend the month of August with them by the seashore. It was a joy for everyone.

Félix took advantage of that stay in Brittany to suggest to Élisabeth to go to Sainte-Anne-d'Auray on the feast of Saint Anne, July 26, a very traditional and always very fervent celebration. A bit surprised by this sudden devotion, Élisabeth accepted with joy. Félix attended the "Grand Pardon" with her; completely at ease in the midst of the people's fervor and hymns, he walked beside her in the long procession of pilgrims who made their way toward the site dedicated to Saint Anne. No doubt he did not join in the songs and prayers. He was there out of slightly critical curiosity, but he said nothing about it. He had gone to accompany his wife, whom he loved and whose beliefs he wanted to respect as he had promised her. He wanted to make her happy.

4

Félix the Magnificent

Félix was bright and cheerful. He was always so elegant, so refined, so neat in his appearance, so slender, his suits, always in the latest fashion, were so well cut by the best tailor in Paris, his black goatee and mustache were so well trimmed, that his friends nicknamed him "Félix the Magnificent". Élisabeth was especially proud of it.

In June 1891, he was appointed a correspondent for a geography journal to which he was to deliver two articles a month; it was exactly what he had wanted and what was compatible with his new life with his wife.

The following year, in 1892, he was offered another position in journalism with magnificent prospects: one of his childhood friends from Reims, the editor in chief of a daily political newspaper, *La République française* (The French republic), informed him that the position of his friend Maurice Ordinaire, in charge of the "foreign policy" column for that newspaper, was vacant.

In fact, Maurice Ordinaire, already senator of Doubs and destined for an important political career, had just been appointed to the ministry as under secretary of state for the colonies.

After a few approaches, Félix obtained the position. He would be responsible for writing sixteen to eighteen articles per month about colonial policy and geography. It was a dream come true and one that must undoubtedly open a royal path to the future colonial career about which he cared above all else.

The editorial office of the *La République française* newspaper was very lively. Every day Félix met men of high political standing such as Delcassé or Poincaré. Maurice Ordinaire would become one of his closest friends.

This daily publication, *La République française*, had a large circulation. It was read in all the intellectual circles and, more particularly, in the political and financial sphere. Founded by Gambetta, it was the voice of the "opportunist party" and showed the strongest anticlerical biases in France. This orientation was not at all displeasing to Félix, who had begun to find it difficult to support the climate of piety in his household. Furthermore, access to the management of the newspaper, with all the meetings and relationships that stemmed from it, fulfilled all his wishes and all his aspirations. The daily association with prominent politicians, each of them more anticlerical than the last, exhilarated him and only increased his aversion and his disdain for religion. He said nothing about it . . . or so little that Élisabeth did not perceive it.

One year later, Félix, as the columnist responsible for colonial questions, joined the staff of the *Le Siècle* (The century) newspaper, which was just as prestigious and anticlerical as that of *La République française*. Professionally, he was fulfilled.

In that same year of 1892, Élisabeth's health strengthened; she was happily able to attend her sister Amélie's wedding to Doctor Duron, a profoundly Christian young man who would very soon become a brother to the Leseurs and the attentive doctor of the whole family.

The birth of this young couple's first baby, a little Marie, to whom Élisabeth would be godmother, was an immense joy for her and at the same time a profound sadness. In front of the image of her sister hugging her little daughter in her arms with such joyful tenderness, Élisabeth measured her disappointment and her sorrow at never knowing, in her turn, the happiness of having a child of her own. Her doctors had confirmed it for her. From now on, this little Marie would be as dear to her as a child of their own.

In 1893, for the first time since Élisabeth's illness, the Leseurs embarked on a journey. A tempting opportunity had presented itself. For Félix, it was an unhoped-for escape after all those years of sickness and confinement near the bed of a sick person. For her, it was a liberation.

The Dominican college of Arcueil organized its annual trip to Rome under the leadership of the director, Father Didon, a Dominican famous for his athletic achievements, his dynamism, and his Lenten sermons at Saint-Philippe-du-Roule, which would later lead to his being sent as an exile to Corbara, a Dominican monastery in Corsica. Consequently, he was a well-known, but also controversial, strong personality in Christian circles. Some family and friends would perhaps join the pilgrimage. Félix's mother and several of her friends from Reims had registered for it. Understandably, Madame Leseur offered to accompany the young family. She did not yet at all suspect the anticlericalism of her son because he had never dared to reveal it to her. Father Didon would guide the pilgrims throughout the visit in Rome; he had even been able to obtain a special audience with Pope Leo XIII for the last day.

After Rome, Élisabeth and Félix would separate from the pilgrimage to Reims. They would personally extend their stay in Italy to visit Naples, Florence, Venice, Siena, Verona, and Milan. It was a magnificent plan of tourist travel that would allow them to discover Italy with its artistic treasures and incomparable landscapes. They were both enthusiastic in advance. After that trip, Élisabeth would say that Italy had so much charm for her that she could have loved it as a living being whom one never stops wanting to see again.

Félix, however, had never considered that in Rome Élisabeth's religious faith would blossom.

Up until then, he had known that his wife went to Mass and prayed often, but, for him, it was without major impact on his own life. Ostensibly, it had seemed almost insignificant to him that his wife was pious, especially after having had the education that she had received. In reality, deep inside himself, all those signs of piety annoyed him enormously, and he looked forward to pulling out smoothly and quickly from Élisabeth's heart the roots of a faith to which she seemed, to him, a prisoner.

By this trip, he had even secretly hoped that the splendors and riches of the Vatican would turn her away from her piety. He had not considered that the evocation of the courage of the martyrs facing persecutions, of the tortures of Peter and Paul, and of the history of the early days of the Church would give a new vigor to his wife's faith and, even less, that her presence in Rome, in the heart of Christianity, would anchor her even more in her very sincere beliefs.

Faced with the enthusiasm mixed with the reverence and prayers of his wife, little by little, Félix felt hostility rising in himself. He had the impression that his wife was escaping him, that she was walking on a path to which he had no access, that she was turning away from him. Recalling this pilgrimage, he would later write:

I had begun this detestable struggle against her beliefs in a deaf and insidious way at first, a struggle that I had to carry out openly and actively in the following years, particularly in 1896, 1897. At the time of our marriage, I had declared myself to be very respectful of the Catholic faith and religion, and I sometimes even accompanied Élisabeth to Mass. But that was all. I was not practicing. To be honest, I attached no importance to beliefs that I did not share and that left me perfectly indifferent. Why had I changed my attitude? How had I lost the religious sense and become skeptical, antireligious? . . . With the turn of my mind, I had tried to look for reasons for disbelief, just as a true Christian seeks his reasons to believe. The history of religions had always interested me, and I drew weapons from the exegesis of combat against the Catholicism I had learned to hate. I was exclusively nourished by all the adversaries of the Church and modern writers: Strauss, Havet, Renan, Sabatier, Réville, Loisy, Houtin, and others. I had built up an abundant library for myself of Protestant, Modernist, and rationalist works, and I was passionate about those systems of denial. If, at the beginning of my marriage, I sometimes accompanied Élisabeth to Mass, very quickly I arrived at impatiently tolerating at my side beliefs other than my negations. Neutrality is either a myth or a deception.[1]

After that trip, which had been like an explosion in their relationship, Félix became a little more aggressive every day toward religion. His hatred for Rome and Vatican politics was reflected in his articles. For example, we read, in his words, in *La République française* on September 11, 1893:

. . . Everywhere and without end, the pope uses his recovered moral authority to decide the fate of political questions. The danger is great for the civil societies that face an elusive power driven by interests and ideas opposed to the fundamental principles of the modern state. The danger is all the more urgent since the enemy is politically shrewd, cautious, and prudent. That is why we have believed it appropriate to report it. Our governments, responsible for defending the liberties that the Revolution has passed on to us, cannot have too much

---

[1] Élisabeth Leseur, *Lettres à des Incroyants* (Paris: Éd. J. de Gigord, 1928), 108.

vigilance or energy to deploy to fight against this disturbing return of the clerical spirit.[2]

When evaluating the summary of his life, he would later write: "I took Élisabeth for the object of my reverse proselytizing, first insidiously, but little by little with more clarity. During the first years, I obtained no results; the exceptional religious formation of her childhood was still too alive; but toward the end of 1896 and the beginning of 1897, I succeeded in awakening certain doubts that became more defined."[3]

It is certain that Félix had lost the faith for many reasons. But why did he want to tear it completely out of his wife's heart? Several hypotheses are possible because no one really knows the depths of souls. Did he want her closer to him, harnessed to the same struggle, in his atheism and anticlericalism? Did he want to change her in turning her away from the traditional education of her childhood? Or was he simply jealous of the profound private life that she lived by his side without his being able to share it? When he married her, she was a very wise little girl, even a sick girl. He made of her a brilliant and fashionable woman of the world; he made her discover political life and initiated her into his professional life; he made her understand that the faith received in her family was a convention connected with a social class; in a way, she was something of his creation. Did he want her to be a new and liberated woman whom he could flatter himself to see completely as his own work, as his success?

It is surprising that neither one of them in their writings reports heated discussions or arguments in their relationship at that time. Perhaps there had been some, but certainly very few; their life together seemed sufficiently exciting for that not to have been the case. Élisabeth possessed an unusual tolerance and willingness to listen to the ideas of others. She would later write in her diary that controversy, especially within a couple, seemed completely pointless to her. Only the testament of a happy, joyful life, especially one given for others, could be useful in the eyes of unbelievers.

---

[2] R. P. Marie-Albert Leseur, *Vie d'Élisabeth Leseur* (Paris: Éd. J. de Gigord, 1931), 108.
[3] Ibid.

In his editorial office, Félix daily encountered the leading figures of the Paris elite, and he inevitably led a dizzying social life. As a journalist, he was often given invitations to the theater, the music hall, and to concerts. Those were the years of "La Belle Époque" when new theaters opened their doors, when Paris sang and danced, when frivolity triumphed in all the shows.

Élisabeth was fascinated by this new life. She accompanied her husband everywhere: to fashionable restaurants, receptions, comedy shows, parties, balls, and even cabarets. The two danced so splendidly that it was impossible not to notice them.

They often met with friends, especially with the Hennequins. They laughed, they drank, they heartily enjoyed themselves; Élisabeth was beautiful, and she knew it; she was always very elegant and wonderfully groomed. Félix wanted to give her expensive jewels to adorn her even better. Sometimes she kindly refused because, she said: "With the price of this jewel we could provide for many people", but he offered it to her anyway because he was proud of her beauty.

She was a credit to her husband: her conversation as a cultivated and interesting woman made her appreciated in all the salons. Félix was flattered to be able to introduce his pretty young wife to politicians, writers, and artists. He knew that they admired her for her erudition, still uncommon in the women of her generation, and for her sensitivity to all forms of art, painting, and music, and for her knowledge of literature.

Élisabeth was never bored during those evenings. On the contrary, she quickly acquired a taste for those associations of intellectuals who were sensitive to art and amusing, for those late nights, for that life that was so different from her austere youth.

Late in the evening or early in the morning, when the shows and receptions had ended, Félix had to return to the newspaper office in order to learn the information from the Havas agency; he collected the latest news necessary for writing his article for the following day. He did not return home until around two or three in the morning.

Most of the time, at the end of an evening gathering, a ball, or a show, Élisabeth accompanied him. She did not like to leave it, but she liked above all to share her husband's interests and concerns so as to understand him better. He had taught her to be fascinated by everything that happened in the world. She had repaid him well. On his side, he enjoyed sharing those moments with a wife who was open to the great problems of the world and capable of advising him in the writing of his articles.

In the silence of a Paris deep in sleep, an intense life, accessible only to the initiated and enthusiasts, bubbled up every night at the end of these long hallways of the editorial office immersed in darkness. For Élisabeth, it was a rich and new life, an opening to the source of the profound movements that shake the world, and all this in union with the man she admired and loved.

Félix was buoyed by a secret satisfaction: he hoped that this life full of worldliness and intellectual enrichments would divert his wife from a remnant of piety that he could not stand anymore.

And indeed, he soon detected the first effects of this whirlwind of activities. Very quickly Élisabeth no longer had the time, or even the desire, to go to Mass every day or to pray for a long time as she had done before. She now lived in a world so bubbling and fascinating that she had other concerns.

Although far removed from evangelical images, Félix knew well that when we detach, even slowly, a shoot from its vine full of sap and life, it does not take long to dry out. And that was exactly what he wanted. And that is what happened.

He would later write: "The war that I waged against Élisabeth's beliefs found very favorable ground in this chaos."[4]

But all of that unfolded in silence. Élisabeth, intoxicated by this new life, was content to observe joyfully the intensity of her social activities without suspecting that it was all secretly part of a premeditated plan.

Both were very much in love and happy with the admiring commotion surrounding their relationship. If they had regret or sadness over not having children, at least they had in common their interest in this nocturnal and exhilarating life-style. The busier their social life, the more anchored in Félix was the idea that religion, and especially Catholicism with its meditations, its penances, and its austerities, was a hindrance to real life, to human happiness, and

---

[4] Ibid., 110.

therefore a hindrance to be opposed. Besides, did he still have to fight it? Happily, Élisabeth now seemed to him so far from all of that past!

In 1894, Félix's colonial dream materialized. By ministerial decree, at the request of his friend Théophile Delcassé, recent minister of colonies, he was appointed a member of the superior council of the colonies.

This nomination filled him with joy because it corresponded perfectly to the aspirations he had had for many years. But . . . it collided with a considerable family obstacle: it implied an obligatory residence in a distant colony. Perhaps Sudan? Perhaps Tonkin? Maybe somewhere else? How could he announce such a faraway departure to his wife? And above all, how could he announce it to the Arrighi family, to Élisabeth's mother, a widow, so concerned for her daughter's health and not at all ready to see her leave for the other end of the world?

Long, often difficult, family conversations ended in convincing Félix not to embark on such an adventure: Élisabeth was not in a condition to go live in such hot countries deprived of hospital facilities in case of a relapse.

Félix eventually gave in to the family's arguments and to his own common sense. With death in his soul, he gave up this appointment. It was an enormous sacrifice, but a magnificent proof of love for his young wife and for his in-laws, who were aware of the magnitude of the renunciation they had imposed on him.

In compensation, the Arrighi family, moved by his sacrifice, offered him another position. Élisabeth's uncle was the director of an important life insurance company: Le Conservateur. He was going to retire in a few months. He would agree to have Félix join the board of directors straightaway with the prospect of soon becoming director. It was a prestigious and lucrative position. The offer was tempting. Félix accepted.

5

A Life of Wealthy Intellectuals

The year 1895 was marked by two events that, once again, would bring about significant changes in the life of the young couple.

On January 1, 1895, Félix replaced Uncle Alexandre and joined the management of Le Conservateur. He was thirty-four years old. He was in the prime of life. He had matured; he had met the most diverse notables both in his profession and in his social gatherings. His bright and competent personality had won him a large number of connections in the political and financial world, where his opinion was always appreciated and considered trustworthy.

At this end of the century, life insurance companies were living through their golden age. The depression that had followed the defeat of 1870 had given way to a period of wonderful growth without inflation. The currency was stable; private reserves in cash, securities, or gold were entrusted to life insurance companies, which were experiencing an unprecedented boom. It was a position with heavy responsibilities that was entrusted to Félix. It was also a position with a high salary.

His five years at the editorial office of *La République française* had opened up many horizons for him, as much from a historical as from an economical perspective; he had had to learn about foreign policy leading almost daily to making a judgment about Russia, Italy, or Germany. He had formed many friendly relationships in the political and financial worlds. His conversations with Élisabeth, his personal reflections, his reading, had enabled him to take a more humanitarian perspective on colonial problems. He had also done much reflecting.

The Leseur couple had become prominent figures among the Paris elite. They were invited to social gatherings where the great names in politics and economics met. For them it was a whirlwind of prestige that completely seduced Élisabeth, ever so admiring of her husband. After the months of sickness, fatigue, and the chaise longue, it was also for them a brilliant and exciting new life in which every outing resulted in a pursuit of elegance where their youth and beauty were noticed.

Félix would later write: "At that time, I attended to foreign and colonial policy; I wrote, I collaborated with influential leftist and anticlerical daily newspapers. Our customary acquaintances consisted of politicians, publicists, journalists, doctors, academics, scientists, men of letters, musicians, playwrights, artists."[1]

Élisabeth now no longer had either the time or the desire to concern herself with the faith of her youth. Her mind was elsewhere. Her husband had told her so often that religion was the recourse of poor minds that she had begun to adopt his views. The great intellects, with whom she mixed at receptions and with whom she happily conversed, were all atheists and anticlerics as well, very often with brilliant arguments and seductive freedom.

If, up until now, she had still aspired to attend, from time to time, retreats or devotions that deeply annoyed her husband, now she did not think of them at all.

Félix secretly rejoiced to see that the excitement and encounters of the new life that she was discovering, thanks to him, his position, and his connections, monopolized her mind and her time. He tried to increase them in order to immerse her in a rhythm of life and a multiplication of areas of interests that left no room for recollection. Vis-à-vis his friends, he was proud of having convinced his wife and of having made of her a "liberated" woman, completely at ease in an atheistic world into which she was integrated and that she understood better and better.

Alone during the day, she devoted many hours to transforming their large, slightly cold apartment in the rue de l'Université into a pleasant and warm place to relax. At that time, department stores like the Bon Marché and the Printemps, which were still in their infancy, offered to young, delighted housewives an incomparable choice of fabrics, trimmings, and accessories to embellish and

---

[1] Élisabeth Leseur, appendix of *Journal et Pensées de chaque jour* (Paris: Éd. du Cerf, 2005), 258.

decorate every room of their apartment. Élisabeth did not overlook a single detail in transforming their "nest" into a haven of peace and beauty where it was good to live.

With the happiness of lovers, they lived for each other when the two reunited in the evenings. Both of them had an office or a little sitting room with a desk and their personal library. Two very different libraries lined the walls with titles and authors of diametrically opposed ideas. Élisabeth and Félix's great happiness was to discuss books they had read in common, exchanging their points of view, for example, on all the great names of French and foreign literatures. Books played a vital role in the life of this intellectual couple who loved to share their ideas and impressions during the course of their intimate evenings under the soft light of the living room lamp.

The rooms where the two might find themselves together were decorated with art and finesse. First and foremost, Élisabeth wanted to be responsible for the happiness of the man she loved. Not having children, all her energy and her imagination were devoted to him simply out of love. She did her best to provide him with every material comfort so that the evenings at home when they were alone together were happy and relaxing moments. Félix savored and appreciated this intimate atmosphere that his wife tried to create for him.

Later, during a lecture for young women on the duties of one's state in life, her husband would show with simplicity the way in which Élisabeth had understood her duty as a wife:

> Élisabeth was the vigilant guardian of our household, which she knew how to protect from any questionable intrusion as well as from any dubious compromise. But at the same time that she kept it very dignified, she did her best to make it very pleasant. Her personal charm, her great elegance, her rare intellectual knowledge, made this task very easy for her. She also knew how to entertain beautifully, and the friends who formed our circle loved, as she did, its moral value and its intellectual culture. . . . Her affection was always on the watch, inspiring her with all devotion. My selfishness adapted very well to being the center of her existence. She was interested in everything that affected me. She was an excellent advisor in all matters,

and, more than once, I consulted her with some success about professional difficulties; I benefited from her intellectual balance and her
moderation. There is not an occupation, an honest pleasure that she
did not accept for me, and what support, what comfort she brought
me in dark hours. She was naturally good-natured, witty, and delight-
fully cheerful. In a word, always and in everything, Élisabeth adjusted
her existence to the rhythm of mine.[2]

She also devoted a lot of time to her family, especially to her
mother, whom she surrounded with affection, but also to her
nephews and nieces. She and Félix felt very involved in the lives
of their respective families. Élisabeth's correspondence with her
mother-in-law and the care that Félix gave to his wife's mother and
close relatives demonstrate an affection that transcended the bound-
aries of each other's families.

Élisabeth artfully entertained their many friends a great deal in
her renovated apartment through which the figures of the political and artistic world paraded. Félix was proud of his young wife,
so elegant and slender in her long, sheath dresses; he admired her
fine profile enhanced by her smartly raised chignon. But what he
admired most of all was her smile, always so warm that everyone
in her home felt expected and welcomed. He was also proud of
her knowledge and the pertinence with which she participated in
conversations about politics or art.

If the evenings when they did not go out were busy with discussing and reading together, Élisabeth had free hours during the
day. She knew that her husband especially enjoyed their exchanges.
Consequently, she would never cease to expand her knowledge daily
and to read the great names of French and foreign literature.

Élisabeth had had a good education, but at that time, young girls
did not learn Latin. Latin was the language of the Church; this language, called "dead", had been familiar to her from an early age,
but, apart from the phrases in the missal, the language of Cicero
remained incomprehensible to her. With her usual intellectual curiosity, Élisabeth felt, without any religious attraction, the desire

---

[2] "Conférence sur le devoir d'état", in Marie-Louise Herking, *Le Père Leseur* (Paris:
Éd. J. de Gigord, 1952), 39.

to deepen her study of Latin. She simply wished to study the development of the French language from its Roman roots and the essentials of philology. She would have undertaken this approach for any other foreign language because she was fascinated by syntax and authors in general.

She told Félix about this project. He strongly encouraged her in this study, pleased to realize that it was going to monopolize her mind and her time for several years. He emphasized to her that Latin not only was an incomparable cultural agent, but also, with its clarity and precision, Latin gave the mind a certain sharpness and rigor in written and oral expression.

With the decision made in mutual agreement, Élisabeth set to work: she took daily lessons with her old professor from the Cours Désir on the rue Jacob. She worked in the evenings at home; little by little she tackled the great authors in their texts. In two years, she had mastered the language, and, a few years later, she would even be able to give Latin lessons to her nephew.

In that year of 1895, Paris was going through a Russian phase. On the walls of Paris, advertising posters that read "Lending to Russia is lending to France" invited citizens to invest their savings in the building of Russian railroad lines. Literary events welcomed the translations of great authors. All the intellectuals at the turn of the century were fascinated by Russian literature, the works of which filled the display windows of bookstores. Posters depicting daily life in Russia blossomed on the walls of Paris. Élisabeth and Félix both devoured Pushkin, Dostoevsky, Turgenev, Tolstoy, and Gorky. When they met again in the evenings, they talked about them, they exchanged their books; their friends shared the same enthusiasm for these great authors who up till then had been barely known in France.

Translations in French abounded, but they were uneven, often disappointing or inconsistent. Élisabeth regretted not being able to read directly from the original text, from the very source of their inspiration, the works of these authors who revealed to France the soul of Russia and the life of Russians in the nineteenth century. She had learned Latin well, why should she not learn Russian? And, of course, once she spoke Russian, they would go to Russia. She would be proud of being able to be their interpreter!

Again, Félix strongly encouraged her in this project that was stimulating for them both. One through the other, they would have access to an entirely new world where the study of the Cyrillic alphabet alone would present a not insignificant curiosity, the first door opener.

Élisabeth looked for a teacher. It was less easy than finding a Latin professor! She met an elderly lady from Russian high society, retired in Paris, who was happy to teach her language to such a motivated and intelligent young woman. In less than two years, with her excellent memory and at the price of serious work, Élisabeth was able to speak and read Russian. Numerous books in Cyrillic letters, including the complete works of Pushkin, Gorky, Tolstoy, and the novels of Dostoevsky, then filled her library, under the admiring eyes of her husband.

The following year, the Franco-Russian friendship was solemnly sealed by an official visit to Paris by the young Tsar Nicholas II and his wife, Alexandra. This visit was celebrated with grand events followed by a jubilant crowd. On October 9, 1896, the tsar placed the first stone of the bridge that would bear the name of his recently deceased father: the Pont Alexandre III; when this bridge was completed, four years later, it would be the highlight of the World's Fair of 1900 with the Grand Palais and the Petit Palais at the end of it making it one of the most prestigious neighborhoods in Paris, not far from the Champs-Élysées.

Of course, the Leseurs received invitations to attend all the events. Élisabeth wrote to her mother:

For two days, we have been living with the tsar and the empress, and we are getting to know them deeply. The day before yesterday, we went to Maurice's house on the Boulevard Saint-Germain for part of the afternoon, and we saw them leave and return for various excursions; in the evening, we attended the departure for the Élysée with magnificent gala carriages. Yesterday we went to Maurice's house at nine o'clock in the morning to watch them pass by; yesterday after lunch, to the inauguration of the Alexandre bridge for which we had tickets. It was very beautiful: the Seine covered in decorated boats, the senate, the chamber, the songs, the poetry verses, and a delegation of young girls who offered the empress a magnificent silver vase. Would you believe that it had been suggested that I be part of this delegation and that I address a few words in Russian to the empress? The minister of commerce was in favor of this idea; my case was discussed with the council of ministers, and the other ministers were of the opinion that a speech was not necessary. I was disappointed about it. It would have amused me.[3]

Two days later, Élisabeth described to her mother the unforgettable and moving military review in Chalons, where they had attended a parade of seventy thousand men in sparkling uniforms.

In July, their friend Maurice Ordinaire invited them to spend a few days of vacation and a change of scene at Jougne, the town of his childhood where he owned a country house.

Jougne was a charming little village about three thousand feet in altitude between Pontarlier and Vallorbe in the Jura Mountains, surrounded by the magnificent scenery of meadows and pine trees. Félix and Élisabeth at once fell in love with these spectacular landscapes, where excursions seemed within easy reach, and, especially, with the invigorating air that gave everyone energy and health.

So thrilled by the beauty of the place and the warmth of their friend's welcome, they would return to Maurice Ordinaire's home again the following year.

Jougne's charm seemed so great to them that they had only one idea: to settle there and have a "home of their own" there for all their vacations. They quickly bought land on which to build the nest of their dreams. For their whole life, Jougne would be their place for vacations and relaxation, the big house where they would have the room necessary to bring families and friends together during the summer. This house would play a very important role in their lives, and especially in Élisabeth's.

In the midst of these plans, a new accident occurred in Élisabeth's life. That same year in the month of August, after their return to Paris, they went to visit Félix's mother, who was on holiday in Pierrefonds. They were accompanied by Félix's brother, his wife, and his sons. It was a beautiful plan for a family reunion that would turn into a disaster: the carriage with which they were traveling through the forest overturned. Élisabeth was caught under the horse, whose kicking hooves broke several of her ribs. A hematoma then formed

---

[3] R. P. Marie-Albert Leseur, *Vie d'Élisabeth Leseur* (Paris: Éd. J. de Gigord, 1931), 115.

in the pleura, invading her lung and once again putting the young woman's life in danger. It was a serious accident. Élisabeth had to stay bedridden for two months without being able to move. Once again an attentive nurse, Félix surrounded her with his tenderness and care.

Once she was better, Élisabeth, a passionate woman, embarked on new studies.

September 20, 1899: I have begun studying philosophy, and it interests me greatly. This study clarifies many things and creates order in the mind. I do not understand why we do not make it the culmination of all female education. What a woman often lacks is right judgment, the habit of reasoning, the personal and sustained work of the mind. Philosophy could give her all of that, stripping her of so many of the prejudices and narrow ideas that she religiously passes on to her sons, to the great detriment of our country.[4]

Numerous philosophical works were in her library of which those of Father Gratry of the French Academy on *La Connaissance de Dieu* (Knowledge of God) and *La Connaissance de l'âme* (Knowledge of the soul) had a great influence on her.

In several of her writings, Élisabeth gave women a responsibility in society equal to that of men: for her time, she was a trailblazer. It pained her to see women of her generation not undertaking studies and often feeling relegated to a minor role in the marriage or in the family: "Woman, whose immense role and influence the French do not yet understand and that she herself does not always understand, must, from now on, once she is aware of her task, devote her life to it. . . . It is a duty never to stop developing her intelligence, to fortify her character, to become a being of thought and will; it is a duty to contemplate life joyfully and to face it with energy."[5]

In this spirit, she went to Charonne several times a week where a group of organizations, under the name of the Union Familiale, gathered children from underprivileged backgrounds on Thursdays and Sundays with the goal of providing them with an environment

---

[4] Élisabeth Leseur, *Journal et Pensées de chaque jour* (Paris: Éd. du Cerf, 2005), 81.

[5] Élisabeth Leseur, *La Vie Spirituelle: Petits traités de vie intérieure* (Paris: Éd. J. de Gigord, 1922), 185.

conducive to educational support. Élisabeth mainly took care of little girls to whom she taught reading and writing but also catechism; she prepared them for their First Communion and taught them the ABCs of housekeeping; she wanted to train them to become responsible women capable of having a role in their future household or in society.

In the same spirit, after having noticed that the female workers of Paris often had a dangerous and very hard life as a result of their isolation, she rented a big house in Vésinet with twelve rooms surrounded by a beautiful, verdant garden, and, with the help of an association of the law of 1901, she procured for them a calm and restful family life. For the first time this house took the name Foyer de la Jeune Fille (Young girl's home). Based on this model, many others would arise in France in the following years.

6

The Whirlwind of Great Travels

It is impossible to list all the trips that the Leseurs took during that time. When Élisabeth's health allowed it, they left for entire weeks in faraway countries. Félix's dreams had materialized a little differently from his original plans in colonial countries, but he remained just as eager to discover new landscapes, new civilizations. The railroad, which had just come into being, was at their disposal, a magnificent tool that henceforward eliminated distances and opened far-off frontiers.

Félix was now a figure in the political world. In 1896, as a member of the superior council of the colonies, he became an obligatory member of a committee supported by the government: the Mosque Project. This committee planned to build a mosque in Paris. Comprised of deputies, ministers, senators, it was headed by Jules Cambon, governor general of Algeria, and had as its vice presidents Monsieur Delcassé and Prince Roland Bonaparte, grandnephew of Napoleon. It was not just a matter of giving a place of worship to the Muslims living in Paris; the project was much more extensive and completely aligned with Félix's views: around this mosque, a university center would be created, a *madrasa*, where aspiring native public officials from Algeria, Tunisia, and the colonies in general would be able to familiarize themselves with French thought and to understand the national spirit. This imprint would promote a closer understanding between the Arab world of North Africa and metropolitan France.

While the council of ministers had very quickly approved the Mosque Project and had even donated a plot of land for it in the heart of Paris, it remained to find the necessary funds to carry out such a project.

Félix was approached. Everyone knew of his great enthusiasm

for the colonial cause and his unswerving integrity. He received as a mission—a mission of trust—to go to Tunisia and Algeria to solicit the financial support of the Bey of Tunis and other Algerian political figures. It was a professional trip that could turn into a pleasure trip.

Élisabeth accompanied him with enthusiasm. She never left her husband, and she was always eager to discover new horizons with him. For his part, he liked having her participate in his missions because he knew how much she understood and supported them. But to go to North Africa at the end of the century was no slight matter! It was a journey of several weeks over the course of which trains, boats, and excessive heat did not frighten this intrepid young couple.

Outside of work, this long journey would be like a sort of new "honeymoon" for them.

In shared wonderment, they traveled those wild and splendid regions under the direction of the resident general of Tunis and the governor general of Algeria. These two figures opened all the doors for them and had them discover those countries as tourists at a time when tourism virtually did not exist.

It was an enchantment, a discovery of the lands of *A Thousand and One Nights*, Félix would later say. All his life he had dreamed of going to the colonies, and at last he was there. And, moreover, in the springtime, in the most wonderful season when all the flowers were blooming in the vast grasslands and gave the country, before the arrival of the heavy heat, an air of freshness and festivity. Élisabeth was as enthusiastic as her husband. She wrote on April 6, 1896:

> At Carthage, in a carriage, with a superb view of the Gulf of Tunis throughout the whole journey. The weather is wonderful, and under the hot sun we contemplate the beds of poppies, yellow daisies, and brooms that carry out their joyful role in the countryside. There are many olive trees and, around the houses, cactus, which adds a grey note to the radiance of all these colors. We were received at Carthage by Father Delattre,[1] but first it is necessary to tell of the feeling ex-

---

[1] A White Father. [The White Fathers are a French missionary order that serves in Africa.]

perienced when, having climbed the hill that was Byrsa, we were in front of a panorama like the one we enjoyed today. Before us, always blue, the vast and tranquil gulf; behind us, a patch of glowing white, Tunis, always shining under the radiance of the sun that illuminates everything here. And, from distance to distance, other white points in the greenery; these are the Arab villages scattered around the gulf.[2]

Under Élisabeth's sensitive pen, the landscapes come alive.

Both of them considered how much the beauty of all these new images, discovered together over the course of their travels, little by little formed in them a bond of love, a kind of treasure for life in their relationship that nothing would be able to take away from them.

In this Tunisia where the Christians had left so many traces, Élisabeth felt no emotion in front of these high places that had seen the blood of martyrs. Her husband observed it and noted it with pride and satisfaction. Since the beginning of the journey, he had feared that the sight of these countries' Christian memories would lead her to reflect and to turn back to the faith, as this had been the case in Rome. But, to his satisfaction, the memory of Saint Augustine, even though she had once read him, the Christian necropolises in the town of Sidi Bou Said, the ramparts of Tunis under which Saint Louis died, the amphitheater of Thurbubo Majus where Saints Perpetua and Felicity were martyred for their faith, did not move her at all. She was too far now from the beliefs of her youth. And Félix would proudly note this evolution in her inner being:

Of Carthage, she sees only the picturesque side. Even when she re-calls the memory of Saint Louis and that of the martyrs of the am-phitheater, she does it in an almost anecdotal way. Saint Augustine, Saint Cyprian are, we would say, absent from her memory, and these places that played such a large role in the history of the Church in-spire no elevation in her. It is because her mind, under my continued pressure, was "enlightened" as I desired and transformed.[3]

He rejoiced in it, and his explanation was triumphant.

---

[2] R. P. Marie-Albert Leseur, *Vie d'Élisabeth Leseur* (Paris: Éd. J. de Gigord, 1931), 121.
[3] Ibid.

Cut off from family influence, Élisabeth thought only to immerse herself in these splendid landscapes and to share her admiration with the man she loved and with whom she had the joy of discovering these far-off lands.

If Élisabeth's life of faith was gradually fading away, on the other hand, her love and the joy of being together for so many discoveries excited her:

> Our trip has ended, and I bring back from it the most exquisite and unforgettable memory. This good life together, so free, so removed from the suffocating conventions of the big city, so disdainful of prejudices, this constant connection with great and good nature, this contact with a new art and a civilization different from our own, all this makes the trip a particularly good and healthy thing, as good for the body, which it develops and fortifies, as for the mind, which it renews, enlightens, and transforms.[4]

This first project of the construction of a mosque in the center of Paris momentarily failed. It would be taken up again a few years later, resulting in the building in 1926 of the current mosque in the fifth arrondissement.

In 1897, Félix, for professional reasons, had to travel again at length to new destinations. As the director of the Conservateur, he had to go to Berlin, then to Vienna, Budapest, and Bucharest. They would take the opportunity to stay with a correspondent in Moldavia, then they would return by Salzburg, Innsbruck, and Switzerland. A very beautiful trip in prospect.

Salzburg was not yet the tourist city of Mozart festivals, populated in the summer by music lovers. It was still a romantic town, a bit sleepy, surrounded by mountains and hills, on one of the final foothills of the Alps. But our travelers were not unaware that it was in this setting of magnificent landscapes that Mozart had conceived some of his most beautiful musical pages, and, in this respect, this trip was for them like a sort of pilgrimage into the world of the musician.

It was the month of July, also a splendid opportunity for Wagner enthusiasts to attend a few performances at the Bayreuth festival.

---

[4] Ibid., 122.

Once again, Élisabeth was enthusiastic; music, and Wagner's in particular, was experiencing considerable popularity at that time in France. Especially for the younger generation, it represented the discovery and access to a new and exciting mode of musical expression, thanks to the expansion of the orchestra and the use of pagan myths and legends. Ever since their engagement, Wagner's music had already deeply united their two souls, their two sensibilities.

In her diary, Élisabeth paints an idyllic picture of their arrival in Bayreuth, this major music venue, and of their shared emotion at seeing the theater designed by Wagner, a kind of jewelry case dreamed up by one designer for the jewel that was his work. It was a hall unique in the world, without boxes or a balcony, and some chairs arranged in the shape of a fan on a sloped floor. For this young couple, it was a splendid and exciting discovery, but it was also the fruit of a wait they had lived together since their engagement, a culmination that amazed them both.

At that time, when recorded music did not yet exist, the impact of facing a big Wagnerian orchestra, for which Cosima Wagner, the daughter of Liszt, engaged only high-quality artists, was enormous.

It is touching to measure how much both felt an intense emotion and thrilled in unison. It was a complete communion between them. Wagner's music captured their entire bodies. With the same happiness, they listened to the complete Tetralogy twice in a row. Anyone who knows the four monumental works that are *Das Rheingold*, *Die Walküre*, *Siegfried*, and *Götterdämmerung* can imagine what shared passion these eight long performances represented in the space of a few days lived in the greatest intellectual communion.

More in love than ever in the face of their understanding, Élisabeth noted: "For a few hours, we had lived in a dream from which it seemed difficult to extract ourselves. All that there is of the best in us had been stirred. Oh! The beautiful, the good sensations felt there."[5]

They also listened to *Parsifal* twice in a row. Élisabeth wrote:

Listening to *Parsifal* at four o'clock. The whole crowd goes up the long avenue that leads to the theater, either on foot or in a carriage,

---

[5] Ibid., 123.

and the general appearance is very cheerful. The performance of *Parsifal* has us spend a few hours in profound enjoyment. But these impressions are not to be analyzed. It seems to me that that would spoil them. I would simply say that, in this remarkable work, religious sentiment was expressed as I have never seen it expressed in any work, however great, and that we breathe in it a divine perfume of forgiveness, love, and purity that calms and stirs all at once. When, with means as "external", so to speak, and material as those at the disposal of music, one reaches the soul of the audience so deeply, we have truly achieved art in all its strength and beauty.[6]

Certainly, Félix did not expect his wife to find a "divine perfume" in Wagner's music. He did not understand at all, and he rejected this reflection inspired by a spiritual aspiration that he was not at all expecting. For several months, he had believed that the last vestiges of religion had been completely and forever eradicated from his wife's heart. But he was not overly disturbed by it. He noted that, after all, any disbeliever, and even he, could have written those insignificant lines. And he triumphantly added: "At that moment I was winning the miserable game that I had undertaken against her beliefs. The absence of contemplation, the worldliness, the readings I was making her do, the influence of the milieu in which I was making her live, had strongly weakened her faith; she stopped practicing, and her family, witnessing this private disaster, were sorry for it."[7]

He had achieved his goal; he had made her definitively abandon the faith that, for him, only represented the sentiments of women from another time, incompatible with a couple of their own intellectual value.

We can imagine that, having arrived at such a result, he must have had many feelings going through him: certainly arrogance, pride.

Could he, who was on the editorial team of *La République française*, the most anticlerical newspaper in France, founded by Gambetta, then as the director of the Conservateur, at the head of one of the most coveted offices in the capital, in an anticlerical Third Republic, and proud of being so, a friend of Combes, president of the

---

[6] Ibid.

[7] Ibid., 125.

council, at a time when evictions were chasing out priests and nuns, have openly supported having a wife whom neighbors and friends, a few months ago, regularly noticed in his neighborhood when she went to Mass?

He, who in his own life had long since chased away with rage and contempt all the religious sentiments of his childhood, he who, through reflection and readings, considered the faith as "the opium of the people", how could he still accept that the woman he loved and whose intellectual superiority he deeply admired could have believed, not so long ago, in all this nonsense?

A secret feeling of jealousy also weighed on him: his wife, so close to him on so many points, this young woman whom he had so tenderly cradled during her illnesses, whom he had trained in worldly life, in politics, in music, in life itself, could she still keep in her a secret garden from which he was excluded: her faith?

For him, that would be unbearable.

Furthermore, such intimacy existed in their relationship, such complicity on all subjects, that he could not imagine that the remainders of unshared beliefs could still exist in his wife's soul and, who knows, maybe resurface on a day when no one was expecting it. He well knew that more than one person had at one time seen a plant that he had believed to be long since dead grow back magnificently. That was his fear. Without seeming so, he was on the watch for the slightest signs.

Since faith had been passed on to Élisabeth by her family, and especially by her mother, it seemed to him essential to cut off his wife from her family roots, at least to keep her away from them for a long time; under the tempting appearance of long trips and a social life in which she obviously took great pleasure, he detected the dreamed-of means to disassociate her from the family cocoon! This long, silent, but insidious combat was not in vain: certain of coming out victorious one day, his strategies for winning it seemed justified to him.

Since, as a first step, he had managed to turn his wife away from religious practices, he still had to attack and demolish the very foundations of her beliefs in case they had survived at the bottom of her soul.

The second step would then be to demolish these fundamental

foundations of Élisabeth's life permanently, to show her how intelligent men had been able to shatter Christianity and illuminate
their reason in light of rationalist doctrines. And how, with a little
common sense and reflection, they had been led to deny everything
and to make themselves proud apologists of their denial.

He waited for an opportunity. It arrived spontaneously: one day,
Élisabeth confided to Félix that she had nothing really interesting
to read and asked his advice.

Élisabeth's library was well-enough stocked for us to imagine that
this request was, for her, rather loving attention, a gesture of the
heart.

She suggested he choose for her from his shelves a book from
among those he especially liked. Out of kindness? For the sake of
both sharing a reading in common? Out of a desire to enter more
deeply into his intellectual world? To get a better understanding of
his philosophy?

For Félix, here at last was the opportunity! He did not hesitate
long before suggesting books to her that were being talked about so
much around them at that time and were so strongly shocking the
Christian world. He first handed her a work by Renan, a popular
author at the end of the century, who had led so many, even convinced, Christians to lose their faith. He was convinced that, better
than all the others, these readings would contribute to turning her
away from religion once and for all.

Élisabeth carefully read the many volumes of *The Origins of Christianity*. Sensitive to the perfection of style, she also devoured *The
Life of Jesus*, surprised to see that events she had known well since
her childhood seemed distorted or presented differently by an iron-
ical and mocking spirit in which she no longer recognized the true
message of the Gospel. At times, the author's bad faith was so obvious that she was hurt or indignant about it. She did not say anything
about it to Félix.

Renan, who had for many years gone rather far in his studies as a
seminarian, was not completely atheist. In the line of Voltaire and
authors of the Age of Enlightenment, he did not completely deny
God, the architect of the universe, but he angrily attacked the figure
of Jesus, whom he considered to be an arrogant person, "The Son
of God, no less!", or as an impostor; he had created a religion only

fit for the dull-witted, the whiners, and the poor in order to be the instigator and leader of it.

> To whom should we turn, to whom should we trust to establish the Kingdom of God? The mind of Jesus on this point never hesitated. That which is highly esteemed among men, is abomination in the sight of God. The founders of the Kingdom of God are the simple. Not the rich, not the learned, not priests; but women, common people, the humble, and the young. The great characteristic of the Messiah is, that "the poor have the gospel preached to them." The idyllic and gentle nature of Jesus here resumed the superiority. A great social revolution, in which rank will be overturned, in which all authority in this world will be humiliated, was his dream. The world will not believe him; the world will kill him. But his disciples will not be of the world. They will be a little flock of the humble and the simple, who will conquer by their very humility. The idea which has made "Christian" the antithesis of "worldly", has its full justification in the thoughts of the master.[8]

All of Renan's long *The Life of Jesus* is built on such claims. Renan demolishes everything. He is a Voltairian.

Little by little, she understood that the rationalism of Renan consisted in demonstrating that since the time when the crowds followed Jesus, human knowledge had progressed a great deal thanks to the evolution of the sciences: every educated mind must be able to reject the ancestral beliefs intended to give a little morality, happiness, and hope to the ignorant people of our ancestors.

The positivist philosophy at the end of the nineteenth century had little by little invaded the intellectual circles that, following the still very popular Auguste Comte, thought that an evolved human being could not be anything but a positivist. Only the backward or the dull-witted had not yet passed through the two previous phases: the theological phase and metaphysical phase.

Félix, like many of his friends and many intellectuals of his generation, shared this point of view; for him, to have seen Élisabeth so anchored to the faith had for years been more than a suffering: it had been a humiliation. To rid her of her "prejudices" had more

---

[8] Ernest Renan, *The Life of Jesus* (London: Trübner, 1864), 113.

than ever become his objective. In his mind, Renan would take care of bringing this about.

As a matter of fact, Renan did make her think and even think a lot. But not in the way her husband had wanted. She understood the former seminarian's argumentation well; she analyzed it intelligently by trying to grasp the core of his thought, studying the false documents on which he often relied. As she advanced in this long study, she discovered the weakness of his arguments and reflected on a way to refute them, just for herself, for her own beliefs.

She certainly needed a lot of courage to undertake such a task:

—Courage in relation to herself: with the faith no longer having been her concern for some years, she had discovered a new life-style and secular readings that she had enjoyed. She was not unaware that this task would lead her to turn a significant page in her personal life and especially in her marital relationship.

—Then emotional courage vis-à-vis her husband; she knew that he was proud of having undermined the Christian beliefs of her childhood and that he became loud about it in the atheist and anti-clerical world they frequented. She loved him as he was, as he had formed her, as he admired her. She was not unaware that this task would go completely against his opinions and that she was headed for interior suffering.

—Lastly, intellectual courage, because to tackle a work as monumental as Renan's point by point—and many others thereafter—represented a long-term intellectual investment. But nothing would discourage her now.

To undertake this task intellectually, she read. From special libraries she borrowed books that could help her construct solid arguments. She acquired and immersed herself in works like that of Canon Alfred Weber on the Gospels, and that of Robert Hugh Benson: *Christ in the Church*. She read numerous conversion testimonies or stories about crises of faith; she thus arrived at the argumentation for a complete internal and profound reconstruction. She steeped herself very much in the works by Father Gratry, a skilled destroyer of positivism. This priest was also a famous writer who had been elected to the Académie française, where he occupied the chair that had been Voltaire's. The speech he had delivered, supposedly to praise his predecessor, had quickly drifted to the anticlericalism of

Voltaire, which earned him violent criticism from the positivists among his immortal colleagues of the famous academy.

She wrote: "Read with interest *Les Sources* by Father Gratry, and now another volume of his in which I very often encounter my thoughts. They emerge thus, from the depths of myself up to the surface, then return to the depths from which they must then, transformed by God, spring forth into living actions and words."[9]

With the help of these works, Élisabeth examined Renan's arguments point by point. She understood their bias. Not only was she not convinced, but, as Félix would write much later:

> With her independent and very balanced intelligence, her sound judgment, her extreme common sense, and her strong knowledge, she was not deceived by the magic of words, but, on the contrary, was struck by the poverty at their core. She quickly perceived the perpetual wavering, the fragility of contestable and often contradictory hypotheses, the artificial character and the lack of sincerity that she encountered at every bend in this work. She wanted to inspect the sophist's arguments; she referred to the sources; she returned first and foremost to the Gospel, and that was the end of my criminal project.[10]

Words always seem inadequate for explaining the progress of souls and even more so for explaining the progress of faith. But what is certain, however, is that through the demonstrations, reasonings, and explanations of Renan's theories, she felt herself called by her name, just like Mary Magdalen in the Gospel, confused by the death of Jesus, and she recognized him. She would never leave him again.

Félix had never expected this reaction. At first furious, he was quickly disconcerted by his wife's spiritual progress, which, at first, he had only sensed because she did not speak to him about it. He asked her very pointed questions from time to time to see where she stood; he commented on her answers in his own way and reassured himself by noting that no trouble seemed to be disturbing her inner peace.

---

[9] Élisabeth Leseur, *Journal et Pensées de chaque jour* (Paris: Éd. du Cerf, 2005), 90.
[10] M. A. Leseur, *Vie d'Élisabeth Leseur*, 125.

Indeed, not wanting to destroy the harmony of her marriage, she kept quiet about the rise of her spiritual aspirations, which she wrote down, for herself alone, in a notebook:

> For several days, I had a desire for retirement, for calm, an ardent desire to go very close to nature, like the gentle Saint Francis, in the midst of flowers and birds, and to pray, work, meditate in solitude there, or at least (because Félix is always in my solitude) with a few friendly hearts who would leave me to myself and God from time to time. My God, will you one day give me this joy of solitude together, united in the same prayer, the same faith, and the same love? For now, let's chase away these thoughts. God wants something else of me, and when I want to meditate, my solitude is entirely internal.[11]

Little by little, her inner transformation did not completely escape her husband, who redoubled his criticisms with regard to Christianity; he sometimes liked to mock publicly what was most precious to her; he sarcastically nicknamed her "Madame Péchin", from the name of a character in a novel by Anatole France who had the naïveté to believe in eternal life; he invited nonbelieving and anticlerical friends to his home and insidiously initiated conversations about religion, on subjects that would make Élisabeth suffer the most; he chose Friday for his invitations in order to oblige his wife to offer sumptuous meals and, most importantly, to serve meat on the day when Christians abstained from feasting in remembrance of the death of Jesus. He knew that this would be a suffering for Élisabeth, but nothing else would make him triumph more. He scoffed at her charitable works by speaking to her about them with the greatest contempt.

Élisabeth bore everything without saying a word out of love for her husband, whom she loved and who loved her. She had long understood that it would be useless to argue or to rebel. That would only create endless disputes. She offered all her humiliations and her suffering to the Lord so that one day her husband might return to him. Out of loyalty and love for Félix, she continued to accompany him on all his outings, even to shows from which she would have preferred to abstain.

---

[11] É. Leseur, *Journal et Pensées de chaque jour*, 92.

At that time, she immersed herself in the encyclical *Rerum Novarum*, published by Leo XIII in 1891. This doctrine had especially interested her because the pope, in his time, as if he had foreseen the events that would happen in France, had denounced the dangers of the atheism advocated by the socialists, that atheism from which she suffered so much. He had given the full meaning to "man", to the human character, by addressing particularly the fate of workers often scorned and exploited; class warfare could only cause hatred and despair, injustice and exploitation. The economy must be at the service of men, not men at the service of the economy.

With Félix, she could talk about this concept of the human person because it was a language that he understood, their only middle ground under a Christian light that he dismissed.

In 1899, they could at last carry out a plan that had been dear to them for a long time: to visit Russia. Élisabeth now spoke Russian fluently. The prospect of being able to talk directly with the Russians rewarded her for her efforts at the same time that it filled her with pride vis-à-vis her husband, who had not yet heard her use the language of the tsars.

It required a lot of courage, patience, and energy in 1899 to take the train to Paris and then on to Russia. No other mode of transport was then possible. Élisabeth and Félix, passionate about the prodigious extension of the French rail system at the end of the nineteenth century, which had seen the triumph of the railway, had been users of it who could be counted among the most enthusiastic pioneers.

The Paris/Saint Petersburg line, inaugurated in 1896, filled France with pride. The Orient Express, that luxurious train, which claimed to be fast, took fifty-two hours to reach Saint Petersburg after having crossed all of central Europe. The train was not long: only an engine, four sleeper cars, a dining car, and a luggage car. It provided passengers with, if not great comfort as we understand it today, at least external luxury because the spaces intended for passengers were decorated with wall paintings in the latest style. The dining car, where waiters dressed in the Parisian style were busy with menus worthy of the great tables of the capital, enabled meetings and conversations with those passionate about discovering Russia.

As soon as they arrived, Élisabeth and Félix visited Saint Petersburg. They walked along the Neva, discovered the Hermitage Museum in shared wonderment. Both great enthusiasts of painting and fine connoisseurs, they knew how to appreciate some of the most beautiful paintings in the world, collected by Catherine the Great. Both knew that the French writers of the Enlightenment had been guests within those walls. Élisabeth knew by heart in Russian Pushkin's poem dedicated to Peter I, whose equestrian statue *The Bronze Horseman*, in front of the church of Saint-Isaac, captivated them. The capital of Peter the Great amazed them. Without fatigue, they visited the Winter Palace and the blue and white Smolensk monastery. They proudly strode down the Nevsky Prospekt among the elegant Russians.

But the heat and the tours on foot of this relatively vast city tired them. They needed rest and calm in more verdant places since nothing was pressing them to return to Paris.

The proximity of Finland invited them to take a boat and to go spend several days in the country of sixty thousand lakes, in the freshness and the greenery, in order to find relaxation and to discover some magnificent landscapes.

Back in Russia, they still had to visit Moscow, which disappointed them deeply. The city was not at all comparable to the prestigious capital of Peter the Great. It was an oppressive, dilapidated metropolis with an enormous population that was poor, sometimes starving, ignorant, and badly dressed. While a few onion-domed churches gleamed with all their gold, it sufficed to walk a few steps in the alleys to discover hovels in ruins and a climate of poverty, indeed, of misery, that distressed them.

They felt oppressed there. The atmosphere of political constraint created by the diffusion of Marxist and revolutionary ideas, already widespread, did not directly affect them, but their intuition clearly exposed it to them. They decided to shorten their stay.

They regarded the outward manifestations of popular devotion, still well rooted in the people, with a certain disdain. Many quickly made gestures did not seem to express anything from the depths of the soul; these meaningless rites, instead, seemed rather to daze an ignorant population. They were scandalized. Félix, however, was not unhappy to be able to observe and comment at length on the wrongdoings of religion on uneducated populations!

Very disappointed by Moscow, Élisabeth wrote to her mother:

In Russia, I could only write you quick notes, our time was busy. And then, what to recount in a country where everything is watched, spied on. We have left Russia without regrets. We were beginning to suffocate; my God, how good it is to belong to a free people! We cannot imagine a great nation without the press, without liberty, without intellectual life; in the long run, that becomes detestable. I made a collection of notes on Russia, both from what we were told and from what we saw. This unfortunate people, kept in a stupor by alcohol and religion, are truly to be pitied. . . . When we disembarked at Constantinople, we had the impression of arriving in a country of superior civilization and great freedom. . . . Our stay in Constantinople, the excursions in its surrounding areas, on the Bosporus, on the Prince Islands, the days spent in Byrsa, that marvel, in that remarkable countryside of the Olympus of Bithynia, was for us an enchantment that lasted the entire return journey by Smyrna, Athens and Greece, Patras, Corfu, Brindisi, and Venice, where we stayed a week with our dear friends, the Bomparts, the well-known orientalist and Venetian painter, his wife, and his daughter, before returning to Paris.[12]

During this trip, Élisabeth recorded her impressions every day, without communicating them to Félix. When, after her death, he would discover her thoughts in front of the Athenian Acropolis, he would be amazed to see to what extent she had completed, unbeknownst to him, a spiritual path that he believed he had completely destroyed. She had written:

The pure beauty of forms, a fragment of immortal Beauty, has been achieved there; human thought was expressed there in monuments and remarkable works. It is a page of humanity that will never be erased. And yet, all of that: the beauty of forms, the power of ideas, the splendor of art and philosophy, all of that has disappeared in the face of a beauty so sovereign, a Splendor so unique, an Idea so fully true, that humanity no longer recognized them and that the victor was the Unknown God that a little, poor Jew would one day reveal to the wise and the humble, to the Greeks and to all the Gentiles.[13]

---

[12] M. A. Leseur, *Vie d'Élisabeth Leseur*, 142.
[13] Ibid., 147.

As soon as they returned to Paris, their worldly life continued. Because of their position in high society, they received invitations for many events or parties. The stories of their stay in Russia fascinated those around them. They admired this young couple, so pioneering, so intellectual and so united, able to travel to distant countries and bring back from there remarkable memories and strong images that everyone awaited.

The Leseurs organized social gatherings in their home during which Élisabeth, always very beautiful and elegant, was a credit to her husband through the intelligence of her conversation and her knowledge enriched by reading and travel. Her kindness, her amiability, her attentiveness won over all her guests. Her husband was proud of it. No doubt she was applying her knowledge of good housekeeping that her education as a well-bred young girl had instilled in her, but Élisabeth's motives were much deeper.

In reality, her friendliness and her attentiveness to each person went much farther. They were not solely the result of social manners. The reason for them was mainly rooted in the very great respect Élisabeth had for the person. Since Emmanuel Mounier, our contemporaries would say that she had a "personalist approach" to human relationships, which is, moreover, simply an often silent look of love on the heart of the person whom one is facing, a "Christian approach" to every human being, whoever it might be.

She always tried, out of respect for the person, to help her visitors "to be", whatever their opinions, and she did it from deepest part of her soul and her intellect.

All the love that she carried within her radiated in her welcome of the other. That is why the atheism or nonbelief of her friends was not an obstacle for her. She spoke to them about what seemed to her to be important in their lives and was then content to pray for them, which her husband did not know.

So, how surprised he would be when he later read in Élisabeth's diary:

Talked and discussed a great deal with dear friends who do not believe. I love better than others these persons whom the divine light does not enlighten, or, rather, whom it enlightens in a way we do not know, poor little minds that we are. There is a veil between such souls and God, a veil that allows only a few rays of love and beauty to pass through it. God alone, with his divine movement, can lift this veil; then real life will begin for these souls. And I, even though I am worth so little, I believe in the power of the prayers that I constantly say for these dear souls.[14]

[14] É. Leseur, *Journal et Pensées de chaque jour*, 88.

7

A Parisian Couple of the Twentieth Century

1900 was the big year of the World's Fair. Many times, the Leseurs, now important people in the Paris elite, showed the exposition not only to the politicians from every continent invited by the director of the Conservateur, but also to their families and friends who came from all over France; tours were followed by receptions or dinners.

The World's Fair of 1900 was a significant event in the life of Parisians because it disrupted the capital's entire layout, not least through the creation of the first metro line, between Vincennes and Porte Maillot, new train stations like the Orsay station or the Austerlitz station, and new pedestrian routes, like the Place de Alma or the Boulevard Latour-Maubourg. Paris was completely transformed. Hitherto, the narrow streets had been overcrowded with cumbersome Berlin carriages pulled by exhausted horses. Now it seemed to them that Paris, with its wide avenues and underground subways, breathed. The first automobiles made their appearance around the same time as the streetcars. The big transformations initiated by Haussmann had modernized entire neighborhoods; comfort came into the houses with the replacement of the blue glow of gas lamps with electricity, as well as with space and light.

The Leseurs were tireless in this new Paris of which they were proud. Their life was a whirlwind, but a happy whirlwind that fulfilled them both.

In April 1900, they undertook a new great journey that would lead them to Tangiers by way of Spain. The Paris/Madrid line had existed for some years, but, for political and financial reasons, it was still broken up and required changes for passengers. They stopped in every city: in Madrid, where they visited the Prado, in Seville, where they attended the Fair, in Granada, where "the Alhambra enchanted me", Élisabeth wrote, in Cordoba, where they saw the mosque, in Toledo and throughout southern Andalusia to Gibraltar, where they crossed the Mediterranean to go to Tangiers, which delighted them.

When Félix was on the editorial board of *La République française*, he had met Henri de la Martinière, then the cabinet director of the governor general of Algeria.

In that year 1900, Henri de la Martinière was now first secretary of the French legation in Tangiers. He gave them a warm welcome and took them on an excursion to the extreme Moroccan south where very few Europeans had been able to enter until then. Henri de la Martinière knew Arabic perfectly as well as the most splendid sites of the country near the vast desert with sumptuously starry nights.

Thanks to their friend, they could venture into the Atlas Mountains, in the Jbel Saghro, and into magnificent remote regions. They were dazzled by the beauty of the landscapes. Félix wrote: "We left in a caravan with the leader of the soldiers of the legation and some Cherifian soldiers of the pasha of Tangiers, everyone on horseback, except for Élisabeth, who was mounted on a mule."[1]

Who could have thought, during this journey, of Élisabeth's inner journey perched on her mule? When she returned, she wrote in her diary:

> After a five-week trip in Spain, I resume my normal life: but I resume it, I believe, in different conditions. During this trip, I thought and prayed a lot, and I saw clearly into myself and into my life. This life, I consecrated it to God; I gave myself to him in an impulse of my whole being; I ardently prayed for those I love, for the one whom I love above all. . . . Around me are many souls whom I deeply love, and I have a great task to fulfill with them. Many do not know God, or know him poorly. It is neither in polemicizing nor in discoursing that I will make them know what He is for the human soul. Through the serenity and the strength that I want to acquire, I will prove that the Christian life is beautiful and great and that it brings joy with it.[2]

The key to Élisabeth's behavior toward her husband is in these few lines. With him, she never sought to argue, which would have

---

[1] R. P. Marie-Albert Leseur, *Vie d'Élisabeth Leseur* (Paris: Éd. J. de Gigord, 1931), 149.

[2] Élisabeth Leseur, *Journal et Pensées de chaque jour* (Paris: Éd. du Cerf, 2005), 85.

led to useless and fruitless discussions, even quarrels; on the other hand, through her love and her way of expressing it, through her joie de vivre, through her wonder at the beauties of nature, the joys of friendship and travel, she brought him a human witness that he appreciated at the time but that he would not understand until much later. She would note in her diary her most reliable weapons for evangelization, as John Paul II would say much later when he introduced the lines of the "new evangelization":

> To go more and more to souls and to approach them with respect and gentleness, to touch them with love. To seek always to "understand" everything and everyone. Not to discuss, to act, above all, through contact, through example; to dispel prejudices, to show God and to make Him felt without speaking of Him; to strengthen his understanding, to enlarge his soul more and more; to love without tiring despite disappointments and indifference.[3]

While waiting, always very loving and admiring of Félix, she wrote to her mother: "A few good days of joy, caused by a gift from Félix, and even more by the note that accompanied it, a note so full of love that I am moved and happy about it. I do not deserve to be so loved, but I fully enjoy it."

It is easy to see that in their life, at that time, everything externally distanced them from God. Despite this passing of several years, which she would later see as a tunnel, the source of living water in the depth of Élisabeth's heart had not completely run dry, and no doubt God never tired of knocking at her door. Despite her admiration for her husband's ideas, she reflected a great deal, read the authors who could help her, then, with intelligence and an awareness of reality, in silence and meditation she found an inner solution.

After having long absorbed Saint Francis de Sales' *An Introduction to the Devout Life*, she was convinced that a "devout" life was perfectly compatible with the life of a man and woman in marriage.

Little by little she understood that she had everything she needed. She had to build her married life with what she had and not with what she dreamed of having. It was not in a life cut off from her

---

[3] Ibid., 109.

husband and far from his concerns that she needed to live her relationship with the Lord. Nor was it in trying relentlessly to "convert" him, which would quickly cut him off from her. She therefore decided to live her marriage fully as the wife of Félix as he was, with his qualities, his faults, his atheism, his refusals and his rejections, his mockeries, but also with all the love that he showed her every day.

Common sense and love revealed to her that it would be pointless and dangerous for their relationship to wish it otherwise or constantly to deplore what it was. Through thick and thin, she was fully aware that she held the happiness of them both in her hands, that she had the responsibility to make their love grow in new ways every day, adapted to their life.

The shared daily life did not fail to furnish her with opportunities for renewal. She would not make big speeches; she would content herself with witnessing to the fruits that she could bear insofar as she was able: "Through the serenity and the strength that I want to acquire, I will prove that the Christian life is beautiful and great and that it brings joy with it. By cultivating in myself all the superior faculties of the mind, I will proclaim that God is the Supreme Intelligence and that those who serve him can draw endlessly from this blessed source of intellectual and moral light. To give, it is necessary to acquire."[4]

They had received the sacrament of marriage together, even if he had never understood either its grandeur or its worth. But on that day, he had given her his life forever, he had gambled on her love, he had given her the best of himself with absolute confidence in their shared future; therefore, she did not want to betray him or even disappoint him. The love and happiness they shared must therefore be enough for her. They were gifts from God, talents that must be made to bear fruit and not buried.

It was with the help of this sacrament, of which she alone measured the significance, that she had to make the union in her marital relationship grow by managing one day at a time, in the sunlight of love, the events that presented themselves.

---

[4] Ibid., 86.

This way of understanding her marriage was a new idea for her time.

In July 1900, a new long journey had them undertake the descent of the Rhine from Mainz to Cologne and an excursion from Koblenz to Luxembourg; they stayed a week with their friends the Hennequins in their very lovely villa on the banks of the Meuse.

They then traveled to Metz, a German city since the war of 1870. Élisabeth experienced a painful feeling. It seemed obvious to her that it was still a French city by the spirit of its population, by the language of its inhabitants, their way of life, the buildings, and yet it was a town of German barracks traversed by soldiers dressed in foreign uniforms and who spoke German.

With great emotion, the Leseurs visited the battlefields of the war of 1870, planted with white crosses. Élisabeth, whose patriotism had been revitalized, wrote:

> During this whole trip to Germany, one thought never left me: that we are still a great people from a moral and intellectual point of view, the "great people, and it is up to us to remain so always". . . . My duty as a French woman will always be for me as sacred as my duty as a Christian woman, or rather, the one includes and implies the other. Only, I hope that both of them will always be understood by me in the broadest and greatest sense.[5]

---

[5] Ibid.

8

Sorrows and Joys

Élisabeth and Félix shared a deep sorrow in the bottom of their hearts that time did not ease; they would never have children.

It was a lack, a profound regret, a cruel absence in their lives. The ordeal of sterility is always heavy for a couple to bear, especially when they see their families around them fulfilled by the arrival of new births.

Consequently, the Leseurs were especially attached to their nephews, whom they often invited. Of course, they were not the children of their bodies, but Élisabeth beautifully said that they were "the children of their hearts", and both of them loved them as such, watched them grow, shared in their games and their progress, thought of them as their own children; Élisabeth helped them in their studies, had them recite their lessons, took them for walks around Paris, and both of them surrounded them with much attention and affection.

They were very attached to little Roger, a boy of seven, affectionate and funny, the son of Élisabeth's brother.

In March 1901, this child suddenly fell ill. As soon as she learned of his condition, which became hopeless in a few days, Élisabeth never left his bedside. Very experienced, she cared for him with all her love and watched over him, surrounding his heartbroken and tearful parents with her affection.

On Wednesday, March 13, 1901, after only a few days of illness, Roger died in the company of all his distraught loved ones. Élisabeth, deeply shaken by the death of this little boy, managed to bear this grief with faith and simplicity in the Father's love: "It was the peaceful departure for the Hereafter, and the veil that separates the two worlds is very light. Dear little one who is in Light and in Love, pray for us."[1]

---

[1] Élisabeth Leseur, *Journal et Pensées de chaque jour* (Paris: Éd. du Cerf, 2005), 92.

The three months that followed, however, were a difficult trial for the whole family. Félix understood it so well that, to take his young wife's mind off things, he suggested to her a three-week stay in July in Savoy, near Lake Aiguebelette, with their married friends, the Hennequins, whom Élisabeth liked so much.

Maurice and Aimée Hennequin were both essentially agnostic and proud to be so. Their very warm friendship allowed Félix to guess that Élisabeth would be happy and at ease in their home. It was his primary objective.

But that was not his only design; he had a much more insidious scheme in mind: he confidently counted precisely on their friendly hospitality to divert Élisabeth from her pious thoughts and to pull out from her heart the last roots of the faith. Both of them were intellectuals whose conversation would surely fascinate Élisabeth and attract her to them. He was counting on a few insidious comments or a few well-placed mockeries of religion that would leave Élisabeth speechless. They would certainly not be lacking over the course of this visit. It would be a good thing for him.

Contrary to Félix's hopes, no controversial topic, no mockery of the faith came to disturb the joy of friendship and reunion. The smiles of the two young women only strengthened the friendship of the two couples, who would have many opportunities to vacation or travel together in the following years.

Élisabeth was enchanted by that alpine region all resplendent in colors and light under the July sun. The fields of wheat were not yet harvested; in the setting sun, the mountain took on soft hues; the old Romanesque bell towers stood out against the greenery and rang the Angelus. In the distance, they heard the bells of cows in the pastures. In so calming and rustic a setting, Élisabeth revived and rediscovered her strength so well that, as soon as they returned to Paris, Félix, ever desirous to exhilarate her as much as possible, again offered her another trip to Belgium and Holland.

After a reunion with the Hennequins, this time on the banks of the Meuse, a little trip to Belgium would have them visit Bruges, where the charm of the canals and old bridges filled Élisabeth with awe. Even though the beguinage was shrouded by a slight religious but long outdated hue, both of them visited it at length with interest from a historical perspective. They then continued to Holland, its canals, its windmills, its polders.

In Haarlem, Élisabeth struggled to keep up with her husband's pace. At The Hague, she was exhausted, and in Amsterdam, where they had arranged to visit the brand-new Rijksmuseum, her liver disease worsened and prevented her from standing. There was only one solution: to return to Paris as quickly as possible to be treated by Doctor Duron, her brother-in-law, who had monitored her health for years.

Félix was very worried. Since the first attack that had so darkened their "honeymoon", he had known that this illness would eventually reemerge one day. As always, he cared for his wife with great love, solicitude, and also anxiety.

At the end of a few weeks, Élisabeth felt the first effects of an improvement. She had only one thought: to start living normally again and to resume the life of a dynamic young wife.

Courageously, she wrote: "Now life is going to resume. This winter, I want to work a lot on Latin, to take care of some useful but very obscure work, to live from day to day doing my job at every hour. It is the best way, I believe, of doing good."[2]

Her husband's atheism, no doubt less displayed in the face of ill-ness never ceased to haunt her, however: "I have before me a great task and nothing, humanly, to help me to fulfill it. Perhaps one day I will have that great joy of seeing my faith, which is my whole life, understood and shared by those, by the one, whom I love so much. All that this represents of suffering, I offer for the souls who are so dear to me. Nothing is lost, not a pain, not a tear."[3]

In 1902, the house that they had built at Jougne was at last fin-ished. For them, it was an accomplishment and a great happiness. The thick walls of this mountain dwelling would provide them with a stability to which they both aspired. During that time, Élisabeth's illness left her long periods of respite. The setting up and moving in to Jougne were energizing activities, the bearers of projects and joys. They devoted themselves to it with enthusiasm. From then on, they would spend all their summers there surrounded by their families. Now that they at last had a house in the countryside where they could rest and have room to welcome their circle of friends,

---

[2] Ibid., 93.
[3] Ibid., 98.

their married life was necessarily going to take a completely different course.

Élisabeth was so fond of Jougne, a village near the distant blue of the Jura, with its pine forests, its old houses of stone grouped around the church, that she no longer lamented the time of great travels abroad. On July 18, 1902, a few days after moving in, she wrote to her friend Madame Duvent:

> It is absolute calm, and I am writing to you facing our beautiful valley, our pine forests, this whole wonderful view that we have from the terrace and the house. . . . I am becoming a gardener, pulling out weeds, removing stones, and trying to give our garden a less dry appearance than the one it currently has. . . . What gives me profound joy is to have around me all our family, and especially the children, whom I make to work, talk to, play with, and with whom I spend delightful moments.[4]

For many years, the Leseurs' numerous friends would come to stay at Jougne in that very warm and very welcoming house. The love that the mistress of the house put into all her relationships with others was so apparent that the name chosen by Félix: _Élisabeth's Enclosure_, was posted over the entrance gate. Later, Félix would understand that a tree is judged by its fruits and that all these fruits of love were due only to the presence of God in the silence of his wife's heart.

When in Paris Félix came home in the evenings, exhausted by the pace of his professional life, it would be enough for Élisabeth to say to him with her magnificent smile: "Félix, think of Jougne", for him to feel reassured. For both of them, that house would remain an element of calm, of peace, and of stability.

At the beginning of the summer of 1902, Félix had to go to Austria for some ten days to resolve a serious professional matter. At that time, Vienna attracted so many young intellectuals captivated by its beauty and its past that it was a trip the Leseurs would make several times thereafter with undisguised joy.

Vienna, at the beginning of the twentieth century, was the European capital of mind and intelligence. This city of magnificent architecture—the cradle of the Hapsburgs—was then experiencing

---

[4] R. P. Marie-Albert Leseur, _Vie d'Élisabeth Leseur_ (Paris: Éd. J. de Gigord, 1931), 153.

a tremendous passion for literature, theater, and music. It was the point of convergence for all of intellectual Europe. In the literary cafes, they could read all the French newspapers right at their fingertips.

The Leseurs liked to go to the Burgtheater, which gave sumptuous performances. In this capital of music, which had witnessed Mozart's beginnings and had welcomed Haydn, Gluck, Schubert, Chopin, and Beethoven, they had the feeling of fully living their shared passions for the most beautiful musical works, especially the Romantic. Fascinated by this intellectual whirl, whenever they could, they attended the concerts of the Imperial Theater, directed by Gustav Mahler, the renowned conductor.

A few weeks later, Félix's professional obligations led him to return once more to Vienna. Élisabeth, whose health was getting better, very much wanted to accompany her husband once more. She did not have to beg, since he did not like to be separated from his wife, and, to tell the truth, he had never traveled without her.

A little reluctantly, because of the heat that year, they had to leave Jougne in the middle of summer while the house was full of family and guests. Élisabeth's mother would take over the role of mistress of the house.

Juliette, Élisabeth's young sister, a girl full of joy and laughter, accompanied them. She had not yet been to Vienna. While Félix was detained by his professional occupations, Élisabeth would show Vienna to her little sister. They would walk slowly under the trees of the Prater, sample Austrian wines on the terraces of shaded cafes. When Élisabeth felt too tired to visit the vast Schönbrunn Palace, it was Félix who would guide his young sister-in-law to admire the beauties and works of art of the prestigious Hapsburg residence. So, while Élisabeth rested under the shade of the park, Félix would take Juliette up to the Gloriette, at the summit of the hill, to show her the superb view of Vienna streaming with sun and light.

Unfortunately, upon returning to Jougne ten days later, bad news awaited them: an elderly cousin of Élisabeth's, who had stayed in their house for the summer, had suddenly died at their home on the eve of their arrival, overcome by an angina attack. The body had been moved to the great hall of the town hall, where the local people, while waiting for the Leseurs' return to fix the date of the funeral, had organized a veritable chapel of repose; every evening they gathered to pray around the deceased, a vigil in which the whole village participated.

As soon as they arrived, Félix and Élisabeth joined them. Naturally, Félix, without saying a word, attended the prayers and the funeral ceremony in the church of Jougne beside his wife.

Élisabeth, very shaken by all these events, confided her fatigue to her diary. She certainly did not mention it to her husband:

> In returning to Paris, I experienced such a feeling of emptiness, of sadness, and of inner suffering that prayer and divine strength alone could help me to transform it into joy for others and into strength for myself. And, at the same time, I never stopped for a moment feeling within myself, very much alive, the presence and action of God. When I look back and I see the remarkable work accomplished by God within me, this genuine creation of a soul, that He alone could do, I sense what duties this grace that He gave to me creates for me, and I hope, yes, I hope from the bottom of my heart, that, one day soon, He will give the same grace to the dear soul who is close to mine and whom I so deeply love.[5]

She believed profoundly in the power of God in her, a power capable of transforming all the physical and moral sufferings that she felt into joy to give to others; joy that she would give first to her husband, with whom she so intimately shared so many things.

When speaking of him, she was sincere when she said: "A soul close to mine and whom I love so deeply."

Except for faith, he shared everything she experienced. Alas, this peace, this joy, this love of Élisabeth's that were rooted in God fell back on him without him realizing it. It was an action that could be compared to a bountiful dew on a garden that gives life in a hidden way to plants but that remains so discreet that we do not notice it. He found it so natural that his wife was radiant like this!

Without him knowing it, the happiness that Élisabeth brought him every day was for him "the salt of the earth" that, very gently, in silence, gave a good taste to the things of his life.

How could he not be in love with a wife who was so attentive and comforting to him?

---

[5] É. Leseur, *Journal et Pensées de chaque jour,* 99.

9

The Surprises of the Lord's Ways

In February 1903, a young manager of the Conservateur came to knock on the door of Félix's office. He told him at once that he wanted to speak to him about a personal matter.

And without a preamble, he announced to Félix that he intended to be baptized soon. We can easily imagine the surprise of the director, who prided himself on being counted among the most anticlerical figures in France. He was completely surprised and even shocked by this type of confidence from the mouth of one of his colleagues, who probably knew him very little.

Briefly, this young man traced his path for him: he had met a Dominican, Father Hébert, to whom he had confessed his complete ignorance of the Christian faith. From conversations to discussions, Father Hébert had taught him the Gospels and had given him reasons to believe along with a meaning to his life. The Christian faith was now his joy and his support. He ardently desired to receive Baptism.

Félix, taken aback and undoubtedly annoyed, at first gave him a rather contemptuous response:

—You want to be baptized? What a crazy idea! Why are you coming to speak to me about it?

And faced with his interlocutor's silence, shrugging his shoulders, he said to him:

—But ultimately, after all, that is your affair. I have nothing to do with it.

After this not very cordial reaction, Félix expected the disappointed young man to leave his office immediately. But, on the contrary, moving still closer, the man asked this completely unexpected question:

—Yes, my Baptism will be celebrated by a Dominican, Father Hébert. But I need a godmother, and I came to beg you, Monsieur le Directeur, to allow me to address this request to Madame Leseur, whom I know to be Catholic and practicing.

Félix, at first surprised and no doubt a little flattered, remained silent a moment and then answered him:

—Personally, I don't see any problem with that. Ask this favor of my wife yourself. I will not interfere in it.

Élisabeth accepted this role with joy. It was thus that she met Father Hébert, well known among the Parisians because he was the Lenten preacher at Notre Dame, but Élisabeth had never heard him preach: it had always been out of the question for her to leave her husband on Sunday afternoons to go to Notre Dame. Her meeting Father Hébert would be a grace for both of them. He would be her confessor and her spiritual father for eleven years until the end of her life; she would later say that after their meeting, "the solemn feeling of a new life had begun for her." For his part, Father Hébert received that day the grace of being the close observer "of the slow and silent action of Providence in the soul of Madame Leseur".

Father Hébert was eager to celebrate this Baptism. He was very anxious for this private ceremony to take place in the crypt of the Dominican church on the rue du Faubourg-Saint-Honoré. They must not wait. In fact, in 1903, the Combes laws were waging such a savage anticlerical battle that religious congregations had to be evicted from their convents. The Dominicans might be driven out any day; and, indeed, they were, five days after the Baptism.

The Catholic Church in France was going through a painful period.

How did Christians of that time endure this fury of destruction of the Christian roots of France? What an ordeal and what an anguish for them to see the religious driven out of their convents, the churches closed, their beliefs ridiculed! Élisabeth wanted to be the little flame that does not want to go out. "The public events would be saddening if I did not have an indestructible trust in the future of the Church of Christ and a great hope in the future of our country. . . . My God, you alone can transform and save. And to me, small and weak, give a little of your divine strength, and come to me in order to do through me much good for souls."[1]

---

[1] Élisabeth Leseur, *Journal et Pensées de chaque jour* (Paris: Éd. du Cerf, 2005), 111.

Her unexpected role as godmother was a great grace for her. She experienced the feeling of a new existence for herself as well, a kind of new baptism; leaving the celebration, she noted in her diary: "A very beautiful, sweet, and blessed morning. God be blessed for all the graces that he has granted me and for this supreme and immense grace, for the way in which he has arranged everything, guided everything."[2]

During the years that followed, Father Hébert would be her confessor and her spiritual father, "placed on her path by circumstances that were simply and gently providential".

Another important event marked that year 1903. For several months, Élisabeth had expressed to Félix her desire to return to Rome.

He had objected that they had already been there in 1899; no doubt he did not remind her that he had retained a bad memory of it because of her piety, whose external signs he could not bear. For Élisabeth, that trip had been nothing but an ordinary journey of Christian tourists, nothing more. Now she expected from such a pilgrimage something truly more profound, more authentic. She wanted it to be a new point of departure in her life. Her dearest wish was to experience Holy Week in the capital of Christianity.

Félix did not know how to refuse anything to his wife. Certainly, while a trip was always tempting for him, he would still have preferred a less ideologically marked destination. As long as Élisabeth would not dive back into the sources of her faith! Despite a few misgivings, however, he agreed.

The Hennequins would accompany them. With them, at least, they would not risk spending an entire week in a mystical atmosphere. They could visit the Forum, the Coliseum, the museums, and they could savor the Roman cuisine in great restaurants!

A foresighted man, Félix knew that, for Easter, crowds from around the world flocked to Rome and that it was difficult to find lodgings at the last minute. In advance, he rented an apartment in a pleasant neighborhood: Piazza di Spagna, at the corner of the Via des Condotti, at the foot of the church of the Trinità dei Monti. Located in the heart of the city, facing the grand staircase that gave

---

[2] Ibid., 101.

access to one of the most beautiful views of Michelangelo's dome and a panorama of rooftop terraces, Élisabeth would be delighted.

The two couples arrived in Rome on the eve of Palm Sunday, when the church squares were already covered with olive and palm branches for the following day's processions.

By mutual agreement, it was understood that Élisabeth would have all the freedom she wanted to attend the Holy Week services. In reality, she would request only two days for herself alone.

As soon as they arrived, all four of them went to San Paolo alle Tre Fontane, near the place where Saint Paul was martyred. They were especially charmed by the calm and the poetry of the place, the greenery, the silence. Élisabeth would have liked to stay longer to have time to pray and to meditate in that place sanctified by the blood of the martyrs. But Félix and the Hennequins, as tourists, were content to roam around the basilica to find in the verdant landscape the grace and beauty of the pines and palm trees, the gentleness of the sunsets in Rome's sky.

In the same spirit, they would visit all four catacombs of Saint Callixtus buried in the Roman countryside. Élisabeth suffered from visiting such sacred places as a tourist without being able to share her emotion. All four of them would be charmed by the Roman ruins of the Forum and the Palatine.

Two profound memories would definitively mark these exceptional moments for her:

—The papal audience with Leo XIII, for which she had an invitation to the second row in the Consistory Hall. She attended it alone with much emotion.

—And, above all, her morning in the basilica of the Vatican, where she received a magnificent grace: there, in the very heart of Christianity, she was seized by the immense tenderness of God for her:

> I left alone for Saint Peter's, and, after having made my Confession to a French-speaking priest, I went to Communion in the chapel of the Blessed Sacrament. Those moments there were fully, supernaturally happy. I felt living in me, present and bringing me an ineffable love, the blessed Christ, God himself. That incomparable soul spoke

to mine, and all the infinite tenderness of the Savior passed to me in a moment. Never will this divine imprint be erased. . . . He who, as a man, suffered and loved, the One and Living God, took possession of my soul for eternity in that ineffable moment. I felt renewed by him to my depths, ready for a new life, for responsibilities, for the work desired by his Providence. I gave myself without reserve and I gave him the future.[3]

Filled with a profound peace and joy, she then knelt down in front of the balustrade of the Confession of Saint Peter, and there, near the tomb of the founder of the Church, she consecrated her life to God at length in the deepest solitude and silence of her heart. This complete consecration for which she had hoped and prepared for so long would be a culminating point for her in her spiritual life, a source of living water that would no longer run dry.

Then, conscious that faith is a gift from God, that her marriage was also a shared gift from God, she ardently prayed that her husband, this man to whom she had been united before God by an eternal alliance, would return to him one day.

This complete consecration to God, in Rome, would remain for Élisabeth a fundamental step in her life of faith. From that day forward, there would never again be any turning back for her. Henceforward, every event in her life would be transformed into a burst of interior renewal.

In meeting Félix and the Hennequins at the restaurant, she barely touched on the revelation to them of this consecration to God, so luminous and so momentous in her life; right away she met with a response of irony, critical on Félix's part and indifferent on the part of her friends. She was used to irony every time she made a few allusions to her faith, but she always received it as a lance thrust into her heart. She suffered deeply from it, but she always refused to respond to it.

She would later write: "What a terrible thing is irony; to know how to withstand a smile of disdain is the mark of a complete moral strength. How painful it is to feel everything we love, everything that makes us live, misunderstood or attacked by prejudices, hatreds,

---

[3] Ibid., 104.

or else to feel complete indifference for the most important things in life and the soul!"[4]

Once more she considered what she had already experienced so often: such intimate experiences cannot be recounted because words very quickly fail or betray, distort what is far beyond human language. Élisabeth concluded: "But I did not care! The flame of Christ still burned within me."[5]

From now on, that flame would never again be extinguished.

The trip would continue with visits to Perugia and Assisi, in the sweetness of Umbria, where the soul of Saint Francis left Félix and his friends indifferent, but where they would be charmed by the beauty of the countryside, the greenery, and the singing of the birds.

Returning from Rome, Élisabeth experienced extreme fatigue. Félix took her to rest at Jougne, as attests the letter, written on September 3 by Élisabeth to Madame Duvent. This young woman was the wife of a painter who was experiencing a certain renown at that time. Élisabeth met her often because the two husbands had very old bonds of friendship. The Duvents had always noticed and admired Élisabeth's sound judgment, tact, and moderation, as well as her sensitivity to pictorial works. It was therefore to her that Élisabeth confided on September 3, 1903. For the first time, she acknowledged the debilitating seriousness of her illness while drowning it, with the eyes of an artist, in a contemplation of the beautiful images of a landscape ever dearer in her eyes:

> I wanted to write you, but for several days I went through an attack of fatigue and physical sufferings, which I have been used to resisting for many years, so long as they do not exceed a certain degree, but that, this time, forced me to surrender. I had to limit slightly my usual occupations, and with Félix having been able to advance his departure by twenty-four hours, we left Paris Tuesday morning and both arrived rather lusterless. We found wonderful weather, a sun to which we are no longer accustomed, and I am writing to you from our little terrace facing a view that is already making me feel good.

---

[4] Ibid., 106.
[5] Ibid.

The atmosphere is extraordinarily soft and luminous, the crickets are singing madly, the mountain's colors are more varied and more beautiful than ever, thanks to the last rains and to the season. This calm gently penetrates and rests.[6]

Once more, Jougne represented a refuge for them, a rest, and a place where their love united them. They took so much pleasure in each other's company! Félix was so good, so tender toward her, so considerate when he sensed she was tired, that not for anything in the world would she have wanted to irritate him or stir up useless arguments by speaking to him about her interior life.

Even if isolation in her faith was painful to her, she put all her fervor into praying for her husband, and, like the birds of the sky who neither sow nor reap, with the trust of a child, she placed her innermost (or perhaps craziest) wishes in the hands of the Lord.

---

[6] R. P. Marie-Albert Leseur, *Vie d'Élisabeth Leseur* (Paris: Éd. J. de Gigord, 1931), 164.

Juliette, *Une Âme* (A Soul)

In 1904, Juliette, Élisabeth's younger sister, was thirty-two years old. The two were very close emotionally and spiritually. Élisabeth had long confided in her about her sorrow at seeing Félix so scornful of her spiritual life and so hostile to any attempt to soften his ideological positions; for several years, Juliette had joined in her sister's prayers and supplications for Félix to return to the faith.

Juliette was "a beautiful soul": on the day of her First Communion, when she must have been about ten years old, she had said to her astonished family:

"We must not be afraid of death because it makes us meet God!"

Félix felt a genuine affection for his little sister-in-law, who returned it in kind; like Élisabeth, she was cheerful, amusing, spontaneous, and attentive to others; she greatly loved to read, and she spoke about her readings with intelligence and vivacity, which delighted Félix. The regular family gatherings on Sundays encouraged relationships through the sharing of what had been the daily life of each person during the past week.

Juliette was not well. She had been sick for a long time, but in that year 1904, the ailments were getting worse. At the end of a few weeks, she gave her relatives great concern. Her health declined rapidly until the day when doctors diagnosed advanced pulmonary tuberculosis. At that time, this disease was ravaging a good part of the youth. No medicine could overcome it. Without other, more effective means, it was thought that mountains, fresh air, and sunshine alone could eliminate the terrible Koch bacillus that devoured lungs.

Desperate, Madame Arrighi took her daughter to be healed in the sunshine of Southern France, in Italy, and then to Menton, where no improvement appeared. She then accompanied her to Jougne, where they stayed a few weeks, surrounded by Élisabeth and Félix's care. This visit was painful for Élisabeth because she knew that Juliette would not recover. Once back in Paris, Élisabeth wrote on May 3, 1904:

> Have I ever lived through a more sorrowful time in all my life than what I am going through at this moment? This cruel, haunting, perpetual ordeal of Juliette's health and fear of the future, the painful awareness of our poor mother's sorrow, my usual trials, a state of poor health and a very painful strain on body and spirit, all this unites to make of my life, in this moment, a sacrifice that, in silence, I offer to God for Juliette, for those whom I love, and for souls. It is a double and very painful sacrifice, that of my great loneliness of soul. . . . To walk constantly by the side of those dear to me without being able to open my soul a little for a moment, without sharing anything of my inner self, is a very intense suffering.[1]

Félix deeply understood and shared her suffering. In his own way, he tried to give her some joy. An attentive husband, he remembered that his wife had once expressed a desire to have a little desk of her own to benefit from a certain isolation; he knew that she liked to write sheltered from his gaze without him knowing what she was writing. He offered her one, accompanied by a little note full of tenderness.

Juliette would never return to Jougne.

Fearing that her daughter might not breathe a sufficiently invigorating air in Paris, her mother rented an apartment at Versailles surrounded by greenery. Despite that environment, the young woman's condition deteriorated day by day. Furthermore, with half a day of travel being necessary for her sisters to go spend the afternoon near her every day, it seemed very clear that this situation could not continue.

To facilitate travel, a new move at the beginning of the winter settled them at Passy, on the edge of the Bois de Boulogne. The open air, the space, and the majestic trees allowed them to hope that Juliette would breathe better. Most importantly, her sisters would be closer in order to go see her every day and ease her life.

---

[1] Élisabeth Leseur, *Journal et Pensées de chaque jour* (Paris: Éd. du Cerf, 2005), 111.

For the whole family and for Élisabeth, it was an excruciating time. Long pages of her diary capture her anguish and at the same time her trust in prayer, her offering of all her sufferings, her surrender. Élisabeth went to her sister's bedside almost every day; she returned home noting that the moments spent near Juliette were the sweetest of her life: "I love her soul, and she, I believe, understands mine. It is a great sweetness because, among those who surround me, except for Mama, my sisters, and my dear Félix, no one knows my inner self. And yet, my whole Christian life will not be understood by my dear beloved until later, when God will have chased away the darkness and made the light shine for him."[2]

Whatever the difficult situations in her life, Élisabeth offered her sufferings to God so that her dear Félix would one day return to him. How many times did she have to remind herself of the parable of the good shepherd who brings back his scattered sheep and rejoices so much in finding them again! But it was not yet time.

Félix was nothing but love for his relatives in distress: first for Élisabeth, for his mother-in-law, for his own mother, who had double phlebitis at that time and whom he patiently nursed, for his nephews, whom he hosted at Jougne and whom he cared for with affection as if he were their father, for Juliette, whom he often went to see and surrounded with a thousand attentions: as long as she could get out of bed, he took her for drives in the car; over the course of her illness, he had been attentive to her slightest desires, bringing her sweets and flowers, reading to her. And when Élisabeth thanked him, he responded:

—Do not thank me. I do not do it for you anymore but for her because I love her as if she were truly my sister.

And during that time, on March 20, 1905, Élisabeth wrote a supplication that so many people at the bedside of a dying loved one have addressed to God:

> Lord, I cry to you in the midst of an anguish and a sadness the like of which I have never experienced. You alone can save her whom we love and not break these hearts that trust in your Love. You are the Almighty and the All-loving; that which you can do, do it, my God, and give us joy by giving life and healing to my beloved sister.

---

[2] Ibid., 116.

She is for me at once a child, a friend, and a sister, the person, along with Félix and Mama, whom I love more than anything.[3]

Félix was very close to his little sister-in-law during the days of her death agony. To the surprise of everyone, it was he, when he came across the priest in the hallway, who asked him to give the last sacraments to the dying young woman.

Élisabeth recounted the last conversation between Félix and her sister almost on the eve of her death:

That same evening when Félix went to see her she said to him:
—Do you know, Félix, what I did while you were not here?
—No, said Félix, who knew perfectly well.
—Well, I received Extreme Unction and I offered for you a part of what I did.
Félix, very moved and trying to hide it, said to her teasingly:
—So, you do not think I am good?
And she, then, in an inexpressibly sweet tone:
—But just so, so much goodness, so many qualities cannot remain useless.
—Yet you do not want me to become a priest?
Then, intervening and also seeking to conceal my deep emotion, I said to Juliette:
—That's it, he will become a priest when he becomes a widower.[4]

For Félix, it was not the time to smile or to shrug his shoulders lightly. He did not respond because he did not yet know that through the voice of his dying little sister-in-law, the Lord had come to knock at his door.

The funeral took place Saturday, April 15. That very morning, when the moment came to give up, until the resurrection, what still remained to us of our sister, after the farewell of the mother to her very beloved child, it was he whom Juliette had loved like a brother who respectfully picked her up and placed her in her coffin. Nothing is lost here below; it is sometimes from the humblest ear that the most beautiful sheaf is born.[5]

---

[3] Ibid., 119.
[4] É Leseur, *Une Âme* (Paris: Éd. J. de Gigord, 1922), 389.
[5] Ibid., 395.

The months that followed this loss were very hard for the whole
family; Félix and Élisabeth had only one thought: to comfort and
surround Madame Arrighi, inevitably very afflicted. In mutual agreement, they first offered for her to come live with them in their apartment and then, when the summer came, to spend the vacation at
Jougne with them.

Élisabeth felt a great gratitude toward Félix for having, on his
own initiative, suggested this visit to her mother. She admired her
husband's goodness and kindness; on his side, Félix also admired
Élisabeth for her courage in the face of hardship. He had thought
that she would be overwhelmed, inconsolable, prostrate. On the
contrary, she proved to be serene, calm, even smiling; he saw her
continue her life with an extraordinary strength that he could neither understand nor explain, if not by the help of that faith which
he had been fighting for such a long time. He was content to note
her serenity and did not dare to mock her beliefs anymore. If her
faith was helping her so much, perhaps it was not the moment to
try to take it away from her?

On her side, and in the silence of her heart, Élisabeth prayed
ardently that God might at last reveal his light to the man she loved:
"My beloved Félix has worries; Mama, an immense sadness: their
dear souls need mine, or rather—because souls need only God—
I can obtain for them, through my sufferings and my sacrifices,
transformation and life. . . . My God, help the one who, despite
her faults, desires above all to make you known and loved."[6]

In her sorrow and in this internal torment, Élisabeth suffocated
from not being able to speak to her husband and not being able
to open the depth of her heart to him. So, she wrote to him and
placed the letter on his desk. She wanted to give him the key to her
inner peace in the face of suffering, but she also wanted to show
him her gratitude, the Christian dimension of her love that, even
if it was not shared at that level, remained nonetheless the work of
God. All love has its source in the love of God.

June 1904

Thank you for everything and above all for being you. And forgive
me for being me, that is to say, someone who herself is not worth

---

[6] É. Leseur, *Journal et Pensées de chaque jour*, 128.

much and who is only made a little better under the influence of accepted suffering, accepted thanks to help and strength much greater than mine. Because of this, you must be indulgent of the beliefs that time and God have made profound and thanks to which I have not become a bitter and selfish person. Never, you can be sure, will they be a bother for you and for others, and it is so good to put a bit of infinity and eternity into a love such as that which I feel for you and into a life where the hardships, known to you, have obscured and cut off many things.[7]

On November 1, 1905, Élisabeth, despite her sorrow, wrote a meditation on the communion of saints, which later, when Félix read it, amazed him and made him understand once more the source of his wife's strength:

This feast of All Saints is very sweet, it is the feast of those who already live in God, of those whom we have loved and who have attained light and happiness; it is the feast of eternity. And what a beautiful idea to have placed the celebration of the Dead right after this one! For these two days, a vast current of prayer and love circulates between the three worlds: between the Church of heaven, that of the earth, and that where souls wait and atone. The communion of saints seems even stronger and more fruitful. We feel close to us, in God, all souls and all those we love.[8]

Many years later, Félix would find in Élisabeth's drawers a little notebook covered in black moleskin and filled with blackened pages of her fine handwriting. It was a kind of diary about Juliette's sickness with some of her own letters that she had copied, letters from childhood friends, and most of all the spiritual account of that illness. And it read:

Une âme (A soul)! That is how I want to name these pages intended only for those who have known our beloved sister. They are made up of these precious memories that remain, from a human perspective, my sweetest consolation; they seek to make live again for the hearts of friends the person whom we mourn and whom we will meet again one day in eternal life. . . . To speak above all about a soul, about the

---

[7] Félix Leseur, *In Memoriam*, introduction to the 1917 edition of É. Leseur, *Journal et Pensées de chaque jour*, 267.

[8] É. Leseur, *Journal et Pensées de chaque jour*, 127.

beliefs that inspired it, of its humbly heroic efforts toward holiness, would seem a strange thing to those who live on the surface of the spirits. . . . When, on the road of life, we find an exceptional person and, by a rather rare good fortune, can walk with him for a time, there remains for us from this encounter such a sweetness; it leaves in us a trace so profound that it seems to us then that the dear influence with which we are filled will again be powerful and that the seed planted in our depths will blossom for others in a bounteous harvest.[9]

The whole story of Juliette's sickness and death was written in these notebooks; it was a magnificent testimony of tenderness and affection, a real treasure of love for all those around her. But it was also an act of living faith, a radiation of courage, of the acceptance of death by an ordinary young woman struck down in her youth at the end of several years of suffering, a living hymn to God.

All this love given and received could have only one source: the heart of God. But at the moment when he would discover this notebook after Élisabeth's death, Félix would not yet know it. He would read it with tears in his eyes. Yes, he remembered that sorrowful period of Juliette's illness. This notebook evoked for him, first, a past of memories, and, then, it was an example of courage.

It was not until much later, when he published *La Vie Spirituelle* (The spiritual life), that he would consider that a testimony of such greatness and such strength did not have the right to be placed permanently under a bushel. He would publish it under the title chosen by Élisabeth: *Une Âme* (A soul).

---

[9] É. Leseur, *Une Âme*, 253.

11

A Spiritual Motherhood

The more Élisabeth advanced in life, the more she suffered from not having children. All the couples in her family circle or those of her friends had large families. It was a difficult and sad acceptance, compensated for, it is true, by the great love that united her to Félix and by the opening of their relationship to others.

Élisabeth and Félix watched their nieces and nephews be born and grow up with affection and interest, as we can see from Élisabeth's correspondence with her sister Amélie's children, with whom they were particularly close because the families happily gathered around one or the other's table on Sundays.

Thus, Élisabeth loved her nephews and nieces as if they were her own children. They spent the summers together at Jougne, where, in their parents' absence, she took care of them as a mother would. She supervised their grooming, gave them French and Latin lessons, took them on walks. Félix played with them with ease. Through the correspondence, we see him take his nephews for walks or play with the diabolo with them on the lawns of the garden.

It had long been planned that on May 25, 1905, little Marie Duron, her sister Amélie's daughter, would make her First Communion. Juliette, her beloved godmother, had rejoiced about it with the whole family. Then, when Juliette understood that her illness was progressing and that she would certainly no longer be there on May 25, she had asked Élisabeth to replace her with her little goddaughter, but above all not to cancel the celebration because of her death. In dying, she had entrusted to her the mission of helping the first communicant to understand the meaning of the Christian life and the magnitude of the act she was going to perform.

The whole family, still in great mourning, thus gathered at the Durons' house, a few weeks after Juliette's death, to surround the young Marie. Everyone was aware that it was out of the question to be sad on that day. It had to be a day of joy without shadow for this little one; no one must allow himself to give in to sorrow or bitterness in front of her. Félix was the first to try to make a smile bloom on every face.

A few days earlier, Élisabeth had written to her niece: "No, my beloved, not one of us will really miss this family reunion; what your godmother had hoped for, she who was so full of faith and love, was the union of her soul and yours in God. This union will be greater than life would have allowed."[1]

Élisabeth had replaced her role as mother with a deep sense of "spiritual motherhood" for her nieces and nephews.

When she was preparing little Marie for this event, she assessed her responsibility. She reflected at length, then she began to write a few sheets that she would gradually discuss with her. Finally, she recopied in a complete little notebook, which she would give to her, the guidelines for life that she offered her.

On the cover, she wrote: "To my only and dear niece, to my goddaughter through a precious and sacred inheritance, to my little adopted daughter, I offer this testimony of a deep and Christian affection."[2]

In this notebook were inscribed the advice and teachings that Juliette would certainly have wanted to lavish on Marie. It can be considered a true "inner treasure". Later, Félix would publish this notebook under the title *La Femme chrétienne* (The Christian woman).

A few excerpts will suffice to provide an understanding of how profound an awareness Élisabeth had of a woman's duties in her state in life and her role in four specific domains:
—in Christian life,
—in her family,
—in her marriage,
—in social life.

At the very beginning of the twentieth century, the education of women was still in its infancy, even though schooling for girls had been obligatory since the Camille Sée laws, that is, since 1881. Of course, there had been exceptions; women of great intellectual or

---

[1] Élisabeth Leseur, *La Femme chrétienne: Extraite de "La Vie Spirituelle"* (Paris: Éd. J. de Gigord, 1920), 176.
[2] Ibid., 175.

spiritual worth had appeared over the course of the previous centuries, but, for the majority, society was not very demanding of the
fairer sex.

Most of the time a Christian woman was asked to know her catechism well, to go to Mass, and to devote herself to some good
charitable works.

In her family, she was to honor her husband by the way she kept
his house, know how to entertain, to revive a conversation in the
drawing room, to demonstrate a certain culture; she had to know
how to embroider and play the piano. In general, not much more
was asked of her.

A few excerpts of the advice that Élisabeth, in 1905, gave to the
young Marie suffice to convince us of the modernity of Élisabeth's
thoughts concerning a woman's role in life.

First, Élisabeth affirms that a Christian woman is a woman like
any other.

But in life, because she has received "the light that enlightens
every man coming into this world", she has the responsibility to
think of herself as a link in the long chain of Christian tradition
that will last until the end of time.

To this end, she asks her niece not to become "this pathetic thing,
this body devoid of soul, that we call a 'practicing' Catholic": "I
wish, my darling, that you be, from an intellectual point of view,
a conscious Christian and that you know the profound reasons for
your faith."[3]

At that time, when the religious instruction given to young girls
was most often limited to sentimental and sugary explanations of
external rites that resulted in a conventional practice, it was wonderful to hear such a request for a personal deepening of faith.

Élisabeth then recommends that Marie read a lot, to increase always the sum of her knowledge in order constantly to broaden her
intellectual horizon. It was a necessary condition for playing an intelligent and efficacious role in society and in the relationship she
would later form with her husband. How many women of that generation had no intellectual exchange with their husbands because
they were totally incapable of it!

---

[3] Ibid., 186.

Family being the foundation of society for Élisabeth, Marie's role in her adult life would be to strengthen the meaning of and respect for the family everywhere:

> Later, when you, in your turn, form one of your own, you will make your home a warm and lively center of influence, and you will be the conscience of those who live within reach of your influence. You will be a friend, a companion for your husband; for your children, a guide and the image of moral strength. You will possess this precious thing of which, with your dear godmother, we have spoken so often and which she kept throughout all her sufferings: the serenity, the peace that nothing can take away from us, neither hardships nor the worst heartbreaks, because it is from a divine source and because God sometimes even gives it in proportion to suffering, through one of those mysterious compensations, unknown to men, but of which he has the secret.[4]

> Every Christian woman also has a social task to fulfill, and, for you, who will have true worth because of your education, you will have to work with all your strength toward the material and moral betterment of everyone. . . . Be sure, however, that to deal with these very important questions today successfully, in this time of transformation through which we are going in order to work toward the establishment of a new, Christian social order, you must prepare yourself through serious study of these grave problems. . . . Later, you will bring to this collaboration much consistency, devotion, and energy, and little concern for the literal meaning, for the "hateful self", the sense of necessary discipline.[5]

And she gives her a piece of advice: "Never be one of those who want to be leaders and not soldiers, who would willingly create works for themselves alone and only accept good done in their own way, according to their methods."[6]

What practical sense and what understanding of human psychology! One cannot help but think of the number of women who, in the name of charity in "good works", have imposed their authority by making those who wanted to collaborate with them suffer!

---

[4] Ibid., 188.

[5] Ibid., 189.

[6] Ibid., 191.

The following year, her nephew André, Marie's younger brother, made his First Communion in his turn. As for his sister, Élisabeth wrote him a little notebook, perhaps simply to show him just as much affection, but no doubt also to give him a slightly different message. She felt responsible for this boy's faith, especially in that period of his adolescence when he willingly engaged in the Christian life.

From the first lines, she reminds him of her tenderness for her nephews, then she evokes the beautiful image of the parable of the sower in relation to the bereavement that their family has just experienced: "You will understand later that souls like that of your dear little aunt sow holiness in other souls through their hardships. When you become a man, a Christian, you will feel that the good accomplished by you is a flower that has sprouted on fertile soil that someone else has watered with his tears, cultivated through his painful labor."[7]

Élisabeth knew so well the dangers that faith ran in a professional life anchored in a world where Christians will become minorities that she cautions him with wisdom and experience.

She had watched too closely the process of the loss of faith in herself and in her husband not to measure the dangers of it:

> There will come a time when you will suffer, more or less suddenly, the shock of doctrines, of denials. If the shock is not violent, you will, however, feel the influence of the intellectual atmosphere of your times; you will breathe, perhaps without even realizing it, the air that surrounds our modern youth, and one day, you will be surprised to realize that you are intoxicated, that you breathe poorly in the air of faith; you will feel that the external life of your piety no longer corresponds to the profound state of your soul, and, no doubt surprised, discouraged, you will be tempted to leave behind this troublesome shell, as it will seem to you, for the free development of your intelligence. Few minds, especially among the minds of men, escape this crisis of faith.[8]

She gives him two weapons that she analyzes at length: prayer and work. Then she insists on the responsibility that he will have

---

[7] Élisabeth Leseur, *Le Chrétien: Petit traité de la vie chrétienne de l'homme* (Paris: Éd. J. de Gigord, 1920), 202.

[8] Ibid., 209.

to assume later when he enters professional life: to bear witness to a Christian life animated by the Gospel.

One of the last paragraphs is worth quoting because it sums up the whole meaning of Élisabeth's life: considering every person as having a value in himself that must be looked after and considered, no matter what his level:

> Put yourself to work with courage, seeking constantly to discern the true task and the possible good, telling yourself that everywhere, no matter the vocation, there are material or moral miseries to ease, minds to calm, hearts to heal, seeing in all those whom you will meet on your way the soul that is in them and exerting yourself to act on this soul through your examples and by your influence. Throughout this active period of your life, may your motto be always the same: *orare et labore*.[9]

She did not yet know how much importance those two poles, which had become one of the mottos of the Benedictines, would later have in the life of her atheist husband.

---

[9] Ibid., 219.

12

The Leavening in the Dough

The more the years passed, the more Élisabeth cherished her husband. Of course, she still suffered from knowing he was an atheist and so incapable of understanding her, but faith was a subject that they no longer discussed at all.

Élisabeth believed that love was stronger than anything for making him one day understand the sources of her tenderness. Human love can find its source only in the love of God who is all love. It was the only language, that of love, that she wanted to use with him, and it was a wonderful language that he understood, appreciated, and that moved him.

For their wedding anniversary, she placed this little letter on the corner of his desk:

July 31, 1906

My dear Félix,

Perhaps you will not be surprised to find this note, in which I would like to place a little of this tenderness, so great that it is sometimes difficult to express. This anniversary stirs in my heart many things that are still vivid and that quickly reappear at the call of a date, a word, a landscape. Seventeen years ago today almost all of us were gathered, and just now I prayed for those who have left us, and also for those who are close to us. If I give you these lines, it is so that, less fleeting than speech, they will become the expression of my profound love and the testimony of my gratitude for all the happiness you have given me.

I, too, would have wanted to give you only happiness, and often, because of my health, I caused you concern. But you can say that I truly appreciated your delicate kindness and your devotion, and that I gave in tenderness, very fully, what I did not give you in external and worldly satisfactions.

I embrace you with all my heart and renew with joy the sweet promises of seventeen years ago. Despite so many trials and sufferings of every kind, I feel the sweetness of looking back and reliving the years traveled together.

Your wife who cherishes you,

Élisabeth[1]

The Leseurs were now living at 3 rue d'Argenson in a new neighborhood that had been renovated by Baron Haussmann. They had arranged the interior of their house together with refined care and much joy. The proximity of the church of Saint-Augustin, which had witnessed the conversion of the unrepentant Charles de Foucauld, often drew Élisabeth there. She easily went to Mass there. Her husband was perfectly aware of it. But he said nothing about it. She also loved to go sit on a bench in the nearby square in the shade of the tall trees.[2]

Certainly, Élisabeth had for Félix all the care and gentleness of the heart, certainly they had long and rich intellectual exchanges with each other about their reading or about politics, but she knew that certain subjects could never be broached with each other and that they were the ones she held closest to her heart. An entire part of her life had to remain secret and hidden, surrounding her in a spiritual isolation that made her suffer cruelly.

Among their many friends whom they so often invited to Sunday lunch, most were Félix's friends and shared his political opinions. It was out of the question to broach subjects that would lead to hurtful arguments for any of them. But without knocking, thoughts sometimes burst forth, and some, especially childhood friends, were sometimes surprised to find themselves in front of a Félix so aggressive toward religion; much later, one of his friends would write to him: "Certainly, for a friend who knows as I do the fundamental goodness, the virtues of mind that atavism had placed in you, the antireligious mentality you had forged was a troubling matter."[3]

Élisabeth and Félix were a couple open to all political opinions

---

[1] Marie-Louise Herking, *Le Père Leseur* (Paris: Éd. J. de Gigord, 1952), 67.
[2] Now Marcel Pagnol Square.
[3] Élisabeth Leseur, *Lettres sur la souffrance* (Paris: Éd. du Cerf, 2012), 44.

. . . especially if they were close to those of Félix . . . Élisabeth knew well that to speak of her faith, even in a very superficial way, would be a humiliation for her husband and would create unnecessary uneasiness for his friends; occasionally, however, in spite of herself, she would let a few remarks slip out, for which she very quickly reproached herself.

On January 31, 1906, she wrote in her diary:

> I spoke too much of you, my God, since it is true that in this world that no longer knows you, it is necessary to calculate our words when they concern you. A few remarks made about me and the attitude of loved ones have already given me a salutary lesson in humility and recalled me to the duty of silence. And this is the resolution that is going to inspire this meditation for me: silence about my hardships, silence about my inner life and about what God has ceaselessly done for me, silence about my soul, silence about all supernatural realities, about my hopes, and about my faith. I believe that it is a duty for me and that, in awaiting the divine hour, I must preach Jesus Christ only through my prayers, my sufferings, and my example.[4]

With what to compare her reserve if not with the leaven that silently rises in dough . . . or the wild mustard seed sown in the ground that seems to be buried forever and will later become a huge bush under the shade of which it is good to rest.

Élisabeth was always so very respectful of the beliefs of her husband's friends—thus, of their friends—that these friends were not afraid to unite with them in friendship despite their very opposing ideologies. An amusing but significant short dedication written on a business card accompanied the shipment of a book published by Édouard Pelletan, whom Félix greatly admired:

> To Monsieur and Madame Félix Leseur.
> 3 rue d'Argenson. VIII Arrondissement, Paris.

> To [Félix] the sectarian, to the Combist, who combines socialism and conservatism in a pleasant mixture, to the fiercely anticlerical, but also to the good and charming friend. To [Élisabeth] the most precious and "esteemed" of friends, a little reactionary, like me, and

---

[4] Élisabeth Leseur, *Journal et Pensées de chaque jour* (Paris: Éd. du Cerf, 2005), 130.

very liberal . . . like me, we offer this memory of the old France that we both equally love. Félix deems this book worthy of you because it is illustrated with the most beautiful colored woodcuts, those by Pelletan, that have been made in recent years. Best wishes and all our affection.[5]

---

[5] Élisabeth Leseur, *Lettres à des Incroyants* (Paris: Éd. J. de Gigord, 1928), 130.

13

Lettres à des Incroyants (Letters to Unbelievers)

This is the title of the book that Félix had published after the death of his wife; it contains 106 letters, written by Élisabeth from 1901 onward, intended for correspondents and especially for dissimilar correspondents.

The greater part of Élisabeth's time was dedicated to her epistolary activities; she wrote her letters out of friendship at a time when telephone conversations did not exist. The purpose of these letters was to share the joys and sorrows of the people whom she addressed out of a desire to help them and also out of a desire to open her heart about questions of faith that she could never broach with her husband.

In reality, most of her friends, at that time, were unbelievers. Félix did not associate with many others. They received such a welcome at the Leseurs' that a great, faithful, and respectful affection had been woven between them for many years.

During those same years, through her readings, reflections, and meditations, Élisabeth had built for herself alone, in the silence of her soul, a strong and structured spirituality. She realized that her heart was overflowing with all that she had to give; so she wrote several letters a day to share with and help those she loved.

Their close friend the painter Duvent, who had chosen Élisabeth as godmother to one of his children, had so often seen Élisabeth seated in front of her Louis XV desk with her face tilted forward, her long dress, her chignon, absorbed in the writing of her letters to unbelieving friends that he had wanted to paint her in that pose. It was the portrait that Félix would later cherish the most.

Those who, in reading these letters published under the title *Lettres à des Incroyants*, were expecting an inescapable argument or convincing words on the topic of Christian beliefs would be very disappointed. Dialogue between a convinced Christian and an equally convinced nonbeliever has always discouraged many good intentions simply because words do not have the same impact, because a deep conviction that has matured over the years in the depths of the heart does not have possibilities for exact expression; most of the time each person comes out of it as if he had struggled with or failed a test.

Élisabeth never sought to "convert" anyone, and, furthermore, she did not, in her lifetime, convert any of her correspondents. She was much too respectful of the opinions of others. Above all she sought to show, with simplicity and discretion, what was deep within her, what enlivened her and gave her strength in the face of trials and illness. Just a little light of love and sharing placed in the depths of her friends' hearts, without knowing if one day it would grow! No big speeches:

> To make myself everything to everyone. To increase leniency and commitment, to avoid all rigidity, all exaggeration in my words, in the presentation of my ideas, in my attitude. To be imbued with this idea that spiritual nourishment is too strong for many souls, that it must be presented to them with care, it must be given in doses, so to speak. To not want to go faster than God, to know to stay in step, very little steps around certain souls. . . . And to repeat to myself that the hour and the means belong only to God.[1]

What moved Élisabeth in all her demeanor, in all her words, in all her writings, was love. Like everyone, love for her husband and for her family, but also for all those unknown strangers to whom she referred with a word of universal scope: souls. For these "souls" spread throughout the entire world, but for whom she felt responsible, she prayed constantly, she offered all her sufferings.

An initial, cursory reading of *Lettres à des Incroyants* mostly gives the impression of going through Élisabeth's everyday life with her expectations and her sufferings, her health issues, her encounters, her friendships, her stays at Jougne, her discussions with Félix, and many other small, seemingly insignificant details shared with friends.

In reality, a more careful reading makes us discover something

---

[1] Élisabeth Leseur, *Lettres à des Incroyants* (Paris: Éd. J. de Gigord, 1928), 69.

entirely different: all those very simple events lived in the light of the Gospel were like a light that she made shine and that silently illuminated the daily lives of her correspondents.

Élisabeth attracted around her a great number of friends because her smile was radiant, her conversation was agreeable, and her kindness gave warmth like a good fire. Among these women, the majority, being the wives of colleagues or collaborators whom Félix had met in his professional life, were nonbelievers. Like everyone, they had hardships to get through, feelings of melancholy difficult to bear, and also, very often, a certain neurasthenia that Élisabeth helped them combat simply by giving them human advice relevant to their lives, like our psychotherapists do in the twenty-first century.

Élisabeth used the same method with these nonbelieving correspondents as she did with her husband: no speeches, much less arguments, because, as she said, ego comes into play so much in arguments that the dialogue is distorted; a great respect for their beliefs; she sometimes spoke of her faith that gave her life, of course, but she never gave herself as an example. She never spoke about it with rigid claims but, rather, simply, as she would speak of the blessing of sunshine on flowers and the joy that surrounds that beauty.

The basis for all these letters was meditated on at length following her readings of Saint Thomas Aquinas, who always advised first and foremost deep respect for the opinions of his correspondent.

An anecdote, recounted later by Félix, is significant: the Leseurs were often visited by Aimée Fiévet in their home, a young woman passionately interested in philosophy; she enthusiastically took Bergson's courses. The philosopher was then so much in vogue that it was necessary to stand in line for several hours to be able to enter the amphitheater of the Collège de France where he was teaching. All the young women were infatuated with him.

The enthusiasm of this student was such that when she spoke about him, Félix would mock her a little and smile at her juvenile admiration. One evening, after she had gone, Élisabeth said to Félix:

You were wrong to try as you just did to ridicule Bergson in front of this little one. Consider a moment that no one has ever elevated her mind to spiritual realities; yet Bergson explicitly opens her eyes to this unexpected realm. He is the only one who can make her reflect on certain truths. So, she will listen to him as she will not listen to anyone else. I beg you not to try anymore to shatter her poor mirror.[2]

This respect for the opinions of others was the great strength of Élisabeth's human relationships.

Élisabeth wrote:

There are two things that are equally deep in me: the convictions that guide my life and that the work of the soul has made alive and strong, and an absolute and total respect for all conscience and all conviction. For me, what passes between the human being and God is something secret, and no one must touch it with an indiscreet hand. Besides, I feel too imperfect and weak myself to make myself a judge, and I have too much need of help from above to be severe toward others.[3]

The Leseurs often visited very dear and very close friends of theirs: Jeanne and Émile Alcan. They were a non-practicing Jewish couple. He held an important position in the high spheres of international commerce. Both very intelligent, open, and cultured, especially about music and painting, they shared many of the Leseurs' tastes. Lovers of paintings, of beautiful antiques, they were knowledgeable and passionate collectors. Quite as much as Félix, they professed complete agnosticism.

Élisabeth was very attached to the young wife, Jeanne. When speaking of her, she said with admiration: "That is a soul!" Both of them felt close to each other while being separated by a faith they did not share. But they understood each other perfectly, so well that with much simplicity and naturalness, Élisabeth opened her heart and her own faith to her. She also knew how to advise Jeanne in the difficulties of her life, how to encourage her, guide her, and especially how to make her soul grow. She wrote her many letters, which constitute the entire first part of *Lettres à des Incroyants*.

Through these letters, in which Élisabeth expresses a great and open trust in her friend, we understand that her illness, of which she never spoke, was far from being over and that her suffering remained permanent.

---

[2] Ibid., 37.
[3] Ibid., 13.

My dear Jeanne, I thank you for your words, which brought me a sweet and friendly comfort at a time when I was not very bright on the surface or within myself. Indeed, I have just been suffering much for a few days, and, although better, alas, I need and will need to take it very easy. You know how difficult this is for me and how much the decrease in my activities, especially some of them, will cost me. But this will be a duty, and I promised it to Félix and to my family. Perhaps, trying to do good other than as we would like is better than doing it as we will: this idea and the strength that will come to me from above me will make me accept this little hardship, which is merely the continuation of those trials that have not been spared me for the past fourteen years. I must sense in you a very faithful and very trustworthy friend to open before you a little of this painful corner of my life, of which I never speak and that God constantly helps me to bear. Perhaps I must thank Him because, due to a few sufferings, I can better understand and share human suffering, and the little that I am worth comes from it.[4]

Let us take a closer look at the highlights of this letter:
—She speaks in all simplicity to her friend about her evolving sickness; she does not hide it, she does not mask her words, she does not complain.
—Like Mary, she simply says "yes", and it is this "yes" that makes her free to envision in her life something completely different from what she had foreseen: to accept to follow a path other than what one had chosen. For Élisabeth, it is to do good differently from what she had desired and to use her suffering to understand the suffering of others better.
—Contemporary psychologists often speak about the importance of "letting go", which, ultimately, is only the first step in accepting a heavy hardship that is bringing about a change in life.
It was thus that she envisioned her mission with complete interior peace.
Very positive points that we will find in other letters, expressed in slightly different ways, but still with the same perspective.
The simple "yes" to accepting her life such as it was:

---

[4] Ibid., 110.

My days are completely according to my heart. In the morning, a good hour of contemplation from which I draw strength for the day, children's work. After lunch and letter writing, my station for the whole afternoon is on the terrace, stretched out in my chaise longue, facing a beautiful view of which I never tire, surrounded by my books, which are charming companions and that I leave for even more enjoyable conversations; I believe more and more that, chaise longue aside, this family life shared between moments of solitude and hours of activity is what suits me best, the one I prefer to any other. Félix is doing well and is resting.[5]

Envisioning in her life something completely different from what she had expected:

My favorite occupation, my dear Jeanne, is to think of those whom I love, to recall them all; each one of them has his place daily in my best prayers, in the moments that my little ones know well, without understanding them, and call "Aunt Bébeth's meditations". They are the best moments of the day, and if, thanks to God, they no longer have to prepare me for expected sorrows, they serve to make me less "forbidding" for others.[6]

Benefiting from her experience of suffering to understand the suffering of others better:

Since yesterday I have been thinking of the little sick child, of his unhappy parents, and I pray with ardor for these poor hearts in agony. It was for them that I went to Communion this morning and asked for the strength that had been given to me on the day of the ordeal and that I would not have had alone. I cannot express to you the compassion I feel for your sister, for you, my dear friend, and I would like to be close to you to try to soften these cruel hours with my affection. Alas, I know what they contain of sufferings, I have lived them, and I have seen them lived close to me.

Benefiting from her suffering to help others overcome theirs through very practical psychological advice:

The fit of depression you are experiencing will not last long, and you will soon find yourself again in peace, in possession of yourself and

---

[5] Ibid., 154.
[6] Ibid., 169.

quite ready happily to resume your life and your normal occupations.
But this will be the moment to take good care and to arm yourself for
the future, as I told you jokingly, "to reform your life". . . . For this
you must discipline yourself morally; make a life for yourself where
peace of mind and physical occupation counter each other in a way
to make you constantly act on your will, while leaving your deep and
inner self in a habitual and conscious serenity. . . . As soon as you are
completely rid of your present miseries, set to work without delay
and map out for yourself a kind of rule of life from which you will
try never to depart. See clearly what your principal duties are toward
your husband, your children, toward others; also, set aside moments
that you will reserve for a little more recollection, which I believe is
indispensable for good inner balance. . . . When you feel anxiety or
worries, let them stir about without giving them long attention; they
will eventually die of starvation. . . . When you are with others, try
to express yourself without too much constraint, but considering as
much as possible what can bring pleasure or good to others; I promise
you much good from this twofold exercise. My dear, my very dear
friend, I am letting myself be carried away by my affection, by my
ardent desire to do good for your so beautiful, so good and sympa-
thetic "me", whom I love with all my heart and whom I would like
to free completely from these miseries that are such obstacles to her
fulfillment. We will get there . . .[7]

The second part of *Lettres à des Incroyants* published correspondence with Aimée Fiévet.

This young, single woman, from a Catholic family, had been a
teacher, then a school inspector. She had completed a rather brilliant
career, though troubled by severe health issues, as the director of
one of the main upper primary schools in the city of Paris. She was
a strong, intelligent, and courageous woman.

A former student of the Fontenay-aux-Roses school, she had been
very influenced by the ideas of the founder and director of that
school, Félix Pécaud. She had lost her faith, she confidently claimed,
and without any possibility of turning back, but she admired the
convictions of Élisabeth, for whom she had a deep affection, a mutual affection, judging by the tone of Élisabeth's letters.

---

[7] Ibid., 185.

Aimée's mentor, Félix Pécaud, her headmaster, was a sincere, austere, and confident man. He wanted to be close to his students, on
whom he exercised a great influence. They called him "the saint",
not because he belonged to a religion, but because of his unwavering moral rigor. He insidiously preached a kind of deism, a religious
doctrine of such a kind that the majority of his future teachers became agnostics even before leaving the school.

A correspondence at first uncertain, "Madame, having gotten
your address from Mademoiselle . . . I take the liberty of writing you", then friendly, and finally much more profound was established between the two women, who, though so different from
each other, were close in their desire for truth.

Certainly, Élisabeth did not at all share Félix Pécaud's ideas about
faith with which her friend's mind was completely filled. But, out
of respect for this young woman's beliefs, she always tried to find
words that would not hurt or shock her. Also, when she spoke
of Félix Pécaud to her correspondent who admired him, she never
wrote a word of reservation or criticism about his religious theories
and philosophies. She made sure to treat them with much respect
because she knew her friend's sincerity and enthusiasm. For nothing
in the world would she have wanted to tarnish the admiration of
the young woman for her headmaster. To hurt the young teacher
or to show her the least sign of poor esteem would have been for
Élisabeth a sin against love . . . and against tolerance.

Pragmatic, Élisabeth had quickly understood that it was not in
directly confronting her friend that she could touch her heart and
make her understand what seemed to her the most essential: the existence of God and the immortality of the soul. But in evoking the
memory of Pécaud, in recalling his beliefs, in going into what was
most dear to her correspondent's heart, she knew that she would
reach the deepest part of her. A difficult path but a sure path. When
Pope John Paul II introduced, a century later, the concept of "new
evangelization", he also would say that to establish deep contact
with people's hearts, the first step is to have them express what is
the most essential for them in their life in order to be able later to
illuminate it in the light of Christ.

Questions of belief held both an important and a discreet place in
this correspondence, but never under the appearance of intellectual

exchanges or dogmatic affirmations. We could characterize these discussions as a soft light of spiritual radiance, a kind of sun whose rays warm and illuminate, to use the words that would come to Aimée's mind when she later recalled the influence Élisabeth had on her life.

An example: this young woman, to whom Élisabeth showed much trust and friendship and whom she often called "my dear", had attended the Baptism of a baby who was a few days old; she had been outraged to hear the prayers of exorcism intended to expel the devil from this little, completely pure soul. She expressed this to Élisabeth, who replied to her without using a single theological argument. She simply responded to her with an eloquent and luminous image, a simple comparison to an experience within everyone's reach: that of the stained-glass windows in a church. When we look at them from the outside, we see only grey and shapeless fragments; but when we enter inside and light passes through them, everything is illuminated, everything becomes colored and takes on meaning, transformed into a splendid, harmonious, and colorful work.

Little by little, Élisabeth became a light and a strength for Aimée. Like a mother, she often gave her "the keys of the Kingdom" in a simple and loving way:

> Take good care of yourself, dear Aimée; consider that I need your affection and that fraternity of spirit that you know how to make so beneficial. . . . And then continue as you do to transform your sufferings into joys for others and to smile at the happiness that does not visit us. All that life (I say Providence) refuses us, let us rejoice to see it come to others, and let us give them all the tenderness that is in us; there are moments in life when the heart feels a kind of nostalgia for the possessions it does not have. I once felt it deeply for motherhood and since then for many desires of an entirely different kind; my refuge then is close to God, and it is near him that I am refreshed and then endeavor to bring only a smile to others.[8]

The third part of *Lettres à des Incroyants* is composed of a long series of letters to married friends: Yvonne and Félix le Dantec.

The history of the Leseurs and the Le Dantec couple is long, interesting, and touching.

---

[8] Ibid., 224.

The two women, Yvonne and Élisabeth, loved each other like sisters. They had known each other since their earliest childhood; they had grown up together in the same building in Paris: the apartments of the two families were for them a shared apartment. A large part of *Une Âme* is devoted to the intimate and affectionate correspondence between Juliette and Yvonne.

Yvonne had married Félix le Dantec in 1905 at the church of Saint-Germain-des-Prés, just like Élisabeth and Félix. Very soon the two couples genuinely became friends and met often, united by an almost fraternal affection.

Félix le Dantec was an erudite figure in the Parisian world. Very brilliant, at sixteen he had received first place in the entrance exam for the École normale supérieure, then he went on to medical studies, and finally became a renowned biologist, admired by Louis Pasteur, who entrusted him with important assignments. It was in this context that, delegated by France, he spent several months in São Paulo bringing the vaccine against yellow fever there.

He held the Chair of General Embryology at the Sorbonne.

He proudly brandished his reputation as a notorious representative of French atheism, which did not prevent him from admiring Élisabeth's beliefs, the elevation of her mind, and her respect for opinions that were not her own. He wrote to her: "I remain filled with admiration for the loftiness of your nature. If there were only people like you, the questions that divide humanity would never be asked."

The two couples saw each other regularly. Félix Leseur admired this friend, who, like him, read much, and shared with him his readings and a common interest in art books, old editions, etchings, and engravings. The two households had much in common. Yvonne and Élisabeth both had faith. Félix le Dantec's respect for his wife's religious beliefs was for Félix Leseur both a subject of admiration and an example.

He was amused to hear his friend occasionally say jokingly to his wife: "Go and see Élisabeth, then, go take your serenity bath."

It was not uncommon, especially at that time, to meet couples in which an atheist, even anticlerical or freemason, husband and a pious wife did not necessarily form a bad couple. Insofar as each knew how to respect the opinions of the other and did not prevent the other from living according to his beliefs, a life together was possible, even if these divergences did not promote dialogue within the couple. At most, each remained in his isolation and in his roles within the family. The rootedness of marriage in society did not suffer decline. The stability of the family and of the couple were strong points of anchorage in life that very few thought of breaking, let alone for ideological views.

The two husbands, the "two Félixes", as they were called, were equally anticlerical, and the two wives were each as open-minded as the other. Later, Félix Leseur would acknowledge that Le Dantec was even less sectarian than he was and that he respected much more than he did the opinions of others. In fact, he welcomed priests or Christian friends at his table with much amiability and open-mindedness. Also, Félix le Dantec did not at all share Félix Leseur's ideas of splendor and gently mocked him for his concern for comfort and elegance.

Le Dantec had written a book entitled *L'athéisme* (Atheism) which had caused a good deal of commotion and had been put on the Index. His thesis tried forcefully to prove, using metaphysical, moral, and political arguments, that God could not exist, that he was an invention of men. However, during one of his stays in a sanatorium, he met a priest with whom he had many conversations, and through this contact, his atheism softened a bit with time. In Catholic circles, however, he was considered a dangerous enemy of religion. He was one of the inventors of scientism, demonstrating in his writings that a good, intelligent society could only evolve toward an amoral atheism.

Following Yvonne's marriage, Élisabeth and Félix adopted Félix le Dantec, nicknamed "the second Félix", as a brother. Shortly before the marriage of her friends, Élisabeth wrote to him: "My dear Félix, allow me to call you that quite simply, since I do not use a more ceremonious form when speaking about you to Yvonne and since I give you this name in my heart, where you already have a place as a brother."[9]

---

[9] Ibid., 291.

And a few days later she wrote to Yvonne, whose marriage had been delayed because her fiancé had already suffered his first attacks of tuberculosis:

> You are marrying an exquisitely good man who possesses, as I have already told you, a Christian mentality and who loves you. If you are equal to your task, as I am confident that you are, you will, on the contrary, do much good. You will show this noble mind that one can be both intelligent and Christian and can unite with a firmness of principles, which must never be compromised, the greatest allowance for others, and the most sensitive understanding of minds and hearts. It is necessary, for his sake, that you be a person of strong character so that he is able to respect you and to respect the convictions with which you align yourself. As for the rest, it is up to God, and no one would do it as he would.[10]

The whole secret of the *Lettres à des Incroyants* resides in these few lines. Élisabeth's tolerance and understanding of all human beings, regardless of their beliefs, was her strength all her life.

She had undoubtedly been inspired by a phrase that had begun to be repeated in certain Christian circles at that time and that would later result in Catholic Action movements: "Grow where you are planted." The circumstances of life had planted her in an unbelieving environment. Her vocation was to flower there.

Later, she would write to Félix le Dantec, with whom she felt very much at ease:

> Let me to tell you once again, my dear Félix, how delighted I am in not finding you a logical atheist, for you would not be the charming person that we love so fraternally. Is it not strange and impressive to think that, finding a true atheist on my path for the first time, I must observe that his admirable qualities are due not only to an exceptionally rich nature, but also to these "ancestral errors" that give so many souls life and from which mine is nourished. I too, my dear Félix, I do as the apple tree does and yield my humble fruits, but I do not fail to recognize the hot sun that has led them to maturity.

---

[10] Ibid., 307.

It was often through a poetic and pleasant image that Élisabeth discreetly testified to her faith.

After Élisabeth's death, Yvonne and Félix le Dantec would be very close and very fraternal friends for Félix. They often asked him how he could live without her, and they did their best to support him, to invite him to their home, to distract him. Yvonne had carefully kept the letters that Élisabeth had written to her. After having read and reread them—"This is my treasure", she said—she ended up giving them to Félix. Le Dantec said of Élisabeth, whom he came to see very often in the afternoons during her illness: "She was a summit of humanity."

Carried away by tuberculosis, which had weakened him for years, Félix le Dantec died at the age of forty-eight without being reconciled with the Church. To the fury of his sectarian and anticlerical friends, however, he had a religious funeral, and had it knowingly because he had said to his wife: "It is not permissible to take away from those who believe the only means of relief and consolation that remain to them in such grief; I find that criminal . . ."

14

Élisabeth's Illness Worsens

In March 1906, Félix, once again, was called to Vienna to attend a trial in order to defend Le Conservateur. Élisabeth very much wanted to go with him despite her poor state of health. They always had great difficulty parting from each other.

Their cousin Maurice Villetard de Prunière, legal advisor of Le Conservateur, a colleague of Félix but also Élisabeth's relative, accompanied them.

Élisabeth had not expected that memories of her much beloved sister would catch up with her on the banks of the Danube and would sadden her so much.

She wrote to her mother on March 9, 1906:

> You can guess what I experienced yesterday when I arrived. Especially because, something I had forgotten, we caught sight of Schönbrunn from the train. When Maurice said: 'There's Schönbrunn' and I saw the castle and the terrace where I still see Félix and Juliette coming down to join me below, I thought I would not be able to contain myself. And yet, no doubt thanks to the dear and invisible protection of our beloved, I have great peace, and, while finding her everywhere, I feel that she is still close to me in a more intimate way. I am going to Saint Stephen's to be reunited with her and to pray. You will not be forgotten.[1]

Élisabeth, already rather weak during this trip to Vienna, which would be one of their last trips abroad, most of the time concealed her fatigue from her husband. In his absence, she often remained lying down in her hotel room, or she read in an armchair in the shade of the tall trees. She never spoke to him of her fatigue and

---

[1] R. P. Marie-Albert Leseur, *Vie d'Élisabeth Leseur* (Paris: Éd. J. de Gigord, 1931), 184.

welcomed him with a smile when he rejoined her. "Silence is beneficial for the soul, necessary for contemplation, conducive to humility. Remembering Jesus during his life and in the hours of the Passion."

From 1907 onward, Élisabeth's hepatic illness became more and more debilitating. She consulted many medical specialists. Some doctors considered an operation, others did not see the use. All were unanimous in prescribing rest and long hours in the chaise longue for a large part of the day.

An interminable period of sickness and suffering was about to begin then.

After that trip, Élisabeth's life slowed down because of the progression of her illness. Attacks followed one after another, though separated by a few periods of stability where both of them had the impression, for a few weeks, that everything would resume as before.

In reality, as Félix explained at a time when the progress of medicine did not allow for another diagnosis: "Her liver was no longer fulfilling its role as protector of the body against the toxins that arise from chronic injury."

Félix then spoke to the best specialists in Paris: first and foremost Doctor Létienne, a renowned surgeon, whom he had known when he was a medical student.

Was it necessary to consider an operation? The first surgeon he had consulted seemed a little disconcerted by this relatively rare sickness for which there was as yet no precise method of investigation. He did not know what decision to make, and finally, after long hesitations, he gave up considering an operation that seemed difficult to him; he did not hide the fact that Élisabeth had to be very careful because she was already in a serious state.

Élisabeth wrote a long letter to her mother-in-law to inform her about her condition:

My case, moreover, has enormously interested the surgeon, who sometimes apologized for the exclamations that escaped him as if someone were in the presence of a rare and curious specimen. He told me that it was necessary, through rest, to calm the current fermentation of the sick area because, he added, "if later on it became worse and it was necessary to take action, that would bother me, but it would bother even more the surgeon who would operate on me." In short, this surgeon, Doctor Gosset, who is at present the leading one in Paris, has been very thorough; indeed, he has a reputation for that.

Thus, I am going to live the life of a recluse, which will not displease me, except for the activities that must be sacrificed and the trouble of keeping Félix indoors. You are a rare mother-in-law, finding that her daughter-in-law thinks too much of her son; I well understood your sensitive and comforting thought. But, all the same, I will send him from time to time to be distracted at friends' houses or at the Pauls'.[2]

When Élisabeth mentioned a recluse's life that would not displease her, she knew that she had within her many spiritual and intellectual resources to support her. She would have a lot more time and silence to devote herself to it. She also knew that her husband, always so attentive, would be close to her to face this ordeal and no doubt would grow even closer to her. Confronting the illness together seemed less difficult to her.

A few joys, however, came to brighten those somber days. In 1908, Félix was awarded the Legion of Honor. He was very happy to announce this news to her because he knew how proud she would be of him. His work as a politician, economist, and journalist was at last officially recognized. As soon as she learned of this distinction, Élisabeth took up the pen and wrote to the new Knight who was first and foremost the knight of her heart:

Without long fasting, ardent prayer, or armed vigils; here you are
a knight; receive then from my hand,
Between a happy smile and a few sweet tears,
The new ribbon that you can wear tomorrow.

All my heart, filled with tenderness at this hour,
Celebrates you in a burst of pure and joyful pride,
My voice whispers, while I laugh and cry:
We now both carry a cross.

Through your daily labor and your courage
You slowly wove the desired ribbon,

---

[2] Ibid., 185.

And since genius is long forbearance,
You can adorn your heart with the desired emblem.

The cross that I carried and I still carry
Is made of past sorrows and efforts,
But the triumphant God whom all my being adores
Has placed the crucifix before my weary eyes.

May the light and cheerful cross forever illuminate
Days made of work and exquisite kindness.
Then, when I die, place on my breast
The other cross, my love and my only pride.

To my dear husband
To a perfect and devoted companion
To a friend.
In remembrance of March 12, 1908[3]

Everything is said in these few lines, which completely expresses the state of her soul.

---

[3] Marie-Louise Herking, *Le Père Leseur* (Paris: Éd. J. de Gigord, 1952), 69.

15

A Shared Passion: Bibliophilia

Even though Élisabeth's illness sometimes allowed respites of several months, the couple's life was inevitably profoundly changed. Social or theatrical evenings hardly existed anymore. Only parents and close family shared a few, brief, intimate gatherings with them. Both of them judged that their life had to be much more sedentary, but much more interior as well.

Félix, very busy with his professional obligations, went to his office every day; he joined his wife in the evenings. She waited for him and welcomed him with tenderness.

Reading remained an essential occupation for them both, even if their choice of authors was often very different. They liked to discuss their reading in their long moments alone together, except for the ideas that were likely to prompt a dispute.

It was at that time when their social life was almost nonexistent that Félix devoted himself to an art form that had tempted him for years: bibliophilia.

Not only had he always been an avid reader, but he was also an astute connoisseur of rare and valuable books. He had long been friends with Paris' experts like Édouard Pelletan (Helleu et Sargent) and Jules Meynial, who had become excellent friends over the years.

At the time, bibliophilia was a very popular science or passion in intellectual circles and even more so in political circles.

Love of beautiful texts combined with a love for beautiful books regularly brought the elite of the Parisian world together between the multicolored shelves of art bookshops.

It was in this setting that Félix Leseur rediscovered his old friend Louis Barthou, also a great lover of rare editions and autographs. Everything brought them closer: their passion not only for books, for politics, but also for music, and especially that of Wagner, about whom Louis Barthou would later write a biography in 1924. Barthou was also editor of a newspaper less prestigious than Félix's and that had its readers in the Béarn, his native province. Above all, he was an intelligent, dynamic, and very cultured politician. In 1918, he would be admitted to the Académie française, where he would succeed to the chair of the medievalist Joseph Bédier.

Louis Barthou was very brilliant. In a few years he had risen through all the ranks of political life until he later became president of the council and minister of foreign affairs, which would cost him a tragic death in 1934: on mission to Marseille to welcome King Alexander I of Yugoslavia in the name of France, he would be accidentally killed on the Canebière by a stray bullet during an attack aimed at the king.

Félix Leseur and Louis Barthou were, at that time, equally anti-clerical and shared the same fight. It pleased Félix Leseur that Louis Barthou, deputy under the Combes regime, had voted for the 1905 laws for the expulsion of religious congregations. Their discussions were passionate and fascinating on many subjects.

Their learning about limited editions or difficult-to-find copies took place mostly in the shops of rare-book dealers. Between six and seven o'clock in the evening, the bibliophile friends met several times a week with publishers, leafing through sales catalogues, carefully examining original editions, browsing the bookshelves, examining rare bindings down to the smallest details with the help of a magnifying glass. Far from the rowdy life of the streets of Paris, they escaped into the silent world of culture and learning. In the catalogues, they located the valuable book they coveted and that they would purchase a few days later at the sale. With shrewdness and sound judgment they knew how much they could invest in sure values. In this way, Louis Barthou and Félix Leseur both succeeded in collecting valuable works that they looked through together as astute connoisseurs. As the publisher Helleu would later say: "They both loved autograph [manuscripts] and printed [books]."

According to Félix Leseur's catalogue of books published at the time of the dispersion of his library, it seems that, although he had been in possession of expensive old books, he had paid particular attention to the contemporary book and especially to the illustrated book, for which he had bindings fashioned according to his taste by commissioning renowned artists like Boutet de Monvel, Maurice Denis, Sargent, etc.

Among the works he valued most was *La Dernier des Abencérages* (the last of the Abencerrajes), by Chateaubriand, an author to whom Félix devoted genuine worship. The catalogue described it in this way: "Printed on vellum decorated with eighty drawings by Daniel Vierge, followed by a double set of prints printed on paper from China and Japan, bound in garnet Moroccan leather with gold threads and laces, reminiscent of Arab art."

The example of another very valuable work gives an idea of the rarity of the books collected by Félix Leseur: *Les Cinq Poèmes* (The five poems), by Victor Hugo, released on the occasion of the centennial of the poet's birth and published by Édouard Pelletan at Félix's request and according to his instructions with the collaboration of well-known painters or illustrators. The binding chosen by Félix has as its central motif a pine tree whose branches extend onto the book's covers, while in the foreground, on dyed and molded leather, the foliage emerges in the shape of needles from which the cone-shaped fruit are escaping, with their engraved scales in a light brown color; at the top of the composition, through the branches, we see the sky, represented by azure stones, and, at the bottom, successive planes of natural or gilded tin representing a pine forest. This single copy is considered by enthusiasts of luxury bookbinding to be the most perfect example of early twentieth-century art.

This work is without doubt the most sought-after of the Leseurs' library, but many others of great beauty stand alongside it. One could multiply the descriptions of books designed by Félix Leseur, fashioned according to his tastes with vellum chosen by him, with original documents, rare autographs. He entrusted their realization to renowned artists who became his friends.

To be sure, large amounts of money were devoted to these creations. But the Leseurs, through these investments, believed they were fulfilling a duty to society and a mission to art in general. By devoting their surplus to the creation of unique books, they were aware of their participation in upholding the French tradition of luxury books. They were enabling the artists to whom they entrusted their projects to earn a living and to make themselves known. In addition, a beautiful text in a luxury "case" then took on a new richness and beauty for which they felt proud and responsible.

Very well known among the bibliophiles of the capital, Félix Leseur belonged to almost all the societies that, directly or indirectly, pertained to books. He knew all the booksellers of the capital and their associate bookbinders, engravers, and painters.

This passion for beautiful books was an indispensable diversion for him during Élisabeth's long illness. It was also for them a land of both encounters and exchanges. When she could, Élisabeth accompanied him into these temples of rare books, whose atmosphere she also loved, but, as and when her illness gradually progressed, it was he who brought valuable copies home to her.

His great joy was to leaf through the quartos in his library with her in the evening and to hear her appreciate his endeavors. Always very admiring of her husband, she wholeheartedly shared his artistic accomplishments with him in intimate moments contemplating beauty.

Much later in 1926, invited to give a lecture to booksellers, Félix would say:

> It is because I have had, throughout my life, the passion for books. I had amassed an impressive library that was my pride, while at the same time giving me the most personal satisfaction. What hours, those I sought the most, I spent in some bookshops, those on the boulevard for contemporary books, as in those of your confreres who deal more specifically in old books, with art publishers like Édouard Pelletan, who was a great artist, among bookbinders whose talent has contributed to a part of France's influence. I was thus able to appreciate the charm of those long talks where we cordially spoke about everything while leafing through the latest published book or rare volume or caressing the Moroccan leather worked with such taste.[1]

Félix Leseur's library catalogue remains, even today, a treasure consulted by bibliophiles.[2]

---

[1] Marie-Louise Herking, *Le Père Leseur* (Paris: Éd. J. de Gigord, 1952), 73.
[2] Librairie Jules Maynial, Catalogue des Beaux Libres anciens et modernes, Juin 1919.

16

When Love Helps to Accept the Unacceptable

As her illness progressed, Élisabeth remained confined at home. They now lived in a bright and spacious apartment at 16 rue de Marignan, not far from the Champs-Élysées, in the chic neighborhood surrounding the Place de l'Étoile, where new buildings, equipped with a comfort that new technologies placed within easy reach of wealthy individuals, were springing up like mushrooms.

All the same, the Leseurs did not miss an opportunity to escape to Jougne as soon as the weather allowed it and especially during the summer.

Initially, Élisabeth went out two or three times a week to go to Mass in a little chapel that she greatly loved at 23 rue Jean Goujon: Notre Dame de la Consolation. Not only did she love its silence, which was ideal for contemplation and the services celebrated there, but also this chapel carried in its walls a weight of griefs and sufferings to which Élisabeth was sensitive. In fact, it had been built on the ruins of the Bazar de la Charité. Élisabeth remembered how horrified she had been when, as a young woman, she had learned of that terrible fire which occurred during a charity sale where a generous crowd was gathered. It had caused the death of 150 people. Since that day, she had always prayed for them.

When she had the strength for it, she went to her parish: the church of Saint-Pierre-de-Chaillot, which had a completely different appearance then from what it has now. It was still an old Romanesque church from the eleventh century. It would not be until 1922, well after Élisabeth's death, that the façade would be decorated with Bouchard's hieratic statues and the master glassmaker Maumejean would decorate the interior with his multicolored mosaics.

Élisabeth's illness, however, did not allow her to go out every day.

As the attacks approached, it was the Dominican Father Hébert who traveled to her house to hear her Confessions. But out of discretion, he never came without having received a written request, very often from the hand of Félix himself.

Father Hébert did not conceal that his situation often seemed to him very awkward with respect to this couple, ill-matched in their beliefs but united by an obvious, admiring, and tender love. The cordiality of Félix, whom Élisabeth's profound exchanges with her confessor did not escape, bothered him at times: What attitude should he adopt when occasionally in front of a notoriously anti-clerical husband and a wife wishing to give an example of Christian wisdom, open-mindedness, and radiant faith?

Although he was always received with perfect courtesy and even with an increasing friendliness, Father Hébert retained the impression of never having become a familiar visitor of the house or a friend of this unusual household in which he recognized strength despite so many differences. With great discretion, he helped Élisabeth to detect "the slow and silent action of Providence" in her life as a sick person; and, above all, he especially took care to help her keep her soul at peace. He feared that by thinking too much, getting too much into the habit of introspection, she would be tormented by scruples capable of weakening her. It was on this path of peace of heart that he guided her. The "obsession with cleanliness" as Élisabeth told him, was apt to create an inner worry or torment in her, sometimes even feelings of guilt. His priority would always consist in helping Élisabeth find a harmonious and serene human balance.

Élisabeth received many visits, especially around New Year's Day. Smiling, she called them her "social events"; happy to see dear faces again, she feared, however, the scattering that the visits caused and sometimes was almost tempted to avoid them. After a few days, she understood that these people, who traveled for her, did not come out of worldliness. They came to distract her a little from her illness, and, above all, they wanted to show her friendship and to bring her support and distraction in this difficult time. So, she wrote in her resolutions the need to become "a little worldly" out of love for her friends and out of an openness to what was important in their lives. In this circumstance, she was aware that withdrawing into one's self was not only anti-evangelical but that it was also, during a hardship, whatever it might be, the worst of dangers.

Félix easily understood that his wife drew her energy from her spiritual life. From now on, he turned a blind eye to this reality, which was completely beyond him. The time when he combatted her beliefs no longer had a reason to exist. He noticed, without appreciating it, that faith helped her to hold on in a painful time whose outcome, unfortunately, he knew all too well. It was no longer a question for him to make her lose the hope that would enable her to keep standing in the years that remained to her to live. He would later write: "When I saw her so sick, and sick with one of those liver conditions that usually provoke such hypochondria, impatience, and disgust, which she bore with such evenness of temper, I was still struck to see this soul so in command of herself and of her body, and, realizing that she drew this superior strength from her beliefs, I stopped attacking her."[1]

Élisabeth, for her part, began a new chapter in her life. She did not want to suffer it in passivity or to let herself go like a wisp of straw tossed about at the mercy of the storm. In order to face an existence, now so short, so different from what she had envisioned, she considered it a duty now to build herself up internally even more solidly than before. She understood that she would not recover. She knew that the physical deterioration of the sickness would not spare her. With confinement often bringing a sluggishness and a despondency that she had noticed in several people, she was fully aware that she would have before her an obstacle very difficult to combat from day to day and, alas impossible to avoid. She would face it to the end!

She needed a great, personal inner strength to confront this new ordeal that she repeatedly called "the greatest trial of my life". Her main concern was not to burden her relatives and much less her husband.

Almost every day she made notes in her diary of resolutions, or, rather, of definite guidelines that she wanted to follow in the most difficult moments. If she wrote them down, it was so that she could

---

[1] Félix Leseur, *In Memoriam* (introduction to the 1917 edition of Élisabeth Leseur, *Journal et Pensées de chaque jour* [Paris: Éd. J. de Gigord]), 271.

refer to them in case too strong a suffering might make her forget them.

> To avoid as much as possible speaking of myself, of my trials, of my illness, above all of my soul and of the graces received from God. . . . To pray to God to give me more and more the knowledge of souls. Go to them through intelligence and the heart: for this, to strengthen my intelligence, warm my heart. To work and act with serenity.
>
> And now, my God, I offer you the new life open before me. I want, sustained by your grace, to become a new woman, a Christian, an apostle.[2]

She wrote the resolution to hide her sufferings from her loved ones, to work each day not only in her duties as homemaker and wife but also to increase her knowledge through new readings in order to be able to continue to be a good conversationalist for Félix. For her, in her situation, this was the "duty of her state in life":

> In view of a greater good, a higher goal, to watch over even my demeanor, my grooming; to make myself attractive to God. To make my home pleasant, to make it a center of good, healthy influences; to gather there diverse minds and hearts and employ my efforts to uplift them or enlighten them.
>
> In brief: to reserve for God alone the depths of my soul and my inner or Christian life. Give others serenity, charm, goodness, useful words or deeds. To make loved, through me, Christian truth, but to say its name only at an explicit, or at least fairly clear, prompting in order to seem truly providential. . . . To be austere for myself, as attractive as possible for others.[3]

The secret preoccupation with seeing Félix return to the faith one day never left her. Certainly he was perhaps less aggressive now, but he remained deeply atheist. She knew it. Drawing on a very human phrase from the Gospel: "We judge a tree by its fruits", she gave herself a rule of life for approaching potential conversations with him and for making him see the fruits that he could understand of the faith that supported her.

---

[2] Élisabeth Leseur, *Cahier de résolutions*, 144–50.
[3] Ibid., 135.

Duties toward my dear husband first: tenderness that does not even merit being a duty, constant concern to be useful and agreeable to him. Above all observe an extreme reserve on everything that touches on matters of the faith that for him are still covered by a veil. If sometimes a quiet affirmation is necessary, or if I can fruitfully open a corner of my heart a little, let it then be a rare demonstration, wisely done, in all sweetness and serenity. Show him the fruits without the lifeblood, my life without the faith that transforms it, the light that is in me without speaking of the one who brings it to my soul; reveal God without pronouncing his name; that is, I believe, the only form my desire can take for the conversion and holiness of the dear companion of my life, my beloved Félix.[4]

Which did not stop her from noting a few days later:

Very acute suffering from an evening spent listening to him mock, attack, criticize my faith and spiritual things. God helped me to preserve charity within, serenity without; to deny or betray nothing, without, however, annoying by overly rigid assertions; but what this represents of efforts and personal sorrows and what divine grace is thus necessary to my weakness! My God, will you give me one day . . . soon . . . the great joy of a full communion of soul with my dear husband, of the same faith and of an existence oriented toward You, for him as for me?[5]

In her resolutions, she gave the most important part of her days to prayer and meditation on the word of God, the Gospels.

Élisabeth tirelessly read and reread the writings of Saint Teresa of Ávila. This woman, even though from another century and another country, had also led the life of a recluse; for a long time she lived the life of a sick person; she, too, experienced a renewal of her faith through the reading of Saint Augustine; she, too, experienced exchanges of love with God; she also had had a concern for "souls". The perfection that Teresa sought in her spiritual life was a model for Élisabeth and the accessible means suggested by Teresa touched her heart.

In June 1908, a new relapse worsened the state of Élisabeth's health. She had to spend the whole summer stretched out on her

---

[4] Ibid., 142.
[5] Ibid., 167.

bed in their apartment. Félix left her as little as possible. She thanked him endlessly for all the attentions he gave her and expressed her gratitude to him several times a day for so much kindness toward her. For his part, he was more surprised every day in the face of her inner peace, her sweetness, and her attentiveness to all those who came to see her. Often a question forced itself upon him: How could such a sick person, struggling daily with suffering, be so serene? So open to the troubles of others? Was her faith the primary reason for her calm? From where, then, did she draw so much interior strength and peace?

Once she was able to be moved, Félix, at the advice of the doctors, planned to take her to Jougne, whose invigorating air had always put her back on her feet. But she could only travel lying down. Félix did not hesitate to put together, with the help of the P.L.M.,[6] for whom this was not yet the custom, a set of practical solutions so that this trip could be made in the best conditions: a car would come pick them up from their Parisian residence to take them to the train station, where a wheelchair would await them; a special chair-bed compartment would be at their disposal in this train that had never contained one. Félix then asked permission from the management of the P.L.M. and from the federal Swiss railroads for this train to make an exceptional stop at the Hôpitaux/Neufs-Jougne station, the time to lower down the wheelchair. For the well-being of his wife, no measure, however unusual it might be, would be too much for him.

As always, the good air of Jougne, at more than three thousand feet in altitude, and the joy of rediscovering its mountains planted with fir trees and its sweeping landscapes very gently put Élisabeth back on her feet; stretched out on the terrace, she finished embroidering a tapestry for the church of Jougne, a cloth for the Blessed Virgin's altar, begun the previous summer. She would take Félix, on the eve of one of his departures, into the church where he never went to admire it on site.

She stayed three months at Jougne. Of course, Félix's professional obligations prevented him from remaining absent from Paris for three months. He was very upset about it because after so many

---

[6] Paris-Lyon-Mediterranean railroads, ancestor of the SNCF.

hardships already gone through together, he was more in love than ever. He judged the importance or the joy of his presence close to his wife both for her and for him. He would only come back on Sundays; it was then that an uninterrupted family chain was set up to ensure that someone was always available near Élisabeth.

Every departure of Félix was wrenching for both of them, as is evidenced in these excerpts from letters written incrementally by Félix during a return trip to Paris:

> I begin my journey by embracing you at the Pontarlier buffet, as tenderly as I can. It seems to me that just now I have not done that enough.

And a few hours later from Dijon during that same return trip:

> A good trip thus far. With every turn of the wheel I feel sad at being separated from you, and I am truly disoriented. I miss you so much it hurts. I love you. I embrace you.

A few days later:

> My dear beloved,

> How my day seemed long and empty. You are definitely my guardian angel, and when you are not here, I am no longer worth anything. You cannot imagine how essential you are to me.

And again:

> Fortunately this letter is the last one I will write to you, and it fills me with joy to tell myself that tomorrow I will be near you and that I will finally really be able to embrace you. I am overjoyed at this thought.[7]

During that same period, when they were writing to each other every day, despite the uncertainties of the postal service, she wrote to him in her turn:

> What a sad day I spent yesterday, my beloved, without a word from you, because your letter from the day before yesterday only reached me this morning along with that from yesterday. Two days not only

---

[7] These three excerpts from unpublished letters were cited by Marie-Louise Herking, *Le Père Leseur* (Paris: Éd. J. de Gigord, 1952).

without seeing you but without having this very little echo of you that a letter would have been; and then, deep down, I worried a bit. . . . Having risen, I went to Mass for you, and on my return I had the sweet joy of your two letters, which did me good and of which I had great need. I was cruel enough to be happy that you are bored without me; without that, the sharing would not really be fair because every day seems longer than the day before, and I always experience the same feeling of emptiness, of sadness that takes hold of me as soon as you are no longer at my side. My darling, these twenty years of shared life, of close union of heart and mind, have created between us a love, I hope, truly stronger than death, and if I had to live without you, I would bury myself in solitude and the world would become a burden to me. It will not be so, thank God, because, on the one hand, you do not, I suppose, have an intention of abandoning me and, on the other hand, Hippolyte Duron told his wife that you were in perfect health, much better than two years ago, which made me hope to take precedence over you for the great departure.

In four days, I will ready myself to see you. At last! . . . I give you, my beloved, a kiss filled with tenderness and I send you the best of my thoughts, which all tend toward you at this moment. Your Élisabeth.

By the power of their love, they were a magnificent couple. What was the cement of their union that many might envy them after twenty years of marriage and so many hardships already gone through? Without any doubt, a love turned toward the other, a love that was a gift of oneself to the other, a love that was attentive, above all, to the happiness of the other, despite the difficult situation of the moment.

Élisabeth very rarely spoke of her illness. She wanted to be cheerful, bright, attentive to her husband, interested in many other subjects.

For his part, even though he was very close to her to surround and protect her from the inherent difficulties of her illness, he thought only to distract her and to experience with her something other than the sessions of rest and medications.

Without saying a word, he accepted her faith, which she less and less frequently deprived herself of expressing to him and which she situated in a context of love for him. She went to Mass for him? He said nothing and took it as a gesture of love. He understood that she gave him what she could give him, that which was in the innermost part of her heart, even if it was not in his beliefs.

Later he would understand that Élisabeth's contemplative life did not express feelings different from the tears and perfume of Mary Magdalen at the feet of Jesus.

During that stay at Jougne, Élisabeth, very aware that her illness would make her more and more infirm, began a path that was not new, but still better defined and accepted, if not almost with joy, at least in peace of heart:

> It is quite clear to me that the divine will for me is not in action. Until further notice, I must confine myself almost exclusively to prayer and endeavor to possess more the spirit of sacrifice. . . . In prayer, we do not see the result—though certain—of our efforts; we are truly the instrument in the hands of the divine artist. We can remain humble, while feeling the great joy of working for the glory of God and for the good of souls. May my lot and my task, Lord, be here, and in silence may I do only your will.[8]

She defined the contours of the "duty of her state in life" in this way.

Fulfilling the "duty of her state", a value of which we speak less and less in our time, always seemed a primordial necessity for Élisabeth. It was a matter, not of creating new obligations, but of accepting, of living each day well, and of handling with all her human capacities the situation in which the circumstances of life had placed her, as difficult as that situation might be. The circumstances of life, with the arrival of new events, always involve chosen and well-thought-out readjustments.

She indicated the major points of them: "Accept as a hardship this impossibility where I am equally in a life active with charities, relationships, and consistent work and in a contemplative life that the duties of my state, the tastes of those around me, and circumstances forbid me. Do everything I can for others."[9]

---

[8] Élisabeth Leseur, *Cahier de résolutions*, 158.
[9] Ibid., 158.

It was in this spirit that gradually and resolutely she made her way toward a contemplative life: Félix pretended not to know about it, but he sensed her interior life when he saw her in her long moments of contemplation. He could only rejoice about it, humanly speaking, because in Élisabeth's pacifying and loving smiles he felt her incredible acceptance of the illness and dependence at the age of thirty-eight!

He still absolutely refused to understand that her behavior was the radiance of an intentional evangelical attitude: "To put into all my actions, my words, even my gestures, a moderation, a serene gentleness that becomes the constant affirmation of my inner serenity. To show God in this way ceaselessly acting in me to moderate me, calm me, and give me every strength."[10]

The stay at Jougne where they sometimes found themselves alone, in the intimacy of their relationship, refreshed Élisabeth's strength.

Before returning to their apartment in Paris, Félix, always very attentive, wanted to provide some kind of distraction for his young wife, who had just spent long months very confined. He himself needed to be reunited with her in a new environment where the long months of illness could be forgotten. Both of them were aware that distractions or joys were now for them nothing but narrow oases in suffering, but they still had an appetite to appreciate good moments lived together.

One week he took her to the shores of Lake Geneva at Ouchy, where he counted on the long boat rides to make her breathe an invigorating air, without the fatigue of walking. The autumn was still mild, and the trees along the edge of the lake took on the colors of a painter's palette, which delighted them both.

Élisabeth wrote to her mother on October 19, 1908:

Yesterday we were again in a beautiful light; we had the vast horizons of the lake, and we saw a very beautiful sunset from the boat. Eventually good things end here below, and it is quite right that I thank Providence with fervor for all the spiritual and temporal graces that it has accorded me during these three months, and also, or rather next, for its good instrument, my dear mother, thanks to whom some of my joys have come. We had warm and delicious weather by the

---

[10] Ibid., 150.

lake, but not more than at Jougne. On Friday, we took a four-hour boat ride to Villeneuve. On Saturday, we left at ten in the morning, lunched onboard the boat, stopped for an hour in Geneva, and returned at five-fifteen in the evening. On Sunday, we toured the far side of the lake in the boat and left for Paris at 11 in the evening. In the morning, I went to Mass; Félix, with great helpfulness, had found for me, near the hotel, a very private and contemplative chapel, built and maintained by the princess of Sayn-Wittgenstein. I attended the 8 o'clock Mass there and went to Communion with quite a lot of people with great joy for this act of gratitude and homage to God on this Protestant soil. Need I tell you of those, all those, whom I mentioned to him?[11]

Since the worsening of his wife's illness, Félix's anticlericalism became more and more conciliatory. He was evolving. He understood that only Élisabeth's profound faith could help her to accept her illness and to live the few years that remained to her in the best way possible. Without at all understanding this inner strength, or even suspecting its vigor, he otherwise went along with her at least to make it easier for her. For him, his wife's belief represented an acceptable remedy, nothing more. In the situation she was in, it was at least a little ray of sunshine for her. That was the reason why he looked for a hotel near a chapel after inquiring about Mass times, why he agreed to her leaving the hotel before eight to go to a morning Mass where he did not accompany her.

While Félix now understood and appreciated the support that the faith brought to his wife, he was still a complete stranger to the idea that he himself might one day turn toward God; he smiled outright when she told him from time to time that he would one day take Holy Orders. For him it had almost become "the family joke"!

Élisabeth knew that his hour had not yet come. Several times in her writings she mentioned her concern to avoid any religious discussion with her husband that would come to nothing.

---

[11] R. P. Marie-Albert Leseur, *Vie d'Élisabeth Leseur* (Paris: Éd. J. de Gigord, 1931), 190.

17

Discovering Beaune

In 1909, Élisabeth seemed to have recovered some strength.

At the beginning of the summer, an attentive friend, Léon Mahuet, offered to drive the Leseurs to Jougne by car. This way the trip would be made easier. At that time, the automobile was still in its early stages. Those who owned one were few.

Knowing how much his friends liked to travel and considering how much they must have needed a change of scene after such bleak and difficult months, he suggested an extensive detour through the Morvan, Burgundy, and especially Beaune, a town full of history; he knew they would appreciate its old houses, arcades, and cobbled streets, which still testified to the splendor of the residences of the Dukes of Burgundy.

Beaune, moreover, was much talked about in Paris at that beginning of the century. In fact, since 1907, the complete restoration of the tiled roofs of the Hospices, in terracotta glazed with four different colors (red, brown, yellow, and green) that cut out beautiful geometric forms on the roofs like a rich tapestry, had just been finished and was the object of many visitors' admiration. The detour through Beaune was all the more tempting because Burgundian cuisine was renowned and a good meal washed down with the Hospices' famous wine could only be a wonderful diversion for a young woman who had not left her house for weeks.

Élisabeth and Félix were very interested in visiting this old hospital in the heart of Burgundy. This *hostel* that was *de Dieu* (of God) had been built with great care by Nicolas Rolin in the fifteenth century with the goal of giving the very sick the best care and great dignity.

The sight of the vast hall lined with double beds concealed behind red curtains was impressive. We can imagine what Félix must have thought of this fifteenth-century religion expressed in the famous polyptych of *The Last Judgment*. The dying poor, naked, distorted by pain, plunged into the fire of hell! How far it is from the Father's love for us expressed all throughout the Gospel and demonstrated by Élisabeth! The fear of hell has always been a point of ridicule for atheists about Christians, and Félix did not fail to smile at it.

Nevertheless, both passionate about all forms of art, amazed, they contemplated the elegant exterior architecture with its tall roofs covered in thin slate, its gables, its wooden galleries, its arcades, its large courtyard.

While the large sickroom had become a museum, the hospital, however, still existed in a less historical setting. Both were interested in this visit; Félix as a former extern in hospitals, Élisabeth as a patient.

During their visit, they noticed a little eight-year-old girl who was apparently very ill; pale and thin, she was lying on a daybed at a distance against a wall under the galleries of the courtyard. They had placed her little bed outside so that she could breathe the good air and benefit from the sunshine. Approaching her, the Leseurs read such suffering on her face that Élisabeth was drawn to her right away. With tenderness, she leaned toward the little one and spoke a few words to her:

—What is your name?

—Marie.

—Are you suffering very much?

—Yes, very much.

—What can I do for you? I am traveling, but I can, when I return home, send you something that would make you happy.

—Oh, Madame, postcards with views. That would make me so happy.

—I understand; I will not forget my little friend from Beaune's Hôtel de Dieu! I will send you some. I promise.

After Élisabeth's departure, when little Marie recounted this conversation to the nun who was caring for her, but who had not met the Leseurs, the nun smiled:

—You are right, this lady is very kind to have made you this promise; but, you know, when traveling we have little time to ourselves, and we often forget what we promised in a moment of generosity. Do not be sad if the postcards do not come to you, it is quite understandable.

But she did not know Élisabeth. At every stop she bought post-cards and sent them to the little girl with a sentence full of kindness and encouragement written on the back. "A nice souvenir from the traveling lady to little Marie and best wishes for better health. Élisabeth Leseur. July 10, 1908."[1]

From Jougne, Élisabeth continued to send postcards to the little patient who, one day, felt the need to write her a few words to thank her. The nun gave her a stamp and an envelope to send her letter and added a short personal note:

> Madame, I do not have the honor of knowing you, but, all the same, allow me to join my respectful sentiments to those of my little patient. I am deeply touched by your gentle charity with regard to this poor child. Your lovely cards are a ray of sunshine for her; I confess that when, upon receiving them, I see a smile bloom on this young face that usually bears the imprint of sadness and suffering, I myself am happy, and I ask God to reward your gentle kindness.[2]

Little by little, a correspondence was established between Élisabeth and the nun. At her request, Élisabeth sent a doll to the little girl, who, whether a sign of Providence or not, named it Juliette, without knowing of course how much this name touched Élisabeth's heart.

The nun regularly sent news of little Marie until the day when she informed Élisabeth that the little girl had died the evening before like a saint. She had been able to receive Communion for the first time a few hours before in the hospital chapel, where they had brought her bed. Full of love and joy, she had had the happiness of wearing a white dress and a little veil under a crown of flowers. "A beautiful lily to decorate her Paradise", the nun wrote.

The encounter could have stopped there.

This child, however, had been a providential link between Élisabeth and the nun. The correspondence between these two women, so different in their environments, in their vocations, had only just

---

[1] R. P. Marie-Albert Leseur, *Vie d'Élisabeth Leseur* (Paris: Éd. J. de Gigord, 1931), 60.
[2] Élisabeth Leseur, *Lettres sur la souffrance* (Paris: Éd. du Cerf, 2012), 62.

begun that day. They continued to write to each other. The exchange of letters between them, although they had never seen each other, became increasingly personal and intimate until it became a true spiritual direction that lasted until Élisabeth's death.

18

The *Lettres sur la Souffrance* (Letters on Suffering)

Such is the title under which Félix later published the seventy-eight letters exchanged between Élisabeth and Sister Marie Goby from December 19, 1910, to March 12, 1914, one month before Élisabeth's death.[1]

They allow us to follow Élisabeth and Félix in their daily life, in their courage in the face of adversity. They also reveal to us the secrets of a genuine fruitful and profound spiritual "encounter" between a sick young woman and a stranger, a hospital nun struggling with difficulties. Both of them wanted to help each other, to support and to confide in each other because both suffered from spiritual isolation and misunderstanding:

Élisabeth wrote to her:

> Your affection has become the sweetness of my life; until now, my dearest affections have brought me little from a supernatural point of view: the souls that I found on my path mainly needed the very little that I could give them. And now it is in this interior desert, which the great divine spring alone nourished (it is true that it is enough for everything), that I have found the beautiful little clear and refreshing drop that has done my soul so much good. I cannot help thinking that it is the lovely attention, a delicious treat from the good God who wanted a little human gentleness, Christian kindness, and supernatural support for the heart that he alone sustained.[2]

In her turn, the nun wrote to her: "You are, my Élisabeth, a friend for all times and all seasons; but above all you are the incomparable friend at sorrowful times and at difficult and painful seasons."

---

[1] *Lettres sur la souffrance*, along with some unpublished letters of response from Sister Marie Goby, were published in October 2012 by Éditions du Cerf.

[2] Élisabeth Leseur, *Lettres sur la souffrance* (Paris: Éd. du Cerf, 2012), 159.

Total submission to the will of God, abandonment to Providence, and acceptance of the duties inherent to this new stage were the main theme confided by Élisabeth as testimony to her present existence and as a rule of life:

> To accomplish what I consider a duty—works of charity, dedication to others or to the poor—in such a way that no one can take offense by it and it does no harm to immediate duties; never to sacrifice intellectual work and to do it regularly, but to become a little worldly, in spite of my love for my own home, for the simple life, and for solitude, in order to please Félix and those around me; in sum, to carry out the most varied duties without anyone suspecting the pain I might have in reconciling them, to forget myself, to develop what God has given me of reason and intelligence, to banish pride completely, even in its most subtle forms, which I know well, to love strongly and without self-seeking, to desire every day and at every hour, sustained by divine grace, that which is the present duty and never to neglect a duty, however insignificant it might be, that is my task.[3]

It is understandable that the title *Lettres sur la souffrance* (Letters on suffering) might discourage twenty-first-century readers, especially if the suffering is connected to religion. The word "suffering" necessarily assumes a sorrowful hue that repels. In the present culture, where everything seems to be done to suppress suffering and offer a world of leisure and pleasures, seventy-eight letters on this subject might seem too austere to some. For others, Jansenism is not completely dead and still leads some to believe that it is necessary to suffer in order to prove to God that we love him.

They forget that Jesus said: "These things I have spoken to you, that my joy may be in you, and that your joy may be full" (Jn 15:11). Jesus does not ask that, to please him, we should add suffering to our lives; like a father, he says that in the trial of suffering he is with us and that he helps us to live it: "Come to me, all who labor and are heavy laden" (Mt 11:28).

Experience shows that suffering exists, sooner or later, in every life and that no one can deny it. The leisure and pleasures offered

---

[3] Ibid., XVI.

by our society do not erase it; they help us to bear it, to forget it once in a while. Certainly they can distract us, and we will see how in these final years Félix increased distractions and travel for his young wife. Nevertheless, both of them knew that this fatal illness would inevitably lead to the time of separation.

Like all couples confronted by this situation, they faced it one day at a time, speaking of it only a very little with each other, no doubt so as not to take away the hope and courage of the other.

Even though palliative care units and painkillers exist these days, the sufferings of certain illnesses remain cruel; each person is led to shoulder them as he can and with what he is. Élisabeth—and consequently Félix—had been confronted with this trial when they were particularly young. They did not lament; they did not complain. They shouldered it together, supported by each other.

The resolutions and advice expressed by Élisabeth to Sister Goby were often very concrete, very accessible for most sick people, and could be considered a guide for confronting serious illness in the best intellectual conditions and spiritual dispositions:

> Let us both do our task, my little sister, wanting only the divine will and knowing in turns "to act or to suffer" without seeking ourselves, even in the spiritual order and in the subtlest way. Let us be abandoned to the hands of the heavenly Father, to the impulses of the divine heart toward us, and in joy or sadness, consolation or neglect, let us know how to smile and say again: Alleluia.[4]

Throughout these seventy-eight letters, Élisabeth so opened her heart to the sister that she entrusted her with passing on her spiritual legacy to others:

> If God leaves me in this world, I want to endeavor to do more of his work in myself and close to others. But if that were not his will, if he were to shorten the road for me, I would leave to you, as the friend nearest to his heart that I have, the mission to tell those who are dear to me that I offered my trials and my prayers for them and that I asked God for their souls at any cost. Thank you in advance, my dear executor; then again, perhaps I will live to hundred years,

---

[4] Ibid., 152.

and that would be good, provided that, at one hundred years as at forty-four, I can praise God and work for him.[5]

For Élisabeth, as her writings testify, Félix's love was without any doubt the most precious help of all. For her, her faith and the certainty that her prayers for the conversion of her husband would one day be answered were the extremely powerful motivations for her acceptance of the illness. Her trust in prayer dictated for her that her sufferings would not be useless. She endlessly watched for the least sign of hope in her husband's behavior or words. At times, she even seemed to detect a little glimmer of hope in Félix's atheism, which was less virulent at that time when he sensed his wife was sick and weak. She opened up to the nun about it because she knew how much she, too, prayed for this conversion:

> I must thank God because my husband understands some things from a religious point of view that were formerly closed to him. However, it is not faith yet, and this will come from above, the divine hour will sound. Ask that it delay no longer and that this great work of conversion be accomplished as quickly as possible. It takes only a moment for Our Lord to change a heart and to secure it to himself forever.[6]

However, this couple's road of suffering was still far from reaching its end: for a few months Élisabeth had noticed a small growth in her breast and had spoken about it to Félix, who, for his part, was also worried about it, but without daring to believe it was a serious health issue. Élisabeth was already so sick with her hepatitis!

When topical treatment yielded no results, the Leseurs, on the advice of their brother-in-law, decided to consult a surgeon, whose diagnosis was final: breast cancer. It was a brutal shock. It was necessary to operate immediately.

Élisabeth received this news with her usual serenity: "I am very resigned to the divine will", she wrote to Sister Goby, whom she asked to pray for her during the operation. And she wrote to her mother, to whom she hardly dared tell the news: "I have a principle that when good to be done comes to me without my looking for it, it is because such is the will of God."

---

[5] Ibid., 126.
[6] Ibid., 206.

Félix was distraught because, to the normal anxiety at the announcement of such unacceptable news was added the impossibility of staying near Élisabeth during the two days preceding the operation. In fact, he was in the middle of preparing for the annual
general meeting of the Conservateur's shareholders. He had reports
to finish, information to research, a speech to prepare; he could not
shirk these tasks.

Thus it was Élisabeth alone who would schedule the appointments with the surgeon, who would reserve two adjoining rooms
in the clinic at Passy, since Félix would occupy a room next to
hers throughout her hospitalization. The same evening, while they
dined together at Le Dantec, Élisabeth informed Félix of all these
decisions, and he could only admire his wife's organizational ability.

On the evening of April 19, 1911, Palm Sunday, Élisabeth entered
the clinic on the rue de la Pompe. Before leaving her apartment, she
wrote: "I offer you, Lord, this ordeal for the intentions of which
you are aware. Allow it to bear fruit a hundredfold and let me lay
my sufferings, my desires, and my prayers in your heart so that you
may dispose of them as I have asked of you. O Mary, pray for me,
for us, now and at the hour of our death."[7]

Félix was edified by his wife's courage. He knew that she drew
her strength from her faith but was not really seeking to deepen
the sources of living water that sustained her. He always came up
against the idea that it seemed incomprehensible to him to love an
invisible and improbable God. For him, God was still only an abstract entity, a pure concept of the imagination.

He did not know that his wife was offering all her sufferings to
God for his conversion.

He was moved to see that, before entering the operating room,
Élisabeth attended Mass in the clinic's chapel and told him that she
needed the strength of Communion to face her health ordeal. He
said nothing. He watched her leave for the operating room smiling, walking up the stairs, ignoring the elevator whose doors he
opened for her. He was impressed by her interior strength and her
determination. At the same time, he was gripped by the anguish of

---

[7] R. P. Marie-Albert Leseur, *Vie d'Élisabeth Leseur* (Paris: Éd. J. de Gigord, 1931), 194.

knowing she was on an operating table, far from him, struggling with an illness that was incurable at that time.

He was not surprised to see her so strong in the face of this trial. "It is her nature", he thought, admiring her. He refused inwardly to accept that her faith carried her. Moreover, he did not see by what mechanism a belief in an uncertain God could give courage, but he noticed it, and, more importantly, he began to respect it.

In the silence of that clinic where, alone in Élisabeth's room, he waited for her return from the operating room, he began to consider the place of faith in his wife's life. For several months he had stopped fighting it, seeing how Élisabeth drew from it this astonishing energy that she needed to fight the illness.

Near the bed of his wife, who was slowly coming out of her anesthesia, the sound of "the still small voice", in which God manifested himself to Elijah on the mountain, had already begun to touch his heart.

The great love that united them was the source of courage for both of them. They lived for each other, each in his own way.

Deeply moved by all her husband's attentions and by the love and understanding that he expressed during her stay at the clinic, Élisabeth wrote to him as soon as she could hold a pencil:

> It is you, my dear Félix, who will have the first lines written by me after this operation. I would like them to express to you my deep tenderness and this gratitude whose very sweet burden has been further increased during these trying days; my patron, Saint Elizabeth, changed humble bread into roses; you have found a way to transform very personal and very profound sufferings into joy and consolations. Powerless as I am to love you more or to pay my debt of gratitude, I entrust this costly debt to God. Better than I, he will know how to repay you a hundredfold for what you have given me and for the good that you have done me.
>
> My beloved I embrace you with all my tenderness.
>
> Your wife, Élisabeth[8]

A few days after the operation, which would be followed by sessions of radiation therapy, Félix, seated near Élisabeth's bed, offered

---

[8] Marie-Louise Herking, *Le Père Leseur* (Paris: Éd. J. de Gigord, 1952), 85.

to read her one of the books she had brought in her suitcase. She chose *The Little Flowers of Saint Francis*. Félix the rationalist was aware that most of the miracles attributed to Francis in *The Little Flowers* were part of the legend. He had seen some illustrations of them in valuable books. It was amusing, almost charming. Without wincing, he read aloud the miracles of Saint Francis that recalled for both of them the frescos of Giotto on the walls of the basilica in Assisi that they had admired together a few years ago. For him it was more a cultural, perhaps even touching, reading to make his wife happy. But it was not a text that truly affected him.

Both sensitive, however, to the poetry of the text and the humility of the Poverello of Assisi, they exchanged their impressions at length; Élisabeth did not hesitate to compare her meeting with little Marie from Beaune to a "flower" given to her life by the Lord. Félix, surprised, found the image "poetic".

How could Félix the unbeliever react to such certainty? For some time he had become accustomed to the expressions of faith that came from his wife, but how could one now mock or contradict so loving a wife, severely confronted with the trial of serious illness? Félix only knew how to keep quiet or smile at her, but how far he still was from the spirit of poverty, abandonment, and contemplation of Francis of Assisi!

Speaking so often of God to Félix with such simplicity and in such a climate of love was already a big step; she knew that little by little, day after day, she was depositing in the bottom of his heart the precious pearls of an invaluable treasure that he would discover later after her death.

Contrary to what we might imagine, this stay in the clinic was not a hardship. On the contrary, it was a significant time in the couple's life. Later Félix would call it "a happy time". Few visitors came to disturb their communion. They were alone together all day in intimacy and love, far from all commotion and all worldly concerns; in the silence of a room whose windows overlooked a beautiful garden, they had time to talk, to visit with each other, to read together, to exchange their thoughts.

As soon as Élisabeth got better and returned home, friends and family flocked as usual. Not because she had become a center of attention, but because her goodness, her friendship, her courage uplifted minds and hearts. Her warm hospitality, her capacity to listen to others, her kindness, her smile led her visitors to overlook the sufferings she endured and to forget the fatigue that a very sick person like her might feel. Félix, sensing it, would have liked to tell them not to stay so long because it was exhausting for Élisabeth after a serious operation, but he saw his wife giving out so much love in big armfuls around her that he did not dare say anything.

19

Beaune Again

When Élisabeth rallied at the end of July 1911, the visit to Jougne was anticipated with great impatience. Both knew that fresh air and the resumption of everyday life in the countryside she loved would do her the greatest good.

Before the long weeks of chaise longue on the terrace prescribed by her doctors, Élisabeth wanted to make a detour through Beaune to meet Sister Marie Goby at last. An exchange of letters had already brought them very close spiritually, but they both needed a personal meeting, which Félix organized with joy to please his wife.

In August 1911, after ten days spent in Burgundy with Élisabeth's brother, the Leseurs, accompanied by their niece Marie, made a detour through Beaune. They arrived there late in the evening and went directly to the hotel.

Early the next morning, Élisabeth went to the hospice chapel to attend Mass with the nuns. Félix and her niece would join her a little later, and together they would attend the High Mass. Félix at Mass!

Élisabeth wrote to her mother to tell her the story of this meeting:

> As for me, I spent a very pleasant morning: at a quarter to seven, I was at the hospital and received Communion with the nuns, among whom was my unknown friend; there is nothing more beautiful than these nuns in white with their winged headdresses all around the holy table in this very charming chapel. At the end of my Thanksgiving, one of the nuns came up to me and took me away. It was Sister Goby, and I had the joy of finding in her everything I was expecting; she led me into a little room and made me take some hot chocolate and croissants. Then we talked and attended their High Mass. Then, after a few moments that I spent alone in a lovely and quiet garden, we

spoke again at length. I returned to the hotel, had lunch, and then all three of us returned at one o'clock to the hospital, where Sister Goby, who genuinely inspired Marie and Félix, gave us an extensive tour of the hospital before and after Vespers. It is a marvel and exudes extraordinary charm. All three of us attended Vespers, and Félix was delighted with the beauty of the spectacle presented by the nuns, the religious setting, and the simple beauty of the chants. Then we said our very emotional goodbyes.[1]

This encounter with the one who would increasingly become her confidant had great importance in Élisabeth's life. Both women knew that they would undoubtedly not see each other again and that only their spiritual life and their correspondence would closely connect them.

In fact, despite Félix's promise to return there every year on their way to Jougne, they saw each other again only once: the following year, not in Beaune, but in a clinic in Dijon where Sister Goby was in treatment for her eyes. But their increasingly intimate correspondence would connect them until Élisabeth's death.

Three points, which Élisabeth mentions, marked the still hesitant and fragile steps of a change in Félix's attitude. Can they be seen as a beginning? Undoubtedly not. Perhaps simply out of politeness? Out of friendliness? Out of a desire to please?

—He participated in the religious services in Beaune. Hostile until then, it seemed that his sectarianism of yesteryear had given way to a new and cordial tolerance.

—He enjoyed conversations with Sister Goby and the friendship that she showed them. Félix, the brilliant intellectual, inspired by the conversation of a humble nun!

—He was sensitive to the beauty and quality of the religious chants during Vespers.

If he continued to remain on an amiable and aesthetic plane, he did not yet know that God was again knocking at his door. But Élisabeth realized it and "kept all these things in her heart".

Humanly speaking, their relationship was completely harmonious: the illness brought them closer together. A gentle tenderness united them as well as a rare intellectual union. Félix knew that Élisabeth

---

[1] R. P. Marie-Albert Leseur, *Vie d'Élisabeth Leseur* (Paris: Éd. J. de Gigord, 1931), 200.

was going through long periods of physical suffering, but as soon as he approached her, she smiled at him and took an interest in him, without complaining. He admired her. For his part, he multiplied his attentions and thoughtfulness. She still admired him so much.

Élisabeth, sensitive to all his acts of generosity, nevertheless felt a permanent sadness deep in her heart. She could not express to her husband what was most important to her in these years of great illness. She felt alone in her spiritual life, which was so essential to her. It was only with the nun from Beaune that she could share her innermost thoughts.

Very regularly during that summer of 1911, Élisabeth wrote to her from Jougne, calling her more and more often: "My dear sister". She spoke to her of her health, but even more often she spoke to her about her spiritual isolation:

> What is truly hard for me is to live in the midst of hostility or religious indifference, to breathe a moral atmosphere where my soul cannot thrive, to be spiritually isolated despite dear and precious kindnesses, whose sweetness I do appreciate, still not to be able to obtain for dear ones the light and the life of the soul. I sometimes tell myself that these much-desired joys of union of heart with those around me will not be given to me here below and that I will savor them only in eternity once the good God has willed to accept my final oblation. . . . I endlessly hope that my prayers will be answered . . . that my dear husband, so good, so tender, will be converted and sanctified. You will help me to obtain all this, won't you, my friend?[2]

And she would later add in her resolutions: "To practice silence more than ever regarding my spiritual life, my sorrows, my health. Silence is the sure guardian of humility."[3]

And a few days later: "My God, will you give me one day . . . soon . . . the immense joy of a full communion of soul with my dear husband, of a same faith and of an existence, for him as for me, completely oriented toward You?"[4]

Her spiritual isolation was absolute. Only the correspondence with Sister Goby allowed her to open her heart and confide in her.

---

[2] Élisabeth Leseur, *Lettres sur la souffrance* (Paris: Éd. du Cerf, 2012), 147.

[3] Élisabeth Leseur, *Journal et Pensées de chaque jour* (Paris: Éd. du Cerf, 2005), 166.

[4] É. Leseur, *Lettres sur la souffrance*, 167.

With time and the exchanges of increasingly intimate letters, deep spiritual bonds were formed between Élisabeth and the woman she now called "my beloved sister" and to whom she confided everything. She told her that at the moment of Communion she prayed with her and that she envied her ability to approach others with, ultimately, the identity of a nun.

She, in order to reach the heart of others, had to wrap herself in a "veil of worldliness" in order not to seem disturbing or embarrassing to her close family or friends who were generally unbelieving or half-hearted in their approach to her.

And what to say about her conversations with her husband!

Allusions to Félix's agnosticism and their inability to communicate about her spiritual life were recurring. And yet . . .

During the year 1912, it seemed that a glimmer of hope appeared on Élisabeth's horizon, until then so dark in the face of her husband's attitude. In a letter written to Sister Goby a few days after Christmas, she informed her with joy that Félix had accompanied her to Midnight Mass.

In another letter she wrote to her: "As for my dear husband, he is stirred internally, and if God really wants to be generous in his graces, he will take this soul completely to himself."[5]

---

[5] Ibid., 194.

20

The Grace of Lourdes

At that time, Élisabeth was not spared trials. With her state of health worsening, she was no longer able to find the inner peace necessary to pray and to devote to God the time she would have wished. She realized she was going through a period of drought and aridity.

Félix was often absent the whole day, still very absorbed in his profession. Élisabeth had to help her mother, who was stricken with chronic bronchitis. She now seemed weakened by age and bereavements.

It was then that her twelve-year-old nephew, Maurice, the son of her sister Amélie, who had already been ailing for months, was seriously injured while playing with a small toy cannon. The wound became infected; the child had to be carried to the operating table three times with an amputation in sight. It was a family shock. Élisabeth, very attentive to everyone as usual, valiantly bore each one's sufferings in her prayers in union with Sister Goby, whom she had asked to join in her supplications. She promised to go on a pilgrimage to Lourdes if the child were healed.

A few weeks later, Maurice was completely recovered; Élisabeth wanted to fulfill her promise without delay. She herself was experiencing a period of respite without knowing how long it would last. It was thus the time to go to Lourdes. She wanted to thank God and the Virgin Mary for all these blessings.

She left by train on June 19 with her sister and little Maurice. Félix accompanied them. He did not hide the fact that he undertook this journey more to accompany his wife, who was still rather weak, than for pleasure.

In fact, he had already been to Lourdes thirty years earlier and still remembered its contemptible and ridiculous displays. For him it had been total rejection. Fully steeped in Zola's sarcasms about

Lourdes, he had perceived only its negative side. He had been exasperated by the vendors of rosaries, statues, and other vulgar trinkets who abounded around the Grotto. This commercial spirit exploiting religion had appalled him.

But faced with Élisabeth's joy and her nephew's recovery, he did not utter a single objection to undertaking the pilgrimage. The child was cured, Élisabeth was doing well at that time, she had made a promise: it was natural to keep it. Moreover, she was no longer in a condition to travel without him.

Madame Leseur, his mother, delighted by the idea of seeing her son at last undertake a pilgrimage, asked him to pray for her in front of the Grotto of Massabielle. She would so much have wanted to see this son, who had renounced the beliefs so rooted in his family, return to the faith. Her request greatly amused Félix. He responded to her: "A few words in haste, as we are departing, to tell you that you can count on me. I will make the prayer you ask of me. But you know, it will be worth what it will be worth. The prayers of your heretic of a son must not have much weight, but it will be made wholeheartedly."[1]

At their return, in a long letter to her "dear sister and friend", Élisabeth described her enthusiasm for the town of Bernadette. She described for her the services at the Grotto, the processions, the singing: "It is truly a remarkable sight, that of these sick people who bring a summary of all human miseries there, of these nurses so full of compassion; and what a surge of ardent faith, of burning charity; how we felt, for a few days, far from all human pettiness, elevated higher than that which passes and causes suffering."[2]

Félix followed his wife at every step, but what did he think about it? Completely skeptical, he reckoned at first that many factors contribute to create a kind of artificial magic around this pilgrimage: the Grotto, the bells, the spring from which Bernadette drank, the singing, the sick. Undoubtedly, he was touched, as anyone would be, at the sight of so much physical misery, but it was solely the infirmities of the sick in their wheeled stretchers that moved him.

---

[1] Unpublished letter from Marie-Louise Herking, *Le Pére Leseur* (Paris: Éd. J. de Gigord, 1952).

[2] Élisabeth Leseur, *Lettres sur la souffrance* (Paris: Éd. du Cerf, 2012), 221.

Nothing else. For him, even if the atmosphere was carefully studied to bring certain people to prayer, it remained a controlled, fleeting impression to which he did not even seek to pay attention.

During the benediction of the Blessed Sacrament in Rosary Square, pressed by the crowd, he found himself by chance in the middle of a Spanish pilgrimage next to a young priest, completely paralyzed, stretched out in a wagon.

At the moment of the blessing, the archbishop of Barcelona stopped in front of this poor young man to bless him in a very fatherly way; this gesture, both solemn and ridiculous to the atheist he still was, strongly struck Félix. Internally, he was outraged. How could anyone not understand that it was criminal to give a hope of healing to a quadriplegic? And this in the name of religion! How was this young man not revolted, as he himself would have been if he had been in his place? Why make him hope for a miracle that would not come? In his eyes, it was scandalous.

While ruminating on his indignation, the movements of the crowd caused him to lose sight of that young priest. Then, all of a sudden, he turned around and discovered him there, near him. He hardly dared look at him, he was so convinced he would see him dismayed and disappointed. To his great surprise, he saw a magnificent expression of joy and peace on his face, indescribable, supernatural. A kind of transfiguration. At the time, he did not understand. Then, undoubtedly aided by grace, he asked himself a question: "Might there not be something incomprehensible or great at Lourdes anyway, a special grace so that all these sick, so gravely afflicted, leave with such joy and serenity despite their disappointment at not being cured?" For him, however, it was an idea to reject, so irrational that it seemed ridiculous to him.

He recounted this episode to Élisabeth. Inwardly, she rejoiced at his astonishment, not to mention at his emotion. She realized that he had still been captured by the supernatural atmosphere of that place, since she would write to Sister Goby: "My husband was moved by the great sights of Lourdes. I asked the Blessed Virgin for his conversion, and I also asked for it as a special gift to the heart of Jesus, at the end of this month."[3]

---

[3] Ibid., 222.

A few minutes after the blessing of the sick on the esplanade, Félix went to the Grotto, caught up in a group of pilgrims. From afar, he caught sight of Élisabeth on her knees on the ground in such an attitude of prayer that he had the impression she was as if lifted off the ground. It seemed to him that her prayer was, according to her expression, "a true flight toward God". She was supernaturally beautiful, radiant as he had never seen her before, and for the first time he experienced a deep feeling of admiration for his wife's faith. He did not yet know that God makes use of the hands, faces, and words of others to speak to the heart of each person. He did not at all imagine that one day he would be able to abandon his agnostic position. That would be the denial of himself, of everything that he had been in his life until then: a strong mind does not allow itself to be moved by prayers that have no meaning!

During that same time, Sister Goby, at Paray-le-Monial with her community, was praying fervently for Félix. Élisabeth would have very much liked to join her. She even wrote to her to ask for the address of a hotel, but Félix was eager to return to Paris. For him, Paray-le-Monial was nothing but a big, ridiculous fraud and not worth the trip. God's hour had not yet come.

21

Summer 1912

In April, Élisabeth wrote:

> By divine grace, I will make myself more gentle, more loving, constantly and solely concerned about others, their pleasure, their welfare, occupied above all with their souls. This in all humility, effacing myself and making my whole spiritual life a life hidden in Jesus Christ.
>
> Then, I want more and more to radiate outwardly the joy, the holy, gentle, and ineffable joy of Jesus. My immense frailty does not allow me to try to accomplish this except at the cost of many efforts. . . . I want to devote this year to the conquest of the souls who are dear to me, especially through prayer and suffering. My husband, my mother, my dear nephews and my niece, my sister, all my dear loved ones, these are the ones I want to give to Jesus at all costs: this will be my goal, and, furthermore, with these much beloved souls, I want to give them the same means to Our Lord.[1]

Despite the deterioration of her health, she wanted to remain until the end the beautiful wife chosen by her husband, whom she did not want to disappoint. How many in her situation would have neglected their appearance! But she had a lofty conception of woman, and she continued to believe that her primary duty remained to please her husband.

She also gave herself very concrete rules of love in order to be for others a silent reflection of the radiance of God's love for them: "Affability, gentleness, constant concern to understand the most diverse minds and to bring them true sympathy, forgetfulness of myself hidden under a smile, the gift of my heart, of my intelligence,

---

[1] Élisabeth Leseur, *Journal et Pensées de chaque jour* (Paris: Éd. du Cerf, 2005), 192–93.

to the service of souls, leniency toward others serving as a veil to my severity toward myself: these are what charity will make me practice."[2]

At the end of the month of July 1912, the state of Élisabeth's health was sufficiently satisfactory to contemplate a departure, welcome in that season, for Jougne.

Between Paris and Jougne, Félix planned a stop in Dijon for a few days' meeting with Sister Goby, hospitalized in a clinic of the city to treat her eyes.

Since there were no longer community rules for her, she had the leisure to eat in the restaurant with the Leseurs, who took her for a car ride in the afternoon.

Félix drove. The two friends, happy to be reunited, chatted in the back seat. Félix heard Élisabeth utter aloud what he had never yet dared to admit to himself.

She calmly announced to her friend her premature death, Félix's conversion, and his entrance into religious life. Great silence and great emotion greeted these revelations. Félix said nothing; he was, moreover, much more upset by the calm with which Élisabeth announced her impending death than by the almost laughable prediction of his entrance into a monastery once he became a widower!

Élisabeth's death was the deadline he feared most in the world. How could he imagine life without her? It was the first time she had mentioned it so openly. Admittedly, both had secretly been thinking about it for a long time, but should the care, the good air of Jougne, the rest, not over time have a beneficial effect on her? Besides, she was far from dying; her health seemed to return at the same time as her strength and her zest for life. And hope is always the strongest!

As always, the house at Jougne was hospitable during the summer. Family and friends came one after another; Élisabeth received them with much affection and thoughtfulness. A few hours of chaise longue on the terrace did not prevent her from joining in visits to the Jura mountains in the afternoon in the car.

She wrote to Sister Goby: "We have some friends here at the moment; so I am quite busy and have little free time. It is a sacrifice

---

[2] Ibid., 163.

for me who so much loves good moments of solitude and for whom meditation is a necessity of the soul; but this activity is my duty at present; thus, I can only choose to surrender myself, entrusting to Our Lord the task of doing his work in me while I accomplish my daily task."[3]

No guilt over the lack of time for the spiritual life, no crippling scruples, complete availability to others, profound hospitality without regret: "[What you do] to the least of these my brethren . . ." was without a doubt more essential for her during those weeks than spending time meditating. It was the momentary "duty of her state in life".

When she had a little time, she read the life of Saint Bernard, impressed by his austerity and his tenderness for those who approached him. He gave meaning to suffering, the lot of all human life, but he considered it to be the bearing of spiritual gifts from God: nothing great is done without it, it obtains everything and "digs the bed through which the great river of grace passes in order to go to souls." This is what she lived daily.

It did not trouble her to realize her illness immobilized her more every day. She wrote: "To accept as a trial this impossibility of living equally an active life through charitable works, relationships, and regular work and a fully contemplative life that the duties of my state in life and the tastes of those who surround me forbid me."[4]

Despite the clouds on the horizon, Élisabeth and Félix envisioned happy projects with confidence and joy. The following year, on July 31, they organized a big family reunion at Jougne to celebrate their silver wedding anniversary. Twenty-five years of marriage, love, and beautiful plans carried out together truly called for a beautiful family celebration. All those they loved would be numerous around them, surrounding them, and already they were both thinking about the invitations and the organization of the day that would mark the crowning moment of their relationship.

At the end of the summer, Élisabeth had regained her strength. Félix suggested a new trip with their friend Léon Mahuet: the Italian

---

[3] Élisabeth Leseur, *Lettres sur la souffrance* (Paris: Éd. du Cerf, 2012), 190.
[4] É. Leseur, *Journal et Pensées de chaque jour*, 197.

lakes by way of Annecy, Lake Bourget, Little Saint Bernard Pass. A beautiful trip with good weather in the program. The Leseurs were especially fond of Italy. Élisabeth expressed herself well in that language whose musicality she loved. Both of them knew and appreciated its literature; Élisabeth had read most of the great Italian authors in their native language. Both of them knew how to appreciate the beautiful displays of nature as well as those of man's creation, among others, the masterpieces of Italian painting, which they had regularly gone to admire for several years.

The tour of the lakes was magnificent. As if she were not ill, Élisabeth was filled with wonder at the changing colors of the water at different hours of the day, the little Italian villages perched in the mountains, the verdant vegetation of the shores, and the broods of ducklings that dodged in and out of reeds. The boat rides allowed her to breathe an infinitely pure and invigorating air without fatigue. Élisabeth felt herself so renewed that both of them seemed to forget during those few days the trials of the illness.

But the cross was always present in Élisabeth's body. They pretended to ignore it . . . or picked the good moments of the present lived together as precious moments to savor fully.

For Félix, his wife's reflections always remained as amusing, spontaneous, and spiritual. He rejoiced to see her happy under Italy's sky. She wanted to be elegant, smiling, loving. She was a credit to her husband. Before leaving, she wrote in her notebook of resolutions: "To sacrifice nothing concerning the 'duties of my state in life'; on the contrary, to be more attentive to the outside: appearance, keeping house, food, even elegance, to make myself more attractive and to hide my personal austerity better."[5]

For a long time Élisabeth had considered cheerfulness a virtue and at the same time a duty since she knew it was one of the qualities that her husband and her friends valued in her. She gladly recalled that Saint Teresa advised her nuns always to be cheerful. But what a contrast between this external behavior and her writings from the same period, all filled with a spirit of mortification, of detachment from this world, with a spirit of poverty. If Félix could have read

---

[5] Ibid., 193.

these, he would have been completely surprised because nothing in his wife's behavior could have led him to guess such asceticism. It was at that time, when she was at the bedside of her dying mother, that she declared to Sister Goby: "Suffering is so powerful and obtains so much: an hour spent in pain, united to the cross, can obtain more than hours consecrated to good works, to action, and according to these very beautiful words: 'Suffering is also a sacrament.'"[6]

After their return from Italy, little by little Élisabeth's body was nothing but suffering, but it was not to be in vain. She wanted to sanctify it, to give it a meaning, to magnify it. This would be her silent mission to her husband.

Perhaps he would eventually perceive this "still small voice" that never ceased to surround him and bless him?

For Élisabeth, physical pain was not the only suffering to bear. She still could not confide to her loved ones about her spiritual journey, and she continued to feel a deep inner isolation. She carried her cross every day, a very heavy cross.

She turned again to Sister Goby, with whom she found attentiveness and whose understanding she appreciated from a distance: "I too, my dear sister, I thank God for having desired this meeting of our souls; life and duty separate us, but by different routes we walk toward the same blessed goal. A day will come when there will no longer be distance, separation, and sadness. Heaven awaits us, and there, meeting forever, we will find God, we will know him and will be able to love him fully at last."[7]

A half century before Vatican II, Élisabeth already expressed her joyful belonging to the vast people of God where laity and religious, after a shared human journey, would one day meet again in great love.

Then a new source of concerns was added to the others. When they returned from Italy, Élisabeth and Félix made a detour to go see Madame Arrighi in Saône-et-Loire, where she was resting in a nursing home. She was now very old, alone, still scarred by the death of her husband and two of her daughters, concerned about

---

[6] É. Leseur, *Lettres sur la souffrance*, 242–43.
[7] Ibid., 263.

Élisabeth's condition; she was suffering from chronic bronchitis, generally in a poor state, and very dejected. Élisabeth opened her heart to Sister Goby about it:

> My dear sister, I beg you, pray for her a great deal; ask God for health for this much beloved mother, but above all, ask him for peace of heart, supernatural consolations, a faith deep enough to transform her sufferings, a strong and active spiritual life. I suffer from the physical and especially the moral state of my dear mother. Oh! That Our Lord might consent to make me suffer in her place and that he might heal this sad soul by teaching her to love him.[8]

For Élisabeth, the sight of the suffering of those she loved was even more difficult to bear than her own sufferings. Only abandonment to the love of God that gives the necessary strength, the "daily bread", allowed her to accept and to bear this burden. And she made the phrase of Saint Paul her own: "I can do all things in him who strengthens me" (Phil 4:13).

---

[8] Ibid., 246.

22

When Disease Conquers the Whole of Life

In spring 1913, Élisabeth had to stay completely bedridden for fifteen days; violent headaches, dizziness, repeated vomiting raised concern of a painful reprise of liver disorders. But other symptoms revealed lymphangitis, a result of her breast cancer. Félix, very worried, but nevertheless absorbed by his professional obligations, escaped the office whenever he could to come to her bedside.

"My dear Félix is the pearl of caregivers, and his devotion is inexhaustible. May God reward him for his tender care",[1] wrote Élisabeth to her friend the nun, to whom she confided that she was "at the foot of the cross".

Félix summoned the most renowned doctors from the hospitals in Paris so that for a few weeks, with beneficial treatment, the ailments subsided and an almost normal life slowly seemed to resume.

A happy life did in fact resume with the joy of being able to attend together the engagement dinner of their niece Marie on her twentieth birthday. The young man was a brilliant student of the École Polytechnique. The Leseurs were proud of it and welcomed him right away as a new beloved member of their big family. Élisabeth's mother was also present, happy to see her granddaughter take the path of her future with confidence and love.

In July, Félix had to go to Ghent in Belgium for professional reasons. He had never traveled without Élisabeth, who had always accompanied him everywhere. Why should she not go with him since apparently she had been leading a normal life for several weeks? The trip would be short; and, especially after the bad time she had just been through, travel and the fresh air of that maritime region swept by winds from the sea could only be beneficial for her. As

---

[1] Élisabeth Leseur, *Lettres sur la souffrance* (Paris: Éd. du Cerf, 2012), 246.

a member of the jury for the Social Economy Exhibition, Félix would have to meet his professional demands during the day; but during the few hours when he was busy, Élisabeth would go to Saint Bavo's Cathedral to see the famous altarpiece, the "Adoration of the Mystic Lamb". They would promptly return home after this little romantic getaway.

In Ghent, Élisabeth felt very fatigued. The train trip had been too arduous for her. She had to stay in bed at the hotel, but when Félix suggested returning through Brussels, which enticed him, she still agreed to it, undoubtedly to please him. She was exhausted. Did he see it, or did he pretend not to notice so she would not think of herself as a very sick person to whom nothing more was allowed?

Back home in Paris, after fifteen days of much rest, the disease seemed sufficiently subdued for the departure route to Jougne for the family vacation to be considered again. She confided to her friend the nun:

> For some time, the good God has presented me with many trials, and, through much weariness and pain and revulsion of all sorts, my union with him is increasing and I am experiencing that strange mixture of suffering and profound (intangible) joy that made Saint Paul say: "With all our affliction, I am overjoyed." How good he is, our master, and what a friend he is for our soul; with him, truly pain no longer exists, or rather, it is transformed completely.[2]

But she was doing poorly. From day to day the departure for Jougne had to be postponed. Élisabeth's condition worsened to the point that she no longer experienced relief. To reduce the suffering from the heat of Paris at that beginning of the month of August, Félix drove her to the house of some friends in Sèvres. In their garden, in the shade of the tall trees and foliage, she would undoubtedly be more comfortable.

She could stay there only a few days. The need for more specific care required the patient to be moved to a hospital run by Franciscan nuns on the rue de Maurepas. Félix, very worried but self-controlled, had to call an ambulance for the trip. Élisabeth completely surrendered herself to the will of God and, through the

---

[2] Ibid., 318.

great peace that emanated from her, inspired wonder in her husband, whom she comforted.

For a long time she had accepted the certainty of her premature death, followed by the conversion of her husband. Too sick to get up, she again read with interest *Bergsonian Philosophy* by Jacques Maritain. She spoke about it to her amazed husband. Maritain had interested Élisabeth for a long time. She was not unaware that he was agnostic and became profoundly Christian. More than anyone else, she followed his journey. She appreciated his attachment to Bergson. This newly published book bore witness to an evolution in Maritain's thought that she followed with interest.

Maritain's reflections would be Élisabeth's viaticum. Once she was too tired, she laid the book on her bedside table and placed a bookmark on page 317; she did not yet know that she would never open it again, that she would never be able to open a book again. This would be her last reading.

Félix deeply admired the moral strength, the internal peace, and the smile of his wife, despite so many physical sufferings. He knew well that her faith carried her, but he did not understand it; he felt he was only witnessing an event that completely escaped him.

One evening, discussing her belief in the communion of saints and in the afterlife, she told him with a rather solemn authority:

—You will come join me, I know it!

A few days before, she had made him smile when she had declared to him with a certain solemnity: "You are of the seed of a saint!" He had teased her about this prediction, unexpected to say the least, and she had responded:

—I am asking the good God to allow my suffering to make this seed grow, or rather that he will do so himself.[3]

He had certainly forgotten the parable of the sower learned in his youth, in which certain seeds, stifled by the stones in the road and brambles, end up one day sprouting and bearing fruit.

For Félix, the idea that his wife might be lost and might leave him alone one day was unimaginable. His role and his responsibility as a husband led him now to help her to get through that difficult time as best he could. His love, his tenderness, his little attentions

---

[3] R. P. Marie-Albert Leseur, *Vie d'Élisabeth Leseur* (Paris: Éd. J. de Gigord, 1931), 349.

would give her the strength to strive to face suffering and, who knows, maybe even to heal. In any illness with an utterly hopeless outcome, it is not uncommon that, in the bottom of his heart, the person closest still holds on, until the last moment, to a crazy and insane, completely irrational hope.

Élisabeth's letters at that time express on every page what a support her husband's love and attentions were for her. But in reality, despite her frailty and her destitution, it was she who seemed to be the support of her husband, it was she who was the couple's strong point. Every time he went near her and found her smiling and peaceful, he was himself comforted. They "carried" each other.

Élisabeth began a novena to Saint Thérèse of Lisieux for her recovery; Félix laughed at it so as not to lose the habit:

—But it is childish, your little nun is nothing at all.

And she replied to him:

—On the contrary, it is very important, but you cannot understand.[4]

And yet, he took up the pen to ask his mother to join in Élisabeth's novena and to pray for her.

A few days later, a medical examination revealed an irrevocable diagnosis: the cancer had metastasized. It is possible that only Félix was informed of this inexorable news.

But as her disease escalated, there were still periods of remission. A few weeks of unexpected respite allowed Élisabeth to believe she was nearly cured. She wrote to Sister Goby:

> God is good, my dear sister! I realize it more than ever after this painful attack. Coming out of this dark "tunnel", where I have laboriously walked during these last months and where I had such an overwhelming feeling of my powerlessness and my annihilation, I find myself, in returning to fresh air, facing new horizons, and I see that while I was doing nothing but suffer, God was acting in me. And yet, I still have many personal aversions, many profound sufferings, many unknown hardships; but no matter, I have rediscovered the profound sense of the divine presence, the sweet union to the adored Master. And I want to try to do the work he wants of me, as small and as humble as it is. . . . My husband is recovering little by little from the

---

[4] Ibid., 335.

moral shock that he had; my mother is aging and sometimes suffering. The others are doing well.[5]

At home, Élisabeth regained some strength; her health allowed her to go out for a while every day to walk in small steps on the Champs-Élysées on the arm of her husband.

At that time, the Champs-Élysées was a haven of peace and greenery. Magnificent trees shaded the paths on which an elegant and refined population strolled. Ladies wore long dresses and big wide-brimmed hats. Men also all had their heads covered with black hats. A few carriages pulled by horses circulated on the "triumphal" avenue that led to the Bois de Boulogne. A few automobiles and especially bicycles began to be seen. The bicycle was called the "little queen". A new world was dawning. But what the walkers admired most were the lavish private mansions that were erected behind the rows of trees. Thus it was a walk close to her home, gentle and distracting for someone very sick who tired quickly.

Félix, unfortunately, was not unaware that this was a grace period; since the beginning of his wife's illness, he had written on a notepad a daily health report for the attending doctor. Every day he recorded the development of the disease of which, despite her almost unchanged beauty, Élisabeth wore the stigmata on her emaciated face.

When Élisabeth could no longer walk at all, Father Hébert brought her Communion. It was Félix himself who prepared a white cloth, a candle, and a bouquet of flowers. Afterward, Élisabeth's face reflected such peace and such happiness that Father Hébert wrote: "I will never forget this impressive figure in her perfect simplicity."[6]

In her moments of respite, Élisabeth, gathering her last strength, tried to comfort Félix, to smile at him, to show him her love.

In his *Vie d'Élisabeth Leseur* (Life of Élisabeth Leseur), Félix recounts:

> She told me seriously, fifteen days before her death, on an afternoon when I had just returned from the Conservateur and when I was near her bed: "You will come join me, I know it." And since I responded

---

[5] É. Leseur, *Lettres sur la souffrance*, 332.
[6] Introduction to ibid.

that in fact, when I left, I had only one eagerness, to return as soon as possible, she continued with still more solemnity, raising her hand; "Oh no, that is not what this is about; you will come join me; I know it."[7]

One night, all the symptoms suddenly reappeared. As much as the pain allowed her, Élisabeth prayed, often aloud, in front of her powerless doctors and in front of her husband, who could only cry. When the priest, called by Félix himself at the request of his brother-in-law, came to give her Extreme Unction, she was already in a coma. The struggle lasted eight days and eight nights during which Félix deployed all the treasures of his imagination and his love to give her a little comfort, to arrange her pillows, to cool her face, to moisten her lips, to surround her with tenderness.

On Sunday May 3, 1914, at ten o'clock in the morning, she took her last breath.

Félix was shattered. He stayed close to her. When he looked at her on her bed and saw her face, so relaxed, so illuminated by a kind of inner joy, he could not believe that it was all over. He sensed that something of her must still exist somewhere. And he asked himself a question: Perhaps a soul still lives outside its body? How is it possible for so many wonderful qualities, so much intelligence, so many virtues, so much love to be forever lost in the void? How was it possible that she had "abandoned me in this way"?

One question tormented him: Could all the beauty of a life stop at the cemetery? And all this love that Élisabeth had given to him for almost twenty-five years, did it really end with death? Was it annihilated with her last breath? Would it stop at the edge of her grave? If she were somewhere, would she not go to show herself to him, who was her greatest concern? He recalled that Élisabeth, quoting Saint Paul, had sometimes told him: "Love does not fail." In front of this deathbed, a thousand questions assailed him.

Without admitting it to himself, several responses inspired by hope came to his mind, but they seemed so contrary to his rationalism that he could only reject them. "Sentimental feelings of a poor, unhappy man who has just lost what he holds dearest in the world and who is not able to accept it", he thought!

---

[7] M. A. Leseur, *Vie d'Élisabeth Leseur*, 348.

By never ceasing to look upon the bed where she had suffered so much, he was moved by her otherworldly appearance, luminous and calm, which he read, in spite himself, on her face, emaciated by the illness. He was pensive. He placed a rosary in her joined hands. She seemed to be praying again as he had seen her do so often.

He wrote in his notebook: "We placed her on her deathbed, and the expression of suffering from the morning was succeeded by a beautiful expression of beatitude, an exquisite smile. A sweet and very consoling vision to preserve."[8]

And the following day: "The same vision of someone enjoying a supernatural peace. It is remarkable and very consoling to preserve."[9]

Félix asked Charles Duvent, their painter friend, to come draw his wife's face, features that he would never want to forget. Duvent and his wife had a deep friendship with Élisabeth, who had greatly supported them at the time of their son's death. Very distraught to be before so dear a friend on her deathbed, their painter friend drew Élisabeth's features in pencil in his notebook. The emotion is visible in his work; but what is most moving is to see that he been able to convey the essential: the image of a soul appeased with the calm of the hereafter.

Did this peace and joy that Félix seemed to see on her face signify that Élisabeth's soul perhaps was not necessarily dead like her body and that maybe it was in front of the great love of God, as she had said?

Still in his notebook, he wrote: "And facing this sight, I came to wonder if there were not, all the same, something outside of the material world."[10]

But his visceral atheism returned to the surface and did not allow him any hope. Death was the end of everything. Félix was definitively alone, torn apart, as if what was vital for him had been amputated.

He had seen Élisabeth sick for so long, lying down most of the time, so weak, that he had not suspected the extent to which she

---

[8] Ibid., 351.
[9] Ibid.
[10] Ibid., 352.

had been, since the day of their wedding, the solid pillar of their relationship. He had often had the feeling that he was holding her up, when, in reality, it was she who was holding him up. He had not appreciated that it was in her smile that he drew his strength, that it was in her willingness to help him right to the end that he had found his reasons to live, and that it was in her courage that he had kept up his own courage for months, not to mention years.

With her death, everything collapsed. It was as if she had abandoned him to an unknown fate. His life as a new widower was now before him like a dark tunnel at the end of which there was no exit.

The funeral service took place on May 6 in Saint-Pierre-de-Chaillot, their parish. He was in the front row, but he barely heard it. As Élisabeth had wished, it was a very simple ceremony without hangings embroidered with silver teardrops over the doors, as was customary at that time.

All of Félix's nonbelieving friends and colleagues were present, mixed in with Élisabeth's very Christian family. And there, in front of this very disparate assembly, united in genuine and unanimous emotion, Félix had a very strong intuition: he noted that despite their opposing conceptions of death, all the attendants participated in an extraordinary communion of hearts and minds, and this on a level higher than that of our earthly existence. "It is the work of Élisabeth," he thought. "She has brought everyone together." This moved him.

Even the personnel from the funeral parlor were sensitive to the reverence of this large assembly; leaving the church, one of them whispered in his ear: "But who was this person? We have never seen a funeral like this."

He was humanly comforted by so many signs of affection and gratitude. But he was surprised to see some people he did not know at all come to kneel around his wife's coffin, weeping. One of them, a woman he did not know, said to him: "She was a saint. She uplifted all those who approached her." What could he reply?

But his rationalist mind regained the upper hand and reassured him: "At all funeral ceremonies, it is obvious that those who mourn a loved one together do not share the same beliefs. Those who hope for a life near the Lord after death are weak minds who console themselves with this unfounded hope."

So he was deeply distraught, facing an emptiness, a black hole, an intolerable void.

No belief in a life beyond death was able to bring him the least comfort yet.

23

Élisabeth's Spiritual Testament

In a drawer of her desk, Élisabeth had left a sealed envelope on which she had written: "My Spiritual Testament for Félix".

After her death, with great emotion and tears in his eyes, Félix read these lines written in 1905, nine years before her death, when she had understood that she would die prematurely, and slightly revised a few years later:

This, my beloved husband, is my soul's testament. I want you to be, in this regard, my principal, my dearest heir. To you especially and to all those who love me, I leave the mission of praying for me and having others pray for me a great deal. May your works, your alms, speak to God of the one who served him very imperfectly, but who loves him with all the strength of her being, all the affections of her heart. Finish paying, all your life, as much as a poor human creature can, the immense debt of gratitude that I owe to the beloved Father whom my prayers, from above, will make it possible for you to know and love.

Once you too have become his child, a disciple of Jesus Christ, and a living member of the Church, consecrate your life, transformed by grace, to prayer and to the gift of yourself in charity. Be a Christian, be an apostle. In your turn, endeavor to give our poor brothers here below what my supplications and my trials have requested. Love souls; pray, suffer, and work for them. They deserve all our sorrows, all our efforts, all our sacrifices.

I leave you the people who are dear to me so that you might surround them with your consideration and your affection. Throughout their lives, help the children, the nephews and niece, who are also friends whom I love so much. Be their spiritual guide, the friend of their souls, an example for their lives. Help them morally and materially at the time of their marriage or religious vocation. Think of them all as the children of our heart, and never abandon them. To their parents, always be the brother or the devoted loving friend that you are right now, but in a more supernatural way. Even increase your affection, since I leave you mine to impart to them.

If I die before Mother, I do not need to entrust her to you; but it would be a great mission if you want to combine with yours my immense tenderness for this much beloved mother. Regarding your mother, so fully mine as well, I ask you to replace me, too.

I entrust to you, in order to carry it out successfully, "Juliette's project", that is, the erection of a chapel in a poor neighborhood. If the name is not already taken, it should be dedicated to the Holy Spirit; if not, to Saint Thérèse or to the Sacred Heart.

I also commend my various works to you and leave you the task of paying, during your life, my donations or such others that might replace them. To our nephews and niece, I remind them never to forget to deduct a portion for God and for the poor out of what we will leave them.

For my funeral, I desire a simple service, without ostentation of any kind, with strictly religious hymns and no wall hangings at the house or on the exterior of the church. I would like them to gather at the church and for my family and friends, instead of sending meaningless flowers, to have Masses said and to offer some alms for me.

And now, my beloved Félix, I repeat to you my unique and great tenderness. I commission you to repeat to our family, to our friends, how much I have loved them all and how much I will pray for them until the hour of reunion. Near God, where other loved ones already await us, we will one day be eternally reunited. I hope for it through my trials offered for you and through divine mercy.

Your wife forever,

Élisabeth
October 15, 1905[1]

---

[1] Élisabeth Leseur, *Journal et Pensées de chaque jour* (Paris: Éd. du Cerf, 2005), 242.

24

Félix after Élisabeth's Death

Once alone, Félix was in despair. His apartment, so full of the smallest details of Élisabeth's presence, seemed infinitely empty to him. He blamed himself for not having been present enough, for not having sufficiently valued the loftiness of her thoughts, of having made her suffer without realizing it, of having even, at certain times, shaken her in her strongest beliefs. He wrote to a friend: "I reproach myself for not having understood her enough, for not having surrounded her with enough affection. She left me a spiritual testament that is an amazing document and that constitutes a whole life plan that I will endeavor to follow to be worthy of her."[1]

This life plan was very precious to him because it was written by the hand of the one he loved so much; but it seemed so far from his beliefs that, for the moment, he did not see how to follow it.

He was greatly supported by his sister-in-law Amélie and her husband, Maurice Duron, the doctor who had given Élisabeth brotherly care throughout her illness. He ate many meals with them as well as with the Le Dantecs. He was now responsible for both his own very old mother and Madame Arrighi, toward whom he made it a duty to behave like a son.

Since Élisabeth was no longer there, bibliophilia was of much less interest to him. He who was such a keen reader no longer even had the desire to read. He merely skimmed the newspapers. Every morning, he went to the Montmartre cemetery. It was the only place in the world where he wanted to live, near Élisabeth.

One day, when he cried at the home of Amélie, Élisabeth's younger sister, she revealed to him that she possessed a precious document for him: a diary in which, from 1899 to 1913, Élisabeth,

---

[1] Marie-Louise Herking, *Le Pére Leseur* (Paris: Éd. J. de Gigord, 1952), 98.

for herself alone, had written down the events of their lives together and her most intimate thoughts.

Amélie, after having received some confidences from Élisabeth, knew that she had placed so much of her deepest self in it that she had wanted to burn her writings. To hand over Élisabeth's private spiritual thoughts, the story of her soul, to the curiosity of nonbelievers after her death had seemed a sacrilege to her.

Amélie had insisted that she keep it, at least for Félix. He, her husband with whom she had shared her life, should have the right to read the words of her innermost spiritual thoughts. He would certainly be moved by it. And at last, this diary was in her home, at Félix's disposal.

So, she gave him three notebooks bound in black moleskin, covered with Élisabeth's fine handwriting. No one had ever read them yet. At most, Élisabeth had read a few passages of it to her sister.

Back home, Félix, with emotion, began to read these pages written by his wife. He undoubtedly knew a little of the loftiness of her aspirations, but he did not suspect the intensity of her spiritual life.

But above all, he was in awe of the beauty of her writing, even though she had obviously never been concerned with literary studies. It was not in her nature. She had written with the flow of the pen without erasures or additions, as her heart dictated it to her. He who was so used to reading the great authors judged that this set of notebooks constituted a work worthy of a true writer. But, he believed his enthusiasm was inevitably biased!

He felt that she was speaking to him; he saw again moments of their life together that, despite the illness, were still those of happiness. He was captivated by the depth of her thoughts, by her silent love for him, who had been the pillar of her whole life.

But what distressed him the most was discovering the sufferings that he had involuntarily caused Élisabeth, the sacrifices that she had made for him, the offering of so much suffering right to the end so that he would turn toward God. He realized that in their relationship there had been between them something like an impenetrable wall that he had never sought to knock down, and this wall had made them suffer, each in his own way, especially her. He blamed himself.

Stuck in his rationalism, he did not understand right away the Christian significance of these notebooks, which he nevertheless read and reread every day to the point of not being able to detach himself from them. Little by little, they became for him the only daily nourishment that allowed him to hold up in his suffering by giving him the best of Élisabeth's soul. For him, they were the spiritual presence of his wife. At times, he had the feeling that she was speaking to him deep in his heart, perhaps even more than during her lifetime, when discretion and silence imposed themselves on her out of respect for his atheist beliefs.

He began to understand why Élisabeth did not try to convince him through pointless arguments when he read:

> Let us not think that we hasten the coming of the Kingdom of God for souls by our personal action. As long as the divine hour has not come, our efforts will be in vain, or rather they will be but an active prayer, an appeal to the one who transforms and saves. Let us, however, send him this appeal with the humble conviction that he alone will do the task and will bring life to the souls for whom we act and pray.[2]

The day after Élisabeth's death, Félix continued to visit his closest friends. All of them made him understand, in veiled terms, that later on he must think about remarrying . . . that he could not live all alone until the end of his life. . . . Several came to see him at home. They were all rationalists or atheists. Besides these, he did not have many other friends; he encountered them at the office when he had the courage to go there. The intellectual level of these minds was what he had appreciated and admired all his life. All of them were filled with rationalist exegesis, radically hostile to all Christian thought.

At the same time, he was eager to return home in order to absorb again and again Élisabeth's writings, and, in reading them, it seemed to him that she was still with him. She spoke to him. She gave him courage. It was his only consolation. But every day he also wondered how his wife could so love a God whom she had never seen,

---

[2] Élisabeth Leseur, *La Vie Spirituelle: Petits traités de vie intérieure* (Paris: Éd. J. de Gigord, 1922), 3.

whom she did not know, and who was solely an abstract entity, a simple concept of human imagination.

One day his friend Léon Mahuet who, a few months before, had taken the Leseurs on a trip during Élisabeth's illness, came to see him; he found Félix in such a sad state that he pitied him and sought to distract him. He suggested a little road trip. His arguments to convince Félix were lengthy:

> You must leave this apartment, still so full of sadness, sickness, and suffering. This will be a beneficial diversion for you. If you continue to go to the cemetery every day and think only of your grief, you will end up getting sick. I will take you wherever you want; you will choose your own itinerary. We will remain silent when you want to reflect. This rest and fresh air will do you good. Given your present state, it is a pressing and urgent necessity.

Félix was deeply touched by this proposal and the reasoning of his friend. But, precisely the prospect of leaving this apartment now gave him qualms: he felt as if he were abandoning Élisabeth. Furthermore, the car in which they were going to travel was the one in which they had visited a good part of France with such happiness the year before. Would being in it now without her not bring back too many memories?

But finally, giving in to the authority of his friend, he overcame his reluctance. They left Paris on June 9, 1914, a month after Élisabeth's death.

This generous-hearted friend was completely indifferent to everything related to faith. He was neither for nor against. Nothing supernatural existed for him. And the subject was taboo.

The morning of June 11, on a beautiful day, they drove between Uzerche and Tulle in the middle of a forest of magnificent chestnut trees on a road flooded with light. Félix surprised himself by admiring the beauty of the place, the invigorating air, and the mildness of the temperature. He was surprised to see that he felt a kind of inner well-being. Since the death of his wife, he had been convinced that nothing on earth could ever delight him again.

All of a sudden, the memory of a specific conversation with Élisabeth arose unexpectedly in his mind. As if in a flash, he seemed to

see her again before him, and he "heard" her repeat to him internally, with tremendous tenderness: "I am grieved." He did not understand: it was he who was grieving, not she. And yet . . .

He had the distinct impression that Élisabeth was close to him
and that she was speaking to him. He was sure of her presence,
invisible but real. Later, describing this first call to belief in a life
after death, he would write:

> I had the very clear impression that she was there, close to me; I im-
> mediately said to myself: "But she lives, her soul is at my side, I am
> coming to have an almost physical sense of her presence; she spoke
> to me; she held me through a supernatural language." The emotion
> was so intense that it was impossible for me to control it, and I gave
> in to it shamelessly. Then, reflecting on what had just occurred, on
> the will outside my own that this event manifested to me, a genuine
> inner revolution happened within me: "But then," I repeated to my-
> self, "if Élisabeth is living, as I have just had the overwhelming intu-
> ition that she is, it is because the soul is immortal; it is, therefore, be-
> cause God exists, because the supernatural world is the philosophical
> truth with all the implications that entails." A clarity illuminated my
> conscience, and I perceived that all this was not the work of chance
> but was the reflection of a light brighter than that of reason and that
> came from the beyond.[3]

In the afternoon of the same day, their route lead them to Roca-
madour, that old French pilgrimage site on the Way of Saint James
of Compostela; they went up to the church, and there, still under
the emotion of that morning's certainty, Félix bought a candle and
lit it before the Black Madonna, as a gift for Élisabeth.

He was surprised and above all embarrassed by this gesture that
overcame him. Until that day, he had considered it ridiculous or
superstitious, and today it was he himself, the rationalist, who lit a
candle before a statue of the Virgin! Watching the little flame flicker,
he asked himself how he could have been led to light a candle in a
church.

Back in the car, he was a little embarrassed in front of his friend,
but no one spoke about it and Félix's emotion gently subsided.

---

[3] Ibid., 22.

Thereafter, their route was a true "Élisabeth itinerary". But his friend Léon Mahuet was obliging, and he had promised Félix he would drive him wherever he wanted.

The First Stage: Châteaugay

For a long time Félix had promised Élisabeth to take her one day to Châteaugay, near Clermont-Ferrand, where the elderly "Granny" who had raised her and who had been in the service of the Arrighi family for many years had retired. This trip had never been possible. Félix rejoiced to be close enough geographically to ask his friend to make this detour. He felt it was a duty now to fulfill this old promise at last. He had the impression of thus fulfilling a moral legacy. It was a relief and almost a joy for him to speak of Élisabeth with the old "Granny". She had a wonderful memory of her years of service in the Arrighi home. She had seen the birth and growth of the children. She had a good number of anecdotes to tell about the childhood and youth of the girl she repeatedly called "her great love". This made him smile for the first time. It was a good moment when Élisabeth still seemed very much present to him.

The Second Stage: Paray-le-Monial

Félix was not lacking in prejudices against Paray-le-Monial. The cult of the Sacred Heart and the revelations to Margaret Mary, which he described as shams, represented for him a kind of incomprehensible paganism or childish gullibility. He had not kept himself from repeating this to Élisabeth, knowing perfectly well how much he was making her suffer.

He remembered that, in 1904, during a visit when she had accompanied him to Moulins, where he had traveled for professional reasons, she had left him one day to go to Paray-le-Monial alone. She had returned from this pilgrimage with such strength and such gentleness that she had promised herself to do it again, but the opportunity had never again presented itself.

It was not, of course, devotion to the Sacred Heart that attracted him to Paray-le-Monial. It was only the memory of Élisabeth.

In his present situation, it was in the places that were dear to her and with the people she had loved that he felt the best, or, at least, less bad.

But alas, after the anticipation, it was complete disillusionment. Élisabeth was no longer there, and he was disappointed by this town that seemed to him empty and gloomy. While taking a distracted look at the Chapelle de la Visitation, he regretted having come. "What am I doing here all alone?"

Waiting for his friend to finish looking after the car, he entered the twelfth-century Romanesque basilica. An expert in Romanesque art and aesthetics, he was amazed by the beauty of it all. He was alone. He surveyed the large nave; his interest and his admiration for the columns diverted him for a while from his repulsion and his loneliness. While he walked around the choir in the ambulatory, he again felt a kind of interior call comparable to that which he had felt two days before on the road to Tulle: the certainty of Élisabeth's presence near him.

> I had the feeling, even more clearly, of the dear presence; unable to resist, I fell to my knees on a prie-Dieu; Élisabeth, in a way, joined my hands, and, weeping, I prayed, without really knowing how, since I had unlearned all prayer for so long, but I spoke to Our Lord, whose statue overlooked the altar, with the sincere impulse of my soul. I truly had the intuition that he was there, in the tabernacle, and that his infinite goodness was leaning toward me. I remained thus nearly a quarter of an hour, lost in my surprise and my emotion, beseeching Élisabeth to pray for me.[4]

The Third Stage: Beaune

Still affected by emotion and this extraordinary sense of presence, the two friends went to Beaune. Sister Goby welcomed Félix with open arms and tears in her eyes. She, too, was still in great sorrow since Élisabeth's death. She needed to know about her very intimate correspondent's final moments. She had not been able to travel to attend the funeral; she alone knew how much Élisabeth had prayed

---

[4] Ibid.

and offered her sufferings so that her husband would return to the faith. She remained very discreet, but Félix understood. In these places, all still full of memories of their last trip together, he felt less far away from Élisabeth.

The return to Paris brought Félix back to his professional occupations and his usual environment. When he thought back to those two moments, his certainty of the living presence of Élisabeth and his prayer that followed in the basilica of Paray-le-Monial, he wondered if he had not dreamed it. He tried to fight against these supernatural manifestations impossible to believe. He repeated to himself that what he had experienced was a purely psychological feeling, normal in the face of the unbearable absence of a person so loved. He tried to forget those moments that ultimately, for him, had only been moments of weakness . . . unless they were of help . . .

He continued to go to Élisabeth's grave every day and to bring her flowers, the only gift he could give her now. As soon as he returned home, he immersed himself in Élisabeth's diary. It was in her writing and at the heart of her most intimate thoughts that he felt closest to her and better. And above all, the reading of the diary gave him courage for each day. Confronted with his wife's strength of character in the face of illness, he decided that he must also have, out of fidelity, the same strength of character in accepting his grief.

He also began to understand better:

> It was no longer as before. I was closer to her all the same, and, without being won over by the faith, I was often troubled by the thought of the inner life. I stiffened then, I wanted to believe myself as much a materialist as before, but my ideas had received a powerful shock and, although remaining attached to my irreligious or skeptical friendships, the work of transformation was being done without my knowing it, slowly, often despite myself, even though no one around me could encourage it, quite the contrary.[5]

Félix dreaded spending his first July 14, 1914, alone in a festive Paris. The public balls where embracing lovers danced so joyfully and so lovingly in the streets, the fireworks, the common jubilation seemed to him, in his sorrow and loneliness, too great an ordeal.

---

[5] Ibid., 23.

Then, one of his old childhood friends, who had affectionately come forward at the time of Élisabeth's death, invited him to spend a few days with him in Reims during the celebrations of July 14. Félix gratefully accepted. Reims was his hometown, in the shadow of its magnificent cathedral, completely charged with history; it had been the setting of his entire childhood.

This friend was very Christian. He lived his faith with joy in union with his wife; they had a large family of ten children whom they both raised with simplicity and tenderness. Félix and Élisabeth had stayed with them twice in 1910 and 1912, on the way back from Jougne. They had been very warmly received; the two women had talked at length while the men discussed childhood memories and professional concerns; the women had understood each other very well, sharing the same faith and the same love for others. Élisabeth had become attached with admiration and affection to this courageous and loving mother, so close to her in her beliefs and in her way of living her faith concretely. She often expressed her regret at being so far away geographically because she would have liked to visit with this friend more often.

During those few days, Félix participated in the life of this family; he was amazed by the image of these children, well-raised, tender, respectful toward their parents, devoted to each other and at the same time spontaneous and joyful. He considered how important a place the Gospel held in their life. He told himself that he had never seen a testimony like this. And, as always, brought back to the thought of Élisabeth, he told himself that it was thus that she would have liked to live and that she understood life in faith and love.

One morning, he was alone in the living room with his friend's wife. Of course, he brought up Élisabeth's death. It was all he could talk about. It was his only topic of conversation at that time. She listened to him with great attentiveness and responded to him with much gentleness. In her sensitivity, she found the exact words to suit his grief.

She explained to him with simplicity all the consolation and strength that faith brings in mourning. Félix felt comforted. He looked at her and suddenly realized that it was exactly what Élisabeth would have told him under these circumstances. The woman speaking to him was filled with a deep faith, full of strength and self-control; she was completely open to his sorrow. A phrase from the Gospels that he had learned in his youth but had long since forgotten came to mind: "You will know them by their fruits" (Mt 7:16). And so, he said to himself, because the fruits are so perfect, the tree that produced them can only be perfect!

> And the truth of Christ's teaching appeared to me in that living room as on the road to Tulle, as in the basilica of Paray-le-Monial. The supernatural again loomed before me in such a way that it was again impossible for me to avoid it; the friend who spoke to me with so much simplicity, modesty, did not suspect the feeling and the emotion she caused in me. Élisabeth's diary, the fundamental thought that inspired it, had just been transformed into action, and God was once more resplendent before my eyes.[6]

Félix returned to Paris, completely filled with reflections and perspectives in which his horizon became gradually brighter.

He understood that, while he had been closed off for years to his wife's faith, God had perhaps made use of the words, of the heart, and of the faith of this wife and mother placed on his path almost by chance in order to speak to him and finally to touch his heart.

A few phrases that he had read in Élisabeth's diary came to mind; only now did they take on their full meaning; he understood at last the weight of suffering that they had carried. He felt a deep remorse for not having understood her, for having shown indifference and contempt for her personal beliefs, and, above all, for having left her in an emotional isolation whose existence he had not even suspected.

> I ardently prayed for those whom I love, for the one whom I love above all.

> My God, will you give me one day this joy of being alone together, united in the same prayer, the same faith, the same love?

> Yes, my God, I must have, you must have, this honest and good soul; he must know you, love you, become the very humble instrument of your glory and do the work of the apostolate! Take him completely

---

[6] Ibid., 27.

to yourself. From my trials, my sufferings, my sacrifices, make the road by which you will come to this much beloved heart. Is there anything concerning me alone that I would not be disposed to offer you to obtain this conversion, this grace so much desired? My sweet savior, it is between your heart and mine that this pact of love must be made that will give you for eternity him whom I cherish and whom I want with me in your heaven.[7]

---

[7] Ibid.

25

The Great War

July 1914. Since the worsening of Élisabeth's illness and her death, Félix, too focused on his grief, had been less interested in politics. He had had neither the time nor the desire to read the newspapers. However, ever since Sarajevo, history had been on the move! On June 28, 1914, while he was completely lost in his grief, he had not imagined that the shot from a revolver fired at Franz Ferdinand of Austria was going to set all of Europe on fire.

When Félix, cut off from all these events, returned to Paris at the beginning of the month of August, war seemed inevitable and imminent. He was shocked to learn about Austria's ultimatum to Serbia, Germany's threats, Russia's defensive mobilization. A few days later, it was the French who were called to serve. Within his own family, his Arrighi brother-in-law and three of his nephews were summoned.

On August 3, 1914, war was declared.

Félix could not be drafted. He was three years over the age limit. But he would have to remain in charge of the Conservateur, where he resumed office after several months' absence. Such an important insurance company had to remain stable during the storm.

When the German troops invaded France through Belgium and arrived twenty-five miles outside of Paris, the long and sorrowful exodus of Parisians on the roads began.

For four years, France was going to live through one of the most violent periods in its history.

A number of his colleagues at the Conservateur were drafted. Given the urgency of the situation, his board of directors, at least what remained of it, met on August 25.

Everyone was unanimous in entrusting the director with a difficult mission: sheltering the company's entire monetary fund far away from Paris, which was threatened by the German invasion. Félix was going to have to transport to Bordeaux (the safest city at the time, where the government had taken refuge) the large sum of cash deposited by all the shareholders as well as the bearer bonds kept in the company's vaults. It was a considerable amount to carry with him in a discreet, hand-held suitcase. The company could not afford to betray the trust of its clients and risk making them lose the money they had entrusted to it.

With the trains crowded and too dangerous for the transport of such sums, it would be essential to take to Bordeaux the next day a taxi that his company had already reserved for him for this difficult transfer of funds.

What no one had foreseen was that all the taxis in Paris would be requisitioned by Marshal Joffre in order to transport the troops to the front at Marne. It was thus impossible to travel as planned by taxi. Therefore, passengers had to fall back on private "renters". To make up for the lack of taxis, many people offered their improvised services. For them it was a time of prosperity.

Conscious of the difficulty of his mission in a France in complete disarray, Félix, accustomed to taking on responsibilities, quickly organized himself. In advance, he put in place every safeguard so that the journey could be carried out in the best conditions: he procured a travel permit for himself, went to a renter recommended to him, and rented a car for August 31 at seven o'clock in the morning. He carefully prepared a large suitcase in which he buried his securities, his stacks of banknotes, and, on top of everything, Élisabeth's diary, from which he no longer ever dreamed of being separated.

The day of departure, when he presented himself at his renter's house with his suitcase, the latter told him that he no longer had a car available. Since the panic provoked by the events and the exodus that had followed, all his cars had been taken by storm.

The option of the train remained, but all the stations were besieged, all the trains were packed. It would be difficult to move.

Dismayed, Félix realized he was stuck in Paris and probably for a long while; he was distressed about the impossibility of being able to fulfill the mission that he knew to be important to his company and his clients; discouraged and not seeing any way out for the time being, he thought of Élisabeth, who always knew how to help him find a solution in difficult situations; he felt even more abandoned and more alone than ever. And he asked her for her help.

While he was still arguing in the rental office, an unknown gentleman, who apparently just came to get some information, overheard his conversation. He understood Félix's predicament right away. He approached him and told him that he was actually leaving for Bordeaux in a few minutes. A friend had lent him a big car. He had a driver. He had room for him and his big suitcase. The miracle!

Scarcely a few miles after leaving the capital, the trip proved difficult, if not impossible. The exodus had put thousands of Parisians on the road on foot, in cars, on carts, in handcarts to which furniture had been tied up, and exhausted elderly people being dragged by their families. The spectacle of this panicked population in complete turmoil was devastating. They followed a massive, disorganized flow of people to Orléans.

At Vierzon, faced with the congestion on the road, the chauffeur gave up going farther and announced to his passengers he was going to drop them off in front of the train station. They could continue their journey on their own! Good luck!

Fortunately, a train destined for Bordeaux was announced at midnight. The wait on the crammed platform was long, but at last Félix glimpsed the end of his journey. Alas! When the train entered the station and pulled up along the platform, he quickly saw that it was already packed to the steps: compartments and corridors were overloaded with passengers standing, sitting, lying on the floor, pressed against each other. It was impossible to move forward.

All the compartments were full. As the train was pulling out, Félix was finally able to hoist himself into the overloaded baggage car. In a corner, all he found was a large, more or less stable trunk on which he could sit. What an ordeal for someone used to luxury trains and sleeper cars. He had to clasp his precious suitcase, which he did not even dare to place on the floor, very tightly on his knees. He thought of the war, of the thousands of civilians in flight, of so much suffering, past and future, of crusader soldiers who courageously joined the front, of France's misfortunes, of his own misfortune, too, at being a widower, henceforward alone everywhere, no matter what turn this war that was beginning would take. He wanted to cry.

At one point, tossed about by the movements of the train and in this overloaded baggage compartment, he experienced an immense inner distress. Like everyone who has lost his spouse, his thoughts, his appeals, his suppressed tears went toward his absent wife.

To his surprise, he once again felt very strongly and with certainty Élisabeth's presence close to him. He felt he heard in the depths of his heart the voice that he knew so well making him understand:

> If you were able to leave Paris in such a strange way, so unexpected, almost miraculous, do not believe that it was simply to safeguard the material interests entrusted to you. That was only coincidence, chance. The real reason, the purpose of all this, it is your inner self who is at stake here; it was necessary for you to be able to go to Lourdes, where God is waiting for you. Lourdes is the true end of this present journey; you must go to Lourdes, go to Lourdes.[1]

He was stunned. He wondered if he had not dozed off, if this were not a dream. But no, he could not have fallen asleep in such an uncomfortable position. He chased the feeling from his mind. He shrugged his shoulders, stating, almost aloud: "Come now, this is not serious, it is only the impression of a poor widower in distress who is not over his mourning!" He tried not to think about it anymore, but several times he heard repeated in the depths of himself, like an echo: "You must go to Lourdes, you must go to Lourdes."

And for the first time, something became obvious. He had been fighting for too long against faith, against the belief in a life of the soul after death. Why continue such a fierce fight? What was the use? He should surrender now, let go, at last understand what his wife had lived so strongly, and he acquired certainty: "Élisabeth is praying for me. The Lord is holding out his hand to me." And spontaneously, in that baggage car, tossed about by the jolting of the rails, he answered her in the silence of his soul: "Yes, I promise you, I will go to Lourdes."

In Bordeaux, the storm France was experiencing caused him to put aside his resolutions from that night. Finding a hotel room was uncertain. The city was overflowing with helpless refugees seeking lodging. The arrival of the parliament, government, and presidency of the Republic with the whole cohort of public authorities,

---

[1] R. P. Marie-Albert Leseur, *Vie d'Élisabeth Leseur* (Paris: Éd. J. de Gigord, 1931), 33.

journalists, financiers, and artists seemed to him a tragic procession heralding defeat.

This commotion did not facilitate the accomplishment of his mission. All the banks were overwhelmed, and it was impossible to find safes to rent or even to arrange the necessary appointments.

For three long weeks, he had to negotiate with departments that were both present and disorganized, meet with Parisian celebrities, go to missed appointments.

He ran into a few professional acquaintances with whom he occasionally shared dinner, but he met no one with whom he could be open about the transformation that was occurring within him because they all seemed to him completely closed to spiritual aspirations in general and, with even greater reason, to his own. And this was not the time for confidences!

Isolated in that city in perpetual motion after defeat, he visited churches as soon as he had a free moment; it was the only place where he felt almost good.

Two especially attracted him regularly because, as an aesthete, he appreciated these twelfth- and thirteenth-century wonders: Sainte-Croix and Saint-Seurin. Every day, he sat for a long time in the silence of the naves of one or the other: he meditated, still torn between that rationalism he had violently defended for so many years, even within the intimacy of his marriage, and this recent call to a personal Christian life, still so mysterious, so vague in his mind. It would be such a reversal in his life that he did not even see the way! The memory of certain conversations with Élisabeth, the reading of the diary, everyday more than ever, nourished his meditations. It now seemed to him that Élisabeth was directing his reflections and pushing him toward other horizons.

At the end of September, after having succeeded in putting the Conservateur's money in a safe place, he could at last begin to consider returning to Paris with the satisfaction of having accomplished the mission.

So many transformations had been brought about in him in the past few months, so many profound changes, about which he could speak to no one, had turned his life upside down that he felt the need to share them with hearts capable of understanding or listening to him. He also felt the need to receive advice, if only to know where he was, what he must do. Until now, in every situation of his life, he had asked advice from Élisabeth, and she had always guided him with common sense and reason; she knew him well. Even for his professional life, he had asked her advice. But now . . .

Since he was in the southwest, he took the opportunity to go to Meilhan near Marmande. The calm and gentleness of the landscapes along the Garonne gave him rest from the turmoil of Bordeaux and the tumult of events.

In the Bordeaux region, a friend of Élisabeth's had been detained by the war in her beautiful family home where she usually spent the summer. This intelligent and cultured woman was also widowed. She lived with her daughters, but since the war, all three went to the Red Cross in Marmande every day to care for the wounded. All three were fervent Christians and paid genuine homage to Élisabeth's memory.

Félix wanted to meet them to talk about his wife with them, but above all to tell them all about the transformation that he felt within himself and that he still very much doubted. Every day he asked himself if he were not making a mistake, if his thoughts were not simply a normal psychological reaction to the pain of his wife's absence, a kind of compensation. Maybe even a way of finding her again? He no longer knew what to think.

In the evening on the terrace, when the heat began to lessen, while with Élisabeth's friends he contemplated the long sunsets on the gentle hills of that region, he opened his heart to these three women whom he trusted completely. He knew they were capable of understanding and helping him. He presented his objections to them and described to them his difficulties; they gave him advice, encouragement. It was the first time he had dared to express such personal thoughts like that.

In Reims, at the home of the mother of the family who had listened to him so well, he had ultimately spoken only of Élisabeth's death, the pain of her absence, his life without her; but he had carefully avoided addressing the topic of his potential inner transformation because he was not yet sure enough of himself and especially because it had seemed premature to him. Since then, he had reflected a good deal. Now he had gained the near certitude of no longer being under an illusion.

For long hours, he read to Élisabeth's friends passages from the diary, which he always kept close to him. It was the first time he dared reveal his wife's innermost thoughts; it was the first time he had heard his wife's deepest sentiments, which, until then, had still seemed to him to be within the realm of their intimate relationship, resound through his voice in the fragrant air of those mild summer evenings.

As he progressed in his reading, he watched the faces of her friends, he listened to their reflections; they were amazed; they interrupted him to thank him for sharing with them such a treasure that made them grow in faith and love, encouraged them in their spiritual life.

These pages seemed so precious to them, so rich, that right away they told him he did not have the right to keep them for himself alone; they should be published. It would be a way to give the word of God to others, to make it known, to evangelize. And no doubt it is what Élisabeth would have wanted, she who had cared so much about bringing souls closer to God. Why not? . . . One day perhaps . . .

26

Lourdes, Way of Light

Before going back to Paris, Félix kept his unspoken promise to Élisabeth: he went to Lourdes.

It was a hard, emotional step. Lourdes was still completely full of his memories with Élisabeth. Two years ago, they had come together to thank the Lord for the improvement in her health and for the healing of their young nephew. All the sites were still full of images of a happy and radiant Élisabeth; but she was no longer there, and these same places cruelly cried out her absence, rekindled his grief, and seemed terribly empty to him.

Félix wondered: By what mysterious journey was he there for the third time in an emptiness and loneliness that he could never have imagined? Why had he come? Such sadness! To what call had he responded if not that impression—perhaps imaginary—of having heard deep in his heart a voice, Élisabeth's voice, requesting it of him? And now that, alone in front of the Grotto, he contemplated the setting where Christians believe the Virgin Mary revealed herself to little Bernadette, so humble and so poor, he was dismayed. He felt no emotion other than a desire to weep over it, over his unhappiness, over his wife who had died so young, over that love which had given him life and no longer existed, over everything that surrounded him and seemed a fiction to him.

Since his last trip, the misfortunes of the war had fallen on France all the way to Lourdes.

Lourdes did not look at all the same as it had two years before. No more pilgrimages or crowds or processions or singing. The hotels had been requisitioned by military medical services to shelter the wounded brought back from the great battles of Aisne, Argonne, Vosges. Every day medical trains again brought more of them, terribly mutilated and deformed, who were carried on stretchers. The rare pilgrims came alone, like himself, singing on their knees in front of the Grotto the litany of the Blessed Virgin emphasizing "Salvation of the sick", "Comforter of the afflicted", "Queen of Peace"—that peace so much requested in the prayer of each person but the prospect of which, in the face of the heightened violence of the war, seemed an illusion.

Arriving in front of the Grotto, Félix was content to watch and listen to these supplications at length, not without a certain skepticism. He was more moved by the sight of all these courageous young people, wounded or mutilated for life, than by the progression of the pilgrimages he hardly ever saw. In that environment of great suffering, they seemed ridiculous to him.

The next day, still touched by the faith of those Christians in intense prayer, he returned to the Grotto for the last time. Without thinking, he too knelt down on the ground among the pilgrims. In the depth of his heart, he was surprised that he too prayed; he beseeched the Virgin to give him faith, to enlighten him, to make him understand what God expected of him.

Once in a while, little by little, he united his voice to that of the pilgrims who prayed by saying their rosary aloud. It was the first time that this had happened to him; all his life he had proclaimed that the rosary was the recourse of the weak minded, and now, repeating with an unknown crowd these phrases that he had learned on his mother's knee, he felt overwhelmed by a great gentleness, a kind of tenderness from God that seemed to envelop him and, little by little, fill him with joy, a truly profound, inexplicable joy.

Where could this unhoped-for solace have come from in such painful circumstances? His heart's response was without hesitation: it could only come from the Lord who had called him here before the Grotto of Massabielle.

Élisabeth's prayers had been answered at last.

Félix wanted to cry, but this time it was no longer from despair and loneliness, it was from joy, peace, like the feeling of at last arriving in the harbor after such a long and tumultuous journey. And he could only thank the Lord for fulfilling him thus in his new life as a widower. He had thought that he would never again be able to experience the feelings of happiness and peace on earth.

He repeated to himself a powerful saying of Élisabeth's that he had not understood until now: "Suffering creates life." Ultimately, it had the same meaning as Jesus' words: "Unless a grain of wheat . . . dies" (Jn 12:24).

Without Élisabeth's prayers and suffering, would he have come to Lourdes alone? In front of this Grotto that had witnessed so many conversions, he acknowledged, little by little, that a new life had to open for him. He understood with certainty that henceforth faith was going to fill his life and undoubtedly change some of his ways. But in his practical everyday life, at his age, what changes could he envision in his life as a widower and in his professional life?

Upon his return to Paris, he felt completely different. He felt the need to go to Mass regularly at Saint-Pierre-de-Chaillot: he read the Gospel every day and read it with so much emotion and joy that this reading quickly became a genuine and invigorating daily nourishment for him.

He chose from Élisabeth's library the works that she had loved and thus shaped his Christian thought; at the same time that he marveled at what he discovered, he was humiliated to realize all the ignorance, bias, and folly that his attacks on religion had contained . . . and even unkindness toward his wife! He considered how much she must have suffered when she heard him mock all that was deepest in her! He was shocked, felt terribly guilty for having lived for so long close to someone who had offered up so much suffering for him until her death without his being able to guess it. He was just as surprised to see that she had had an inner life of such intensity while he, her husband, who lived with her daily, had not suspected anything of the richness of her soul . . . or very little.

The daily reading of Élisabeth's diary continued to be a substantial nourishment for him, a profound and indispensable emotional and spiritual bond. As soon as he returned from the office, he read the thoughts of the one who was so dear to him. Thanks to her, he thus progressed for several months all alone on the path of light that brightened more every day. But to whom should he speak about his journey, which was still so personal? With whom should he share this new discovery, which was still so fragile? Who would understand that the fierce anticlerical he had been had returned to the Father like the prodigal son or the lost sheep? Who would believe in such a reversal?

One day, after much hesitation, he gathered his courage to go confide his inner transformation to the old priest of his parish Saint-Pierre-de-Chaillot, whom he knew only by sight. The welcome and kind attentiveness that he received from this man, who, while not knowing him, had understood his effort and his humility, comforted him and filled him with gratitude.

No doubt things would have stayed that way if one of his friends, Gabriel Thomas, whom he met by chance at Louis Barthou's, where he was the only Christian in an indifferent, if not hostile, environment, had not spoken to him, without any preface, of his own personal situation: he had rediscovered faith at the end of a long journey.

Félix had known Gabriel Thomas for many years. They had previously met in bibliophile meetings or auctions.

Talking to him, Félix sensed a way open for him to confide his transformation and his hesitations. He found an isolated corner to reveal to him the path he had been traveling in recent months and to ask him for advice.

Two days later, Gabriel Thomas, no doubt a bit of a proselytizer, told him: "I have arranged a meeting for you with Father Janvier. He expects you Tuesday at ten o'clock in the morning."

"But I don't know him", Félix said, stunned.

"Well, you will get acquainted!"

Father Janvier was a Dominican but fairly well-known in Paris. He had a great spiritual influence in the intellectual circles that, after the storm of anticlerical laws, saw returning to them quite a few writers or artists who were no longer afraid to witness to their faith. He had founded the *Fraternité du Tiers Ordre des Hommes* (Fraternity of Third Order Men) for them, where famous names like those of Maurice Denis, Robert Valléry-Radot, Henri Ghéon, and many others regularly met. He had been the confidant and witness of numerous instances of spiritual evolution quite similar to that of Félix.

It was not without a certain apprehension that Félix knocked on the office door of Father Janvier, who warmly received him for more than two hours. Father Janvier immediately understood that he had before him a man of great intelligence, entrusted for many years with serious professional responsibilities, full of humility and goodwill, and who had come from very far away on an almost incredible journey. He perceived the spiritual height of the wife with whom Félix had gone through part of his life, their love, the weight of the sufferings and the graces they had carried together during the years of her illness. He also understood Félix's character. He did not doubt that such a late call to an authentic and well-considered faith would one day come to fruition in a believer's commitment for the, unpredictable for anyone but certainly quite complete, future.

The priest listened attentively to the story of the man in front of him, who was there almost by chance, since brought there by a friend whom he had met at a gathering. But he realized that this chance meeting was in God's plan.

He understood above all the place and role of Élisabeth's love in the transformation of her husband. It was the first time that Félix could thus express himself so freely and intimately. But not everything was easy for him in faith. Many points that he had rejected all his life in light of his reasoning and intelligence still remained true obstacles or real causes of perplexity. Félix would disclose them to his interlocutor over the course of several subsequent meetings.

A few weeks later, the priest suggested to Félix that he go to Confession, then Communion.

Who does not see here the image of the father of the prodigal son who for years awaits his child on his doorstep and runs toward him with open arms when he sees his figure appear on the edge of the horizon?

After these powerful moments, the "returnee", as they say nowadays, went to the chapel that Élisabeth had visited so often on the rue Goujon to pray to her or with her. He knew that it was she who had guided and supported him during those months of grief, distress, denials, hesitations. Despite her absence, he had been carried and guided by her love, and if he had been drawn, almost despite himself, toward a desire for the Eucharist, this could only be thanks to her. If she saw him, she must have rejoiced from the height of heaven. Radiant, Félix at last understood Élisabeth's phrase at the heart of her sufferings offered for him: "You will come join me, I know it."[1]

---

[1] R. P. Marie-Albert Leseur, *Vie d'Élisabeth Leseur* (Paris: Éd. J. de Gigord, 1931), 348.

In a talk that he gave later in Rennes in 1927, Félix, who had become Father Leseur, would testify that things had not been very clear for him. He would admit that in leaving the chapel he had again experienced a feeling of rejection. He was hoping to experience a kind of communion with Élisabeth in faith, but he had felt absolutely nothing but a sense of denial of everything that had been his life, a painful disenchantment, a void: "I was wrong. I had set myself up. I was hoping to gain understanding, and I found nothing."[2]

Convinced of having repeatedly been the victim of his imagination recently, he decided once again that day to abandon everything once and for all. From now on, he was convinced that his so-called spiritual journey was only a mistake due to the pain of having lost his wife. This would only be one chapter in his life. He needed to turn the page. Life had to continue for him now. He was still in the prime of life. He was the director of one of the biggest insurance companies in Paris. He had a future ahead of him. He had been the plaything of his imagination or his grief. He needed to pull himself together and start living again.

As he did every day, he then went to Élisabeth's grave. Waiting for the metro, seated on a bench in the Marbeuf station, he was repeating to himself internally this rational and wise, definitive decision, when, suddenly, he thought he heard Élisabeth's voice in the midst of the revolt or turmoil in the depths of his heart. He felt completely overwhelmed by her love and a great inner peace. And he understood as if in a revelation:

> It would be almost immoral if, after having renounced and fought against God and Jesus Christ all your adult life, you believed that because you went to Confession and Communion you were going to possess immediately all clarity, all consolations. Here it is no longer a matter of your feeling, but of your will, which you must henceforward put in the service of Christ in order truly to gain faith with his grace.[3]

---

[2] Ibid., 354.

[3] Marie-Louise Herking, *Causerie de Rennes, Le Père Leseur* (Paris: Éd. J. de Gigord, n.d.), 119.

He was shaken. Throughout the entire metro ride, he recalled that phrase that had come to his mind so clearly. He reflected. It was a final turnaround. And when, at the end of a long path, he arrived at Élisabeth's grave, his heart had finally been enlightened. He had at last acquired the certainty that he had awaited for so long.

Without hesitation, he decided to go to Communion again the next day and from then on to place his life in the service of this God full of love against whom he had fought so much and who had made use of the precious pearl of his wife's love to call him.

"If you knew the gift of God!" (Jn 4:10), said Jesus to the Samaritan woman. That day it was to Félix that he said it, and Félix, after so many years and so many battles, at last understood the meaning of that phrase.

27

And Then?

Félix was fifty-three years old. He had a professional life at the highest level where his responsibilities and qualifications placed him in contact with leading figures from the world of politics and finance. Even though he had experienced an important and secret reversal in the depths of his soul, outwardly his life continued as before.

Less oppressed by his grief, he enjoyed seeing his friends again. Since he was a good guest and his conversation was always interesting, he was often invited to the best restaurants in Paris for business meals. He always readily accepted in accordance with the advice Élisabeth had given him. But he remained very quiet and discreet about his conversion, unknown to his friends and colleagues.

He continued to read Élisabeth's diary every day. Up until then, it had been the presence, the memory of Élisabeth that he was seeking in its lines written by her hand. Now it was almost a way of life, direction, instruction, a doctrine, and he encountered a love. He perceived the recovery that this reading accomplished in him day after day. It seemed to him that his wife was guiding him very gently by the hand toward God. Prayer, still in its infancy, and careful reading of the Gospel gradually helped him to get back on his feet.

But still much more: through her human love, which had accepted all the sufferings that he had unintentionally inflicted on her, Élisabeth revealed to him God's love for him. He genuinely gained the certainty that he was himself the lost sheep, for whom the good shepherd had left everything in order to go in search of him in the mountains. Or rather, he understood that Élisabeth had been for him the guide that the good shepherd had sent on his path to accompany him over the years on his lost paths and bring him back to him. "If you knew the gift of God!", this gift of God that he had never understood and that he now discovered more each

day. In front of this new manifestation of the divine call, he began
to sense that this call would no longer suffer limitations.

Now deeply convinced that Jesus was "the way, the truth, and the
life" (Jn 14:6), he immersed himself more every day in the books
close at hand, those that now slept in Élisabeth's library. Since they
were selected, read, and annotated by her, he had the impression
that it was she who presented and explained them to him. For several months, in light of these readings of exegesis and apologetics,
explanations of the Gospels, and meditations, his faith strengthened.

Then, there arose deep within him, little by little, the idea of con-
secrating himself to God completely. Since Jesus had said that he
was "the life", a path of renewal might thus yet open for him. Yes,
he wanted to choose life. Until now, he had been a poor widower
convinced that his life had ended the day of his wife's death. And
now, springs of living water were bubbling up in him.

Filled by this love that surpassed him, he remembered a phrase
that Élisabeth often repeated to him at a time when he did not
understand the weight of what it meant: "We love truly well only
in God."

He had at the time greatly benefited from the fruits of the Spirit
evident in her behavior toward him and others: the goodness, kindness, gentleness, helpfulness, but how could he have refused to rec-
ognize the sole source of these fruits?

He did not see how else to respond to this love except by giving
it his whole life, as Élisabeth too had done, but in a different way.
And the sentence his little sister-in-law Juliette had said a few hours
before her death often came to mind: "Félix, one day you will be
a priest."

He also remembered a conversation with Élisabeth at the clinic a
few days after her operation: "When I am dead, you will convert,
and when you are converted, you will become a religious. You will
be Dom Leseur or Father Leseur. You will be Father Leseur."[1]

At the time, he had shrugged and smiled at such a prospect, which
might have been amusing if Élisabeth had not been so sick! He had

---

[1] Élisabeth Leseur, *La Vie Spirituelle: Petits traités de vie intérieure* (Paris: Éd. J. de Gigord, 1922), 56.

thought that it was undoubtedly the recommendation of a wife repelled by the thought of her husband attached to a new woman!

And now, like evidence that pushed him toward a new future, the very powerful words of the apostle Peter to Jesus resonated in him: "Lord, to whom shall we go? You have the words of eternal life" (Jn 6:68).

Deeply determined to commit himself henceforward to this path of light and to consecrate his life to God in a monastic order, he informed himself about the spirituality of different religious orders. The orders of Saint Benedict and Saint Dominic attracted him. He hesitated for a long time between these two congregations, got a lot of information about them, and eventually, day after day, a marked preference for the Dominicans formed in his mind. In fact, he was attracted by the harmony between contemplative life, conventual life, poverty, intellectual life, the study that would be indispensable for him, and the apostolic ministry. This corresponded exactly to the life he now wanted.

His primary concern was to announce it to Élisabeth's family and to his own family. But contrary to his expectations, he realized that his plan met only objections:

> You are not at all made for this life, you who love luxury and wealth so much, you who love to travel so much, you who have fought so much against God. . . . Even if you have changed a little, it is not a reason to change your life completely at fifty-four years of age. . . . You would never stay the course. . . . Why the Dominicans? Of course, this could not be otherwise since you have been influenced by a Dominican, but it is not necessarily reasonable. . . . Clearly your Father Janvier has known you for only a short time. . . . You see clearly that he is recruiting . . . all the orders do the same thing.

It was a family break that pained him without managing to dissuade him.

At that same time, he sought every opportunity to give of himself to others. It was with this in mind that, for a few weeks, he took in his very elderly mother. He knew that Élisabeth would have advised him to have this filial attentiveness. In the evenings, he read to his old, amazed mother passages from Élisabeth's diary and gradually disclosed his plans to her. This woman who had suffered so much from seeing her son become atheistic and anticlerical and who, until the end, had hoped for the miracle that would bring her son back to the faith had no trouble detecting Élisabeth's work.

After a few months, on the advice of Father Janvier, Félix attended his first meeting of Third Order Dominican Men, where he was warmly welcomed. His new "brothers" were not quite the kind of men with whom his profession and social life had accustomed him to socialize. He was deeply touched by their welcome and their open-mindedness. For him, the Third Order was already a first step, in anticipation of what was perhaps the next, which was still very uncertain in his mind: his entrance into the great order about which he still spoke to no one.

The Third Order was composed of laymen who were well-established in life. They were part of the Saint Dominic movement and the Dominican Order, and they wanted to be "preachers" in their own spheres, which were all very different from each other. Prayer, daily reading of the word of God, attendance at liturgical Offices, gatherings for reflection, and regular meetings united them and brought them close. Motivated by shared spiritual aspirations, they were like brothers who gathered regularly to pray together. Seeing them, Félix thought of the first Christian communities described in the Acts of the Apostles.

On Pentecost 1915, a day when the whole Church was celebrating, during a very simple ceremony, Félix, surrounded by his new brothers, put on the white sackcloth habit of the Third Order, which he would wear only during meetings. The rest of the time he would continue his life as usual.

Very few in his entourage knew of his new commitment, which would surprise more than one person in the world of his professional and political relationships. Beginning that day, he would regularly be followed and surrounded by Christians confident in their faith. All of them desired to grow in the spiritual life, to pray, either together or alone in their homes, to study the word of God and to live by it, to bear witness in their lives to their brotherly love animated by the love of God and others. Almost all his new brothers were fathers of families and none of them were contemplating monastic life.

With the arrival of the summer of 1915, Félix went to Jougne. It was the first time he had been alone in that big house all arranged by Élisabeth. He found her presence everywhere, in every corner of the house, on the terrace where she had lain on her chaise longue, in the garden where the plants that she had sown flowered all alone in the sun. When he went to pray at the church, he saw on the altar one of the three cloths that she had embroidered during her long hours of convalescence. He was no longer sad as in the first months of her absence.

He wrote to a friend of Élisabeth's on July 20: "The more I live, the more I am convinced that the dead are the true living, that they are in the light and in full life, and that they are close to us, guiding us and surrounding us. I live constantly with Bébeth, near her, and I prefer seeking out the places where she was happy."[2]

In September, at Félix's pressing invitation, Father Janvier came to spend a long week at Jougne. They were alone together. Every day, they went walking on the grassy paths where they found a magnificent view of the old houses of the village, the valley, and the spruces on the surrounding mountains.

One morning, feeling the moment had come, Félix confided to him the plan he had thought about for some time: to enter the Dominicans. The priest stopped walking, raised his arms to heaven and cried out with an intensity that nailed Félix to the ground: "Ah! Let this go, these are the thoughts of a neophyte! You must drop them!"[3]

And during the whole rest of the walk, he showed him that it would be enormously foolish at his age to change his life so radically: religious life required a flexibility of mind that he could no longer have. He would certainly render many more services to the Church and to the order by remaining in his worldly life and in his profession, which had so much need of being evangelized.

Félix was disconcerted, disappointed, but he also knew that, with his usual tenacity, he would not give up. The words of Jesus' disciples to the blind Bartimaeus strengthened him in his decision: "Take heart; rise, he is calling you" (Mk 10:49).

---

[2] Ibid., 52.

[3] Introduction to ibid., 52.

In the meantime, as soon as he returned to Paris, he continued to socialize with his new friends from the Third Order and to immerse himself in Élisabeth's diary. He read them some passages from it. Everyone strongly encouraged him to publish it, but Félix hesitated: Could he surrender such an intimate spiritual life to an unknown public, reveal to it the isolation of his wife in her faith, which he desired, openly expose their love, their life as a couple? He asked for advice from Father Janvier.

His response was clear: he considered the diary a work of rich uplifting thought and great beauty of style. He admired "the clear and right reason, the abundance of evangelical vigor and the reliability of the doctrine". In his opinion, Élisabeth's writings were deeply evangelizing.

Thanks to Father Janvier's judgment and encouragement, Félix was strengthened in his desire to publish the diary. But before embarking on this venture, he wanted to have the advice of a lay person as well. He then approached one of his friends from the Académie française, Louis Barthou. His judgment was the same. Thus, the diary would be published.

Even though he knew numerous publishing houses, Félix had many difficulties finding a publisher. No one wanted to take on such a commercial risk. Would this overly "pious" book sell? What audience of readers, at a time when war was ravaging families, would be interested in sorrowful remarks, written by a nobody with a life in which no sensational event happened other than a banal situation within a relationship: one person was an atheist and the other a believer.

After several rejections, Félix ended up taking the manuscript to J. de Gigord, a publisher in the rue Cassette whom he knew well, having met him at bibliophile gatherings. After some hesitation, he agreed to print two thousand copies. What more could he have wanted! It was even too much for Félix, who wondered how many years it would take to sell two thousand copies! He did not yet know that in less than a year he would sell thirty thousand copies of it and that the diary would be translated into several foreign languages.

Father Janvier would introduce the work to the reader in an "Open Letter" published at the beginning of the book. Félix would write a preface that he would entitle *In Memoriam* in order to explain the genesis of this work.

Completed on All Saints Day 1917, his preface ended with a call to holiness that his wife would have loved:

> And now . . . I surrender these precious pages to my family, my friends, to everyone. I pray that the Holy Spirit will spread them among souls and help them to bring about in the greatest number the renewal that they have produced in mine. Thus the apostolate work, for which God had destined my dear and holy Élisabeth and that, in finishing, I place under the special invocation of Saint Dominic and Saint Catherine of Siena, will come to fruition and will continue.[4]

For Félix, the transmission of this diary with all the elevations of soul that it carried thus became a principal mission in his life, the mission of a husband aware of the graces received in his relationship and desirous of generously spreading them.

In the spring of 1917, the diary was released in bookstores.

Félix had to arrange the publicity, send the book out for reviews intended to make it known, prepare a list of important clerics, for the most part unknown to him. He felt as if he were still working for and with Élisabeth.

As soon as the book was launched, it met with a triumphant success. In a few months, the first edition sold out; new printings had to be quickly completed; requests poured in.

Then Félix received a great number of letters from strangers. All spoke of their admiration, of the good that reading this diary had done them. Élisabeth was a soul of light; her diary was a lived gospel, a revelation. Priests drew inspiration from it for their homilies; sick people found their strength in it. The agreement of all these testimonies deeply moved him.

Out of loyalty to the memory of Élisabeth, he scrupulously responded to each of these letters. He called this work, which he thought to be of the utmost importance and which took up all of his time as soon as he returned home and late at night, "her posthumous correspondence". For him, it was always Élisabeth who

---

[4] Félix Leseur, *In Memoriam* (introduction to the 1917 edition of É. Leseur, *Journal et Pensées de chaque jour* [Paris: Éd. J. de Gigord]), 275.

was present and radiant. He thus completed and achieved her work "for souls", as she said.

He had the certainty of working with her and for her now. The publishing of this book was the joint work of their relationship: that of his wife before the Lord and that of the one with whom she had shared her life.

28

Félix, Future Dominican

Several months later, the persistence of God's call within him led Félix to repeat his request to enter the Dominican Order.

This time, Father Janvier was less dogmatic. He began to understand that this vocation was not the result of a moment's infatuation or the emotional refuge of a widower, but that it was serious and thoughtful. After numerous conversations and spiritual exchanges, he consented to consider Félix's aspirations and, after several months, finally suggested to him a meeting with the Father Provincial of the Dominicans.

Félix would not understand until much later that so many reservations and postponements were ultimately out of prudence. When detractors would dare to tell him that all religious orders take advantage of men's weakness to "recruit", it would make him indignant and angry. His own experience had shown him the exact opposite and helped him appreciate the reflection and the discernment with which his future superiors had surrounded his vocation.

In 1916, France was still in the middle of the war. Félix had kept his elderly mother with him for several months, but with her condition worsening, he entrusted her to the Ladies of Hope at Versailles. He went to see her several times a week. He talked with her a great deal, and day after day he prepared her for the great departure.

She was amazed to hear her son, whose atheism had made her suffer so much, speak to her with such faith. On February 9, he learned of her death. After his "conversion", death was no longer the inner heartbreak for him that it had been before. He knew that one day he would have the joy of finding her again.

On Pentecost 1916, after a year of Dominican novitiate, Félix made his profession in the Third Order. He was surrounded by all the friends with whom he had walked for a year, but also by friends whom he had known for a long time, like Maurice Denis, whom he had known in the bibliophile circles for having asked him to illustrate rare books.

With this step completed and time having done its work, Father Janvier at last became favorable to Félix's entrance into the Order of Saint Dominic. He had been won by Félix's unwavering commitment and by his proofs of attachment to the order.

But not all the pitfalls were ironed out yet. The priest felt a certain uneasiness about the concrete change of life that was going to happen for a man over fifty years of age.

He asked himself: How would his penitent, used to the grand life of the director of a big insurance firm, who had always lived in a rich and plush apartment, endowed with all the modern comforts, in the wealthiest neighborhoods of the capital, adapt to the austere life of a monastery? How, after having had a staff under his command, would he accept the vow of obedience?

The order could not accept his request before knowing how he would adapt to the discomfort of a monk's cell or to a very detailed Rule to which he had never been accustomed.

So he asked Félix to make a retreat for several weeks at a monastery where he would share completely in the life of the monks and especially the novices. It would be a first experience without mutual commitment.

At Félix's unconditional acceptance, he then suggested a retreat at the monastery of La Quercia near Viterbo in Lazio, Italy. This way he could spend a few days in Rome beforehand and there meet Father Janvier, who was to preach a retreat to the students of the Dominican university in preparation for the recommencement of their studies.

29

Rome

At last Félix began to see the culmination of his plan. In Rome, he stayed at the Angelicum, the Dominican university. It is one of the oldest and most renowned institutions in Rome, whose various branches of education (theology, philosophy, canon law, exegesis) are based on the doctrine of Saint Thomas Aquinas and its applications. It was practically an obligatory path for a future Dominican. For Félix, it was already a first commitment, a true break from his usual world. It was the first time he was going to live according to the constitutions of the Order of Saint Dominic. He considered it a privilege to be able to take his meals in the refectory of the religious.

At the Angelicum, he met young people intending to enter the order, but also famous Dominicans like Father Garrigou-Lagrange, with whom he quickly bonded when the priest confided to him, in the savory accent of his native Gascony, that he also had begun medical school, had also lost the faith for some years, and that he too had experienced a complete conversion. Now he was one of the Thomist professors; he taught the *Summa Theologica* at the Angelicum with fervor and sometimes even with humor, convinced that Thomism was the most important safeguard of Catholic doctrine, the light of souls. Félix in turn explained to him that Élisabeth had been filled with Thomism, that several books on the subject were in her library, and that up until her final days she had been an enthusiast of Jacques Maritain, the beacon of Thomism in France.

Father Janvier had been able to obtain a private audience at the Vatican for Félix. On October 2, 1917, the latter was received by Pope Benedict XV. Presented by Father Janvier, who explained in a few words the journey of Élisabeth and her husband, Félix, very moved, was able personally to present the pope with a copy of the diary. Father Janvier elaborated: "Monsieur Leseur is a member of the Third Order of Saint Dominic." Then Benedict XV stood up, warmly took Félix's two hands in his own, and said to him: "But so am I, we are brothers!" Encouraged by this enthusiasm, Father Janvier continued: "Monsieur Leseur intends to make these connections stronger still by soon taking the habit of the Great Order."

Félix was expecting approval or encouragement, but the pope grew heated and told him forcefully with a kind of fierceness: "Ah! That! No, no, and no." And after a moment of silence:

> No, sir, do not do that! Every time I am consulted about a late vocation like yours, I advise against it with all my strength. We must watch out for the most generous ambitions. Especially at your age, following a conversion that belies a wholly irreligious life, I cannot recommend abstaining and the negative enough. Remain a fervent Catholic in the world: that will be much better from all points of view.[1]

Father Janvier and Félix were disconcerted in the face of such a speech. After a moment of silence, Félix, more determined than ever, dared to speak again: "Most Holy Father, my decision was made with full knowledge of the facts, after careful consideration. It was opposed for three years by my spiritual father. He finally accepted it after making sure that it was not the result of a momentary enthusiasm."[2]

Then, Father Janvier supported his plea. He persuasively put forth the reasons for which, after having fought for a long time against the desire of his candidate, he had finally been won over. The pope listened, then he spoke again with a kind smile: "Well, monsieur, you have a director who knows you and who has great experience with souls; and if he recognized the supernatural reality of your vocation, he who has all the elements of a wise judgment, I have only to endorse it, and I bless your plans wholeheartedly."[3]

Three years later, when Félix had already entered the order, the pope would send, through the intermediary of his secretary of state,

---

[1] Élisabeth Leseur, *La Vie Spirituelle: Petits traités de vie intérieure* (Paris: Éd. J. de Gigord, 1922), 54.

[2] Ibid.

[3] Ibid., 55.

Cardinal Gasparri, a letter of thanks for Élisabeth's *Journal*: "In congratulating you for having responded unconditionally to God's call, the Sovereign Pontiff deeply rejoices to see the beginnings of your religious life made fruitful by works of the apostolate, which is at the same time, and above all, the apostolate of Madame Leseur."[4]

Félix went to the monastery of La Quercia. It was an important place of Dominican life built during the Renaissance. Its name is connected to a legend according to which an image of the Virgin had been found on an oak branch (hence the name Quercia in Italian). Above all, it was one of the great novitiates of the order, well-known to the French because many, including Father Lacordaire, known for his sermons, had completed their novitiate and had been ordained to the priesthood there.

Félix arrived at La Quercia from Rome by train. A young boy came to fetch him from the station, carried his suitcase, and led him to the monastery. Upon arriving, Félix asked him to show him to the cell of the novice master, to whom he was bringing a letter. The boy went ahead of him on the magnificent stone stairs that led to the dormitorium to drop his luggage there. The new arrival was sufficiently knowledgeable about art to appreciate the magnificent Renaissance architecture.

When they reached the top of the stairs, they found themselves in front of a French Dominican priest, Father Boué, who, surprised to see a visitor in elegant civilian clothes in that place reserved for monastic life, questioned him about the reasons for his presence in that place. Félix himself recounted this conversation:

"What do you want, monsieur?"

"Father," I replied, "I come from Rome, from the Angelicum. I come to spend ten days at La Quercia at the invitation of the reverend Father Novice Master for whom I am looking."

"Very good, monsieur, I will introduce you to him."

And very obligingly, he was accompanying us when, stopping suddenly, he continued:

"But would it be indiscreet, monsieur, to ask you who you are?"

"Not at all, Father, I am Monsieur Félix Leseur."

---

[4] Ibid., 1.

At these words, the religious, showing great surprise and raising his arms, cried:

"You are Monsieur Leseur, is it possible?"

And with a completely spontaneous gesture, he added:

"Allow me to embrace you!"

"Very willingly, Father," I responded, surprised in turn.

"Ah! I surprise you, monsieur, and I understand why, but I must tell you that I live with Madame Leseur's *Journal*, it is my meditation book, I share it around me. Madame Leseur is a saint whom I venerate, for whom I have the most sincere admiration, and, without ever having known her, I can honestly tell you, the most respectful affection. It is very nice to see you here."

You will easily understand the emotion that this encounter and this conversation caused me. So, it was Élisabeth who welcomed me at the threshold of this pious house, it was she who was guiding me in the undertaking, inspired by her, that I had come to carry out there and that was going to direct my future once and for all! I was struck by this manifestation of Providence toward me, and I found in it new proof of the extraordinary spread of Élisabeth's *Journal* and of the powerful effect that it had on souls. Moved, I thanked God with all my heart, I told the priest all the good he had just done me, the great joy he had given me.[5]

The planned ten days of retreat at Viterbo extended to several weeks, during which Félix strictly followed the monastic customs. When he returned to Paris, he was more determined than ever to don the white robe of the Dominicans.

---

[5] Élisabeth Leseur, introduction, *Lettres sur la souffrance* (Paris: Éd. du Cerf, 2012), 3–4.

30

On the Determined Path of No Return

Upon returning home to Paris, to his great surprise, Félix found a large number of letters awaiting him.

His correspondents were the enthusiastic readers of the *Journal* and spoke to him only of Élisabeth. The book had indeed sold beyond all hope. It had been translated into several languages. It had spread far and wide.

Some letters, coming from strangers located in many parts of France, mentioned his wife's influence; they expressed their gratitude for the help that Élisabeth's writings had brought to their lives and especially to their spiritual lives.

Others informed him that they were going to begin novena prayers to Élisabeth and asked him to join them. Associations, groups, even convents asked him to come speak about her at one of their meetings. He began to appreciate the spiritual mission of the one he had misunderstood for so many years. Humbly, he responded to each of these letters.

It was undoubtedly during one of his talks at Berne that he met Marie-Louise Herking, a member of the Dominican Third Order, who, over the years, would become a friend to whom he would confide many memories and write many letters; she would affectionately support him during his religious life and even into his extreme old age. Later, thanks to memories of their conversations, letters exchanged and compiled, she would write his biography, from which this book has drawn invaluable information and quoted many excerpts.

He did not lack for work. Before entering the monastic world, he wanted to publish *Lettres sur la souffrance* (Letters on suffering), the correspondence sent by Élisabeth to Sister Goby during the three-and-a-half-year period that preceded her death. These letters, by revealing Élisabeth's profound soul, could touch "souls", as she said, and make them grow in the love of God. Therefore, Félix considered it a husband's perfectly natural duty not to leave such rich and evangelizing texts lying in a drawer.

For this new publication, he undertook to write a long introduction of more than eighty pages in which he published letters filled with admiration from strangers that had been sent to him after the publication of the *Journal*. He then traced the genesis of the friendship between his wife and this nun that had resulted in a profound exchange about their inner lives. During that period, the nun, several times, had gone through crises of darkness and scruples. Élisabeth, with sensitivity and charity, had helped her, brought her clarity, set her back on her feet: genuine spiritual direction, woman to woman, soul to soul.

This project completed, Félix was still missing some letters. Certain information or explanations were necessary. He had to go to Beaune twice.

During a conversation, though focused on Élisabeth, he confided to this nun who had been so close to his wife and so full of her thought his definitive decision to enter the Dominican Order soon. And she responded:

—I knew it.

—???

—Élisabeth had told me that you would become a religious.

—And how did she know it?

—She always knew it. She never doubted it.[1]

Once more, Félix was reassured in his decision, no longer by hopes, but by the certainties articulated by his own wife; he listened to them at length with unconcealed emotion.

Félix was now quite certain that he must enter the Dominican Order. He was sure of never renouncing this call: this new way was going to transform his life into a path of light that his vocation would lead him to impart to those he would meet. His life was going to take on new meaning, it was going to become "rich", but

---

[1] Unpublished letter from Marie-Louise Herking, *Le Pére Leseur* (Paris: Éd. J. de Gigord, 1952), 133.

not in the usual worldly way. He acquired the certainty that all these renunciations to come, which he now had fully weighed, were going to be springs of "living water" and produce "good fruits" in the service of his brothers and of souls.

But in fact, these renunciations represented a big human step that he had not yet taken. He wondered where he was going to draw the strength to give up, in a few days, everything that brought him comfort, well-being, or even interest in his current life.

At fifty-six years of age, how would he adapt to a new life so different from the one he had known until now? Would he have the courage to leave everything, to change his way of life completely? Monastic discipline was not what worried him the most. What was hard was permanently turning the page on everything that had been his life until now, beginning with his apartment—that "love nest" so full of Élisabeth's presence, her furnishings, the desk where he had so often seen Élisabeth busy writing, their living room furnished with the taste and love of his wife—his comfort, his travels, his freedom, his friends, his profession that fascinated him.

There was also the Montmartre cemetery, where he went every day to place flowers on that precious grave. Who would look after his wife's grave now? These visits had become an indispensable ritual for him that balanced him. How could he imagine his life without that presence, however sorrowful, in that corner of the earth that had now become his second home?

He would have to break all his habits, say goodbye to the general meetings at the Conservateur, to the almost daily meetings with his colleagues who had become friends, to the important financial responsibilities, to his managerial office, to professional dinners in the fashionable restaurants of the capital.

The walks in Paris, the long hours in bookshops leafing through the latest published books, the bibliophile gatherings where he came across artists and authors would no longer exist for him. Friends would certainly be surprised by it. They would miss him.

One sacrifice seemed especially painful to him: parting with his library, where, since his youth, he had lined up the books he loved; each one represented a choice, a favorite, a center of interest. In his living room, shelves lined the walls to the ceiling. He was so attached to all these books, each of which represented a memory, that they had become familiar and constant presences to him, almost his second identity.

Élisabeth's library that he valued so highly seemed to him perhaps even more difficult to abandon than his own. All the shelves were filled with books that she had read, loved, annotated in her own handwriting. They were still her presence, the life of her mind, true relics. How could he separate himself from them forever?

How could he also let go of all the art and deluxe books for which he himself had designed the sumptuous bindings to his own and Élisabeth's taste and for which he had invested a fortune? These books were his pride and also somewhat his self-realization. Must he give them away, sell them to strangers who would never understand with what love and care they had been conceived?

There was also the big house in Jougne, arranged and decorated entirely by Élisabeth in a shared enthusiasm, whose walls contained the memories of so many warm and joyful celebrations, a true emotional heritage that it was also going to be necessary never to see again?

So much tearing away!

The sacrifices that his new life was inevitably going to bring were considerable, crippling even. Only Élisabeth could give him the courage to leave everything, but her smile was no longer there to encourage him and guide him on this painful path.

Before taking the big decisive step, he again felt the need to return to Lourdes. Was it not at the foot of the Grotto that he had found the faith again? It was perhaps the only place in the world where he would draw the courage to take this big step that now seemed to him, despite all the renunciations that it would involve, the only path of light that he wanted to consider for the rest of his life.

He spent two months there: May and June, 1918. He stayed in a monastery, voluntarily leading a monk's life in silence, prayer, and meditation. And there at last he could say, in the depth of his heart, the definitive and unconditional "yes" that he had been preparing for so long.

In a talk that he gave much later, in 1926, he would testify: "In 1918, Élisabeth led me to Lourdes, where I went to stay to give some mature deliberation to my religious vocation that would lead me to the Order of Preachers whose Queen and Mother is the Blessed Virgin. I returned from there a submissive servant, a spiritual child of Our Lady of Lourdes forever."[2]

Summer 1918. The war entered into its final phase. Foch won the second battle of the Marne. All France was glued to the news. They began to glimpse the victory that would not be final until November 11. Train travel became easier, and Félix went to Jougne. He knew it was the last time.

He did not, however, have time to indulge in melancholy. He decided to publish new writings found in Élisabeth's desk after her death. He was so completely unaware of most of them that their discovery had at first been a shock and very emotional for him. Then, the beauty of these texts having brought him wonderful enlightenment and a certain edification, he thought of sharing them and making them known to Élisabeth's readers, already so numerous.

For him, these texts would constitute a new and different manifestation of his wife's evangelization, a new outreach of their "relationship"—yes, he really said of their "relationship": Élisabeth in heaven and he on earth, but both of them still harnessed together to the same task in the now shared concern of being "the salt of the earth and the light of the world" (Mt 5:14–16).

He had been strengthened in this decision by the public reading he had given either in religious communities, to priests, to religious, or to friends. Their reactions had been unanimously encouraging. Everyone, and especially the men and women religious, had been astonished to read these meditations from the pen of a woman of the world living in an essentially secular environment. Her faith in the efficacy of prayer was a testimony all the more precious because it was her own, previously anticlerical, husband who came to read them these texts in their respective communities.

The manuscripts that he had prepared for publication at J. de Gigord were nine in number.

Five among them had titles given them by Élisabeth herself: *Litanies de la conversion* (Litanies of conversion), *Retraite spirituelle de chaque mois* (A spiritual retreat for every month), *Prière au Sacré-Cœur*

---

[2] Ibid., Conférence sur la Vierge et Lourdes, 135.

(Prayer to the Sacred Heart), *Tout petit traité de l'espérance* (Little treatise on hope), *La Paix chrétienne* (Christian peace). The other four had been given by Félix: *La Femme chrétienne* (The Christian woman), *Le Chrétien* (The Christian), *Appel vers la vie intérieure* (Call to the interior life), *Conseils pour l'organisation et le développement de la vie spirituelle* (Advice for the organization and development of the spiritual life). And he added to it the manuscript of *Une Âme* (A soul), dedicated by Élisabeth to the memory of her sister Juliette. In fact, the little volume of *Une Âme*, previously published in a small edition mostly intended for friends, had completely sold out, and he had been asked for it repeatedly.

To organize all these manuscripts, Félix placed them under a general title: *La Vie Spirituelle* (The spiritual life). He himself wrote a long introduction in which he outlined his spiritual journey thanks to the love and faith of his wife. He requested a preface from the archbishop of Paris, Cardinal Amette. The latter, after having compared Élisabeth's life to the words of Jesus about the grain of wheat that bears fruit in abundance once it dies, ended his text with a beautiful image: "We radiate our soul, so to speak, and when it is a source of light and warmth, other souls are illuminated and warmed by its mere touch. We give, sometimes without knowing it, that which we carry within us."[3]

A few strong ideas underlie these different works.

Spiritual Retreat

To have a deep spiritual life, a certain discipline is necessary and requires reflection. It was in this spirit that Élisabeth wrote her *Cahier de résolutions* (Notebook of resolutions).

For example, she recommends making a little interior retreat every month, to consecrate a special day to God in silence and prayer.

This time of meditation will enable us to be certain that our actions bear fruit only when ripened and prepared before God.

In all her writings, Élisabeth's essential objective was to bring to God or to bring closer to him those who were dear to her. It was

---

[3] Élisabeth Leseur, *La Vie Spirituelle: Petits traités de vie intérieure* (Paris: Éd. J. de Gigord, 1922), introduction, ix.

for her a duty, an apostolate, an evangelization. This gave meaning to her life.

Every day, she chose a person among those she loved and dedicated her day to her: she prayed for her in silence or she offered up her sufferings to God for her. Conscious that only the visible fruits of a life in God, first and foremost love and respect, were evangelizers, she considered words and speeches futile.

The Call to the Interior Life

This is the title given by Félix to a collection that Élisabeth had written for her mother after Juliette's death.

Madame Arrighi, despairing after the death of her two daughters Marie and Juliette, and because of the illness of the third, Élisabeth, spent all her summers at Jougne with the Leseurs always surrounded by a large part of the family. There were easily twelve to fifteen people at table. To show them her affection and to help them, Madame Arrighi went to a lot of work taking charge of all the housekeeping. Élisabeth regretted that her mother was tied solely to material tasks. She would have liked her, who was so Christian, to have time each day to pray and to meditate in order to accept better the grief and fury that the death of her two daughters had caused her.

Élisabeth felt responsible for her spiritual elevation. She would have liked to persuade her to abandon herself to God: it would be a more positive path for her. So she wrote a few pages for her, and she gave them to her the day when she and Félix left Jougne; Madame Arrighi would have the time to read them during the three weeks she would remain to close up the house in preparation for winter. A few excerpts allow us to understand a daughter's guide to her mother, dictated by affection and the desire to see her less unhappy:

> I know well that your nature despises contemplation and that the word meditation frightens you. . . . We must take the first steps to encounter the good God; but if we persist in seeking him thus, one day he will repay us a hundredfold, and very sweet is the reward bestowed on our labor. . . . I think I love you enough to know you well and that the two things that you lack the most are perhaps, from a

human point of view, the will to discipline yourself and, from a religious point of view, complete trust in God, the spirit of abandonment and joy. What I want to repeat to you, however, is our gratitude for everything you have done for us, our very great, very deep filial tenderness, and the union of our hearts in a dear memory, in the love of our Juliette and in the hope of meeting that dear person again who waits for us; this reunion will come quickly because nothing is long in life, and we can await with serenity that which we are sure, God willing, of possessing one day.

It is on this beloved name that I leave you, confiding to your invisible guardian angels the care of your dear soul and giving you, dear Mother, in the name of Félix and myself, the best, the most tender kiss.

Your eldest daughter,
Élisabeth
August 31, 1907.[4]

These were recovered writings that Félix wanted to have published before entering the monastery under the general title of *La Vie Spirituelle* (The spiritual life). In rereading and annotating them, he discovered, in this review of his wife's most intimate thoughts, additional and motivating reasons to support him in his decision, which had now become final: to give his whole life to the Lord by abandoning everything that was not him.

His work completed, he left Jougne forever, by car, without looking back. Henceforward it would be his nephews who would take over the house.

"The marvel of a house is not that it shelters you or warms you, or that you own its walls. But that it has slowly instilled in us its provisions of sweetness",[5] Saint-Exupéry would later write. That is what Félix thought.

These "provisions of sweetness", or these memories of love, contained in the walls of his old house, naturally could never be erased from his heart, and they would always remain deep within him. But

---

[4] *Appel à la vie spirituelle*, viii.

[5] Antoine de Saint-Exupery, *Wind, Sand, and Stars*, trans. Lewis Galantière (New York: Harcourt, 1967), 74.

he would draw from all this love, received and given, the strength necessary to go farther and take the big step.

He stopped at Arbois in Franche-Comté at the home of a friend whom he had met in the Third Order Dominicans, Robert Valléry-Radot, the son-in-law of Louis Pasteur. He and his wife Marie-Louise still lived in the big house surrounded by vineyards where Pasteur had his laboratory, not far from the church with the rounded bell tower. It was a place both moving and restful at the edge of the Cuisance, a pretty river with a refreshing current.

Valléry-Radot had undertaken a work somewhat similar to his own: he was also trying to collect and publish Pasteur's writings. So he was especially interested in Félix's work and expressed his desire to become acquainted with passages from Élisabeth's writings.

It was in the scientist's laboratory, where they had invited a few friends for the evening, among whom was their parish priest, that Félix read them passages from the manuscript that he always carried in his briefcase. In that old stone dwelling, still so full of the presence of Pasteur and of his fruitful research for medical science, he noticed with emotion that, through his voice, the best of Élisabeth's very simple heart resonated in those walls filled with the scientist's presence and seemed to touch his listeners.

His mission to Élisabeth now seemed complete to him. All that remained was to take the manuscript to the publisher.

On July 22, 1919, on the feast of Saint Mary Magdalen, so dear to the Dominicans' heart, he wrote at the end of his introduction to *La Vie Spirituelle*:

> As of now, I am going to enter into the great silence of the Dominican novitiate.
>
> Later on, if my superiors deem it useful and appropriate, I will be able to devote myself anew to the apostolate of my dear Élisabeth and to begin publishing other manuscripts; to start with, the very considerable, very beautiful correspondence that she left behind, as I have already said in *Lettres à des Incroyants* (Letters to Unbelievers.) But I am no longer my own, and I will gladly submit to the directions that will be imposed on me. May I be permitted, however, to say today how happy I am to have been able, thanks be to God, to erect to the memory of the sweet saint whose action was so invisible in everything that has gone before, the sole monument worthy of her, by

publishing three of her books: *Journal et pensées de chaque jour* (Journal and thoughts for every day), *Lettres sur la souffrance* (Letters on suffering), *La Vie Spirituelle* (The spiritual life). Inspiration rises progressively in each of them. *La Vie Spirituelle* is the pinnacle, and, upon handing over the remarkable pages that comprise this new work to the public, I pray to the Holy Spirit to bless them as he blessed those of the previous two, to ensure their wide distribution, to make use of it for the conquest and sanctification of a great number of souls. Once again, I place the apostolate that emerges from these pages under the special invocation of Saint Dominic and Saint Catherine of Siena. They have, moreover, so effectively protected the first two volumes that I cannot better show my gratitude and how much their patronage has become even more precious to me today than by entrusting this one to them.[6]

---

[6] É. Leseur, *La Vie Spirituelle*, 94.

31

Renunciations

On November 11, 1918, the bells of all the churches in France rang to announce the end of four years of a nightmarish war. In the jubilant streets of Paris, people embraced and rejoiced together at the same time as so many women in long black mourning veils grieved over their heroes killed on the fields of horrible battles.

As soldiers returned to their homes, where normal life seemed to resume for an utterly exhausted country, a new life began for Félix.

It was now time to rid himself of everything that had been his life until then. Despite his absolutely irreversible determination, he did not hide that these were very painful moments to experience.

He terminated his lease for the beautiful apartment in the rue de Marignan, so empty now to be sure, but so full of Élisabeth's presence and memories of her life and illness.

He gave away or sold his paintings and furniture.

For the books, he had his bookseller-friend Jules Meynial come to his house. He entrusted him with compiling a catalogue of his library, developed with so much joy and enthusiasm over so many years. Each work represented for him a quest, a purchase, an interest, a reading, and, most of the time, a conversation with Élisabeth.

But what was even more difficult was seeing the big quarto books go, those for which he had spent a lot of time designing costly bindings. They were his work, his creation. He knew they would be scattered in sales at the discretion of bibliophiles who, for the most part, over time, would be unknown to him. It was deeply wrenching to see them pass through the doorway of his apartment forever, stacked in moving boxes.

He gave Élisabeth's furniture to the Dominican nuns in Paris. They would make a kind of sanctuary with it.

He entrusted her complete library to J. de Gigord in order to avoid a dispersion that he thought would be regrettable.

He also had to provide for his succession at the Conservateur. For some time, his prolonged absences had given a large part of his responsibilities to the deputy director. But his official and permanent resignation was needed to ratify a situation that had become difficult for the whole staff. In that environment, in part indifferent or anticlerical, the majority were stunned by the decision of their employer, whom they had great difficulty imagining in the austerity of a monastery in the white habit of the Dominicans.

It was also necessary to announce this new life to friends and say goodbye to them.

Some of them had been very close during Élisabeth's illness and had greatly supported him once he was alone. While the closest among them had sensed his spiritual development, none of them had ever imagined an entrance to the monastery at fifty-six years of age in a renunciation of everything.

Later on, Félix would love describing his last dinner at the Barthous. When they sat down at table and Félix made the sign of the cross, Louis Barthou told him with a smile: "What you just did there was very chic!"

For more than twenty years the Leseurs had had two maids, Annette and Maria, who were both very attached to Élisabeth, whom they had known since before her marriage. They had followed her illness and death very closely and thought they would continue to be in Félix's service during his widowerhood. They were full of kindness toward him.

To the latter's surprise, they did not show great astonishment at the announcement of his decision. They simply told him: "It was obvious that there had been changes in your life. . . . In a monastery, no one will make you the food that you love!"

This had made Félix smile; touched, he had responded: "There's a good chance that's true!"

For him, so used to good food and fine dinners, this was no small sacrifice.

The farewells to his family and to Élisabeth's were the most difficult. His brother Paul and sister-in-law in Reims were in deep mourning. Their son had been killed the previous year in aerial combat; Félix had been a solid support for them in that situation. His departure distressed them as much as it distressed Félix.

Madame Arrighi, who was very old, had always been so connected to the Leseurs' life that she felt she was losing her daughter twice; the Durons, Amélie and her husband, Élisabeth's doctor for many years, were also on the verge of tears; the nieces and nephews, now married but so filled with memories of their shared vacations at Jougne in the affection of the Leseurs, could hardly believe this was an important page turning in their own lives as well.

All these visits took a few weeks. Félix went to each of their homes to say goodbye. With all of his friends, these were certainly painful moments, but they in no way affected his decision.

And the day of departure at last arrived. Annette, the cook, had prepared an exquisite meal. She placed flowers on a little table, one of the few surviving pieces of furniture in that apartment which had been so luxurious not long ago but was now nearly empty. Félix tried to be cheerful, to joke, but it was an excruciating moment for him.

When, for the last time, he crossed over the threshold of "their" apartment with his little suitcase in hand, he felt so alone, so abandoned, so stripped of everything that had been his life, that his legs gave way; he had to sit a long moment on the edge of the sidewalk near his building, like a poor, homeless beggar before regaining his strength and his courage to go to the Gare du Nord.

Later, he would confide to one of his friends: "My heart was beating so fast, as if it were going to break, that I thought I was going to die."[1]

Seeing Félix leave everything for this new life, we cannot help but connect this step with the one Jesus had proposed to the rich young man: "And Jesus looking upon him, loved him and said to him, 'You lack one thing; go, sell what you have, and give to the poor, and you will have treasure in heaven; and come, follow me'" (Mk 10:21).

---

[1] Unpublished letter from Marie-Louise Herking, *Le Père Leseur* (Paris: Éd. J. de Gigord, 1952), 139.

32

The Novitiate

At the end of this long road of renunciations, a light pointed brilliantly to the horizon for him: the love of God. It would never leave him again.

It is remarkable and awe-inspiring to consider the action of grace in a heart that, a few years earlier, had not been at all disposed to receive it. Élisabeth had written in her *Pensées de chaque jour* (Daily Thoughts): "The action of God in the soul: something elusive, profound, strong, that we do not fully understand until the divine work is accomplished. . . . Let us not believe that we hasten the coming of God's reign in others by our personal action. So long as the divine hour has not come, our efforts will be in vain, or, rather, they will be but an active prayer, an appeal to the one who transforms and saves."[1]

The divine hour had at last rung for Félix.

Since the anticlerical laws of 1905, there was no longer a Dominican novitiate in France. The government of the time, in which Félix had many friends, had expelled the religious from French soil. The novitiate had found refuge in Kain, a few miles north of Tournai in Belgium.

The Dominicans had undertaken construction in a former Cistercian monastery built in the thirteenth century. It was now a beautiful and vast building in the middle of the countryside, surrounded by willow trees[2] at the edge of a small river, and for that reason they called it Le Saulchoir.

When he rang at the door of Le Saulchoir, after having declined to give his name, Félix asked to meet with the master of novices. It

---

[1] Élisabeth Leseur, *Journal et Pensées de chaque jour* (Paris: Éd. du Cerf, 2005), 226.
[2] "Saule" means willow tree in French.—TRANS.

was a great relief for him, now completely freed from every material aspect of existence, to reach his new life at last.

Father Berger came to meet him. It was the first time he had received an almost sixty-year-old novice with such a journey. He was impressed, but he also knew that conventual life would be such a change for him that the new arrival would inevitably have to go through difficult times.

In that year of 1919, after the war, in which the majority of young men had been drafted, some forty novices had just entered or were going to enter the monastery at the same time as Félix. Monastic life would be difficult for those, too, who had lived through four years of trench warfare.

Father Berger went ahead of Félix to the cell that would be his for several years. Small, bare, with walls whitewashed from top to bottom, it was furnished with only a board covered with a straw mattress to sleep on fully clothed. What a contrast to the plush apartment he had left the day before!

He then led him to the refectory: a large hall, also painted white, furnished with long wooden tables with benches on only one side so they would never face each other during meals.

The silence that filled this great house was impressive, startling for an ear used to the tumult of Parisian life.

Father Berger introduced to him the other novices, his new companions: they seemed to him young enough to be his sons!

The next day began a week-long retreat in the most absolute silence and recollection. Special spiritual exercises were designed to prepare the novices, still in civilian clothes, for the clothing ceremony, which was to take place at the end of the retreat. Everyone was eager to wear the white robe that would henceforth be the sign of their belonging to this great Dominican family. They would henceforth be "Preachers", whose primary vocation would be to "contemplate and convey to others what they contemplated". To meditate, to pray, and to give.

The constitutions specified: "The habit of the order is composed of a white tunic with a white scapular and hood, with a black cape and hood as well as a leather belt with a rosary."

The whiteness of the habit symbolizes joy, the message of light into which the novice wants to be initiated during the long years of study that he undertakes from that day forward. It also signifies self-effacement in a brotherhood where all wear the same clothing as a sign of poverty, common to all.

In that year of 1919, the clothing ceremony took on a particular solemnity because of the exceptional importance of the number of novices: forty men from diverse backgrounds, lined up in the choir, who affirmed their will to give themselves to God by observing the three vows of poverty, chastity, and obedience.

After putting on the white habit for the first time, a visible sign of a new identity transfigured by the presence of God, they embraced each other because, from strangers to each other, they had now become brothers. A great and new family.

For more than seven centuries, an immense line of preachers animated by the same desire had preceded them. As their names were called, each one inscribed his in the register of the "elect" who had worn the habit. From that moment, each lost his civilian first name to accept one carried by one of the members of the Dominican family. Henceforward, Félix would be named after his spiritual father: Brother Marie-Albert.

For a year, Brother Marie-Albert would strictly lead the life of every novice. A brother would wake him a little before midnight with a *Benedicamus Domino*, to which he would respond *Deo Gratias*, in order to go sing Matins in the great silence of the night. A few hours later he would have to go to the choir for Prime and adoration followed by sung Mass. He would also have to go to Chapter to confess, prostrated on the ground before the novice master, his breaches of the Rule. His whole day would thus be regulated until Compline in the evening with the singing and procession of the *Salve Regina*. When Élisabeth told him "One day you will be Father Leseur", no doubt she imagined her husband converted to the faith; she probably pictured him in the Dominican habit; but had she foreseen so many life changes, so many renunciations?

Despite all his good will, it was a difficult time for Félix. He would not hesitate to acknowledge it later. One does not abolish the habits of a comfortable past of almost sixty years in a few days, even if only the rhythm of the hours of sleep. When they came to wake him up at midnight to go sing Matins, his whole body remembered that it was at this very hour that he was used to going to bed in a heated room on a good, comfortable bed! At the end of a few weeks of rudimentary food, he missed the good little meals of former times terribly. He did not conceal that the "perpetual abstinence" was difficult for him or that the lack of heating made him suffer.

And yet, not for anything in the world would he have wanted to consider a softening of this Rule that he had chosen of his own free will.

Various instructions from the novice master punctuated the days. Every day, he commented on a few points of religious life, emphasizing the spirit of the order and the Rule. Félix had always enjoyed intellectual life. He immersed himself with interest in the thoughts of Saint Thomas, especially since Élisabeth herself had made him one of her favorite studies.

He also had to get used to cleaning his cell and certain parts of the monastery. He who had never held a broom or made a bed often worried about not knowing how to perform this task correctly. He must have opened up about it in a letter to his friends the Barthous, because Madame Barthou responded to him in November 1919: "And the sweeping? Are you making progress? No, I cannot see Louis cleaning his room, he would be comically clumsy, and, moreover, he wouldn't have the grace!"[3]

No doubt Brother Marie-Albert had real graces, but nothing, however, was easy for him in that apprenticeship in a monastic life that was so austere compared to all he had been living for fifty-six years.

Supported—he was sure—by Élisabeth's prayers, he devoted himself fully and scrupulously to his new duties.

Then a special responsibility for him was added to the daily Rule. Since he had been a medical student, they entrusted him with the responsibility of being the nurse for the novitiate. He fulfilled it with great gentleness and love for his brothers; he had been so used to caring for his sick wife that he easily remembered all the gestures that calm or give comfort.

Rediscovered letters, however, enable us to understand what a difficult inner struggle this new life was for him: "Sometimes the

---

[3] Unpublished letter from Marie-Louise Herking, *Le Père Leseur* (Paris: Éd. J. de Gigord, 1952), 144.

past makes an infernal uproar in my mind, even though I am no longer attracted to it." "I feel I am on the margins of the community, an amateur novice, and yet I do not listen to myself. . . . It is the ultimate test."[4]

He, so used to a bustling life for so many years, often felt he was wasting his time. "What am I doing here?" was probably his recurring question, which, at the end of a few months, changed to: "How much longer am I going to endure this regime?" To remain kneeling on the stones of the chapel for a long time, never to eat meat, to spend winter without heating, little by little became increasingly heavy physical hardships each day.

At the end of four months of strict observance of the Rule, he fell seriously ill: double phlebitis. At that time, the only way to stem phlebitis was complete immobility. For him, this meant confinement to his cell day and night. A trip to a hospital would have cancelled the four months already spent at the novitiate, which would have involved starting the whole course over after his recovery.

For two months he remained lying up on his board, more isolated than ever, but above all disappointed to note that he was not able physically to withstand the austerities of the novitiate, while the youngest ones seemed to bear them cheerfully. He tried to keep his smile and good humor when a brother brought him his meals, and in the silence of his cell, he joined in the offices in chapel.

Correspondence held a large place during his days; he continued to receive letters from readers of Élisabeth's books. According to the rule that he had always set for himself, he did not leave a single letter unanswered.

The other novices greatly admired him. They appreciated his kindness, his smile, his brotherly cordiality. Of course, he did not play ball with them during recreation, but he spoke with anyone who wanted to approach him. They then saw his warmth, but also his knowledge on every subject, his experience; they said of him: "He is a living dictionary!" A dictionary they consulted as often as possible and that kindly, and often with humor, gave the expected responses.

---

[4] Ibid., 145.

On September 23, 1920, at the end of the novitiate, Brother Marie-Albert asked to make his "simple profession". He wanted to commit himself for a period of three years, during which he would pursue his studies of philosophy and theology at Le Saulchoir, in this house that had now become his own.

The profession took place according to custom during the conventual Mass. After having been prostrated on the ground with his arms in a cross, having asked for "the mercy of God and that of his brothers", and having stood up, he placed his hands in those of the master of the order, or his representative, to establish a physical connection with him symbolizing the spiritual bond that would henceforward unite him to the Dominicans for the rest of his life.

He undertook those years of study with courage and joy; philosophy had always greatly interested him; he had always read a lot and reflected a lot, and recently he had read all the philosophy books in Élisabeth's library.

For three months, he carried on everything with zeal, but at the end of three months he could no longer keep up the pace. Despite all the notes that he took and that blackened his notebooks, he was discouraged.

His superiors advised him to take advantage of the visit of the Most Reverend Master General, Father Theissling, to Le Saulchoir to ask for a dispensation, which deeply humiliated Brother Marie-Albert, but was wise. Considering his knowledge of philosophy and his exceptional general knowledge, he was from then on exempt from philosophy studies. As for theology, he would study it alone in his cell, under the direction of a theology instructor.

A few weeks later, as a sign of gratitude, Brother Marie-Albert sent Father Theissling Élisabeth's three books accompanied by the following letter, in which are already outlined the direction of the ministry for which he dared to hope. He already knew that it would also be the work of Élisabeth, of their relationship, united for eternity.

The publication of Élisabeth's three volumes, the talks I was asked to give about them before entering the order, the considerable amount of correspondence that they inspired and that does not diminish— far from it—the frequent visits from strangers constitute a kind of real and active ministry while awaiting the true ministry that will be given to me once I receive the priesthood, if God grants me this extraordinary blessing. . . . I try my best to respond to your goodness and to become ready to receive ordination as soon as my solemn profession has made it possible. I must tell you I yearn for that moment with all my heart.[5]

At that time, he asked permission to hang the photograph of Élisabeth's portrait painted by their friend Duvent on the wall of his cell; at every moment he was working or praying in front of her.

It was the reproduction of the oil portrait that Duvent painted in 1900. This beautiful work gives a good idea of the interior and meditative look that characterized Élisabeth.[6]

When he met with any difficulty, he looked at her face, he knew she was there. He wrote: "I live with her, through thought and through prayer, much more intimately than during her life."[7]

In 1922, he wanted to publish *Lettres à des Incroyants* (Letters to Unbelievers), which has already been discussed at length in the chapter about Élisabeth writing them. After having requested a preface from Father Garrigou-Lagrange, he himself wrote a long introduction of almost eighty pages, which plunged him back into their shared past, still so present.

From the outset, he emphasized the love with which Élisabeth addressed her unbelieving friends: no harsh judgment, no lessons to teach, no antipathy, no hostility. With sweetness, generosity of spirit, understanding, listening to what was important to the other person, silence, and prayer. Moreover, it was through love that Élisabeth had revealed to him the love of Jesus Christ:

We were speaking with Father Hébert one day about Élisabeth's *Journal*, which had been out for several months and whose rapid and extraordinary dissemination had provoked much astonishment. "I was just speaking a short while ago", the priest told me, "about Madame Leseur and her book with a very distinguished man of my acquaintance, who holds a very important position in French industry, and

---

[5] Ibid., unpublished letter, 150.

[6] R. P. Marie-Albert Leseur, Avant-Propos, *Vie d'Élisabeth Leseur* (Paris: Éd. J. de Gigord, 1931), 6.

[7] Unpublished letter from Marie-Louise Herking, *Le Pére Leseur*, 152.

the criticism he made of it to me was very unexpected. He was surprised, scandalized even, by the complete tolerance, by the eminent charity that the book revealed, and he concluded, reproachfully: 'this woman has no hatred'! As if that diminished the appeal of the *Journal*."

Here we have certainly a reader who did not imagine that we can profess any other feelings than indignation and anger for people who do not embrace our ideas. He would gladly have condemned them. Nothing, however, is more contrary to the spirit of Jesus Christ. Let us recall the parables of the lost sheep, the lost drachma, the prodigal son, the pardon accorded to Mary Magdalen, the episodes of the adulterous woman, of the Samaritan woman, and so many others. All of his teaching is summed up in the love of God and neighbor: "Love one another." He had only severity and condemnation for the professional excommunicators of the time, for the hard-hearted Pharisees, egotistical and evil hypocrites.[8]

To publish *Lettres à des Incroyants*, Father Leseur had to go to Paris briefly where he had the joy of seeing a few of his friends again, including the Barthous, but the Paris that he rediscovered in his white robe was no longer the Paris of "Monsieur Félix Leseur", director of the Conservateur. He almost felt like a foreigner, far from that world, that noise, even from all those everyday or political concerns. He was anxious to return to his brothers and his conventual life.

Preceded by a foreword from Father Garrigou-Lagrange, *Lettres à des Incroyants* would be released in bookstores in 1923, accompanied by a portrait of Élisabeth seated in her living room in front of her little desk decorated with a bouquet of roses; featured on the cover was one of the key phrases of the message her husband wanted to convey: "I want to love, with a particular love, those whose birth, religion, or ideas put them at a distance from me; these, above all, are the ones whom I need to understand and who need me to give them a little of what God has given to me."[9]

---

[8] Élisabeth Leseur, Introduction, *Lettres à des Incroyants* (Paris: Éd. J. de Gigord, 1928), 4.

[9] Cover of the 1923 edition of *Lettres à des Incroyants*.

33

The Solemn Profession

On March 23, 1923, Brother Marie-Albert was permitted to make his solemn vows. The ceremony, one of the most moving in the Christian liturgy, is a major event in the life of a new Dominican, the final act of long years of study, but above all the departure, still uncharted, for a new life.

It was not without strong emotion that Brother Marie-Albert considered that he in turn was taking his place in that long continuity of apostles, established so strongly and so simply from Peter, the humble fisherman of the Sea of Galilee.

At that time in his life, Brother Marie-Albert did not know what duties would be entrusted to him in the Dominican Order. But he knew that respect for his tastes and personality would be a priority in his superiors' decisions.

His ordination was set for the following July 8. Since entering the novitiate, he had been waiting impatiently for this moment, but as the date approached, he wondered if he were truly worthy of it.

He humbly admitted it a few years later in one of his homilies:

> The sense of my wretchedness, of my unworthiness in contrast to that of the transcendence of the priesthood, held me back, overwhelmed me, would have easily, it seemed, driven me to flee, to give up. But God is good and stronger than we. When He wants us in his service, He knows how to take us despite everything. His call becomes more compelling, his light brighter, his mercy more considerate. He dispelled my scruples and gave me the immense happiness of being completely his.[1]

The ordination celebration was held on French soil, at Lille, in the church of Saint-Maurice. It was the bishop of Lille, Monsignor

---

[1] Sermon de prémices, 1926.

Quillet, who consecrated his hands and gave him the power to speak the words of the Consecration and the forgiveness of sins.

This ceremony is moving for every young priest who consecrates his life to God. But for a man of his age, with a past so hostile to religious life and so far from suspecting that such an event would one day occur in his life, it was truly a marvel. Only Élisabeth, in her faith, could have imagined it.

When, with his face against the ground, fully prostrate on the cold pavement of the choir, he heard the long litany of saints sung for him, his emotion expressed his enthusiasm and his joy to enter officially into the communion of all those saints whom the congregation begged to intercede for him. And among those saints whom they invoked, he knew well that his Élisabeth was there, infinitely present at this celebration. His faith gave him the certainty that, in the presence of God in her eternity, she prayed for him as much as when she was on earth: "Saint Élisabeth, my wife, pray for me, pray for us."

All the priests present, friends or teachers, each in turn, then placed their hands on his forehead as a sign of their brotherhood and their protection.

The following morning, he said his first Mass at Le Saulchoir. Those who knew Father Leseur well knew that he often described how he had felt a strong emotion when he held the Body of Christ in his hands for the first time. He had almost experienced a physical collapse when he spoke the words. If he had not had the certainty of Élisabeth's presence at his side in that moment, he still wondered, several years later, how he would have been able to endure that strong inner shock.

To commemorate that day to those who came to support him, Father Marie-Albert offered each one a souvenir image. In memory of his place of Baptism, Reims, he had chosen a sculpture that he admired on an arch of one of the doors of the cathedral: Christ bent under the cross, the symbol for all Christians of redemption through suffering. How could he not make a connection to his personal journey, his own birth in the faith and a new life, thanks to the cross that Élisabeth had carried for him for so many years? On the back of the image he inscribed a sentence taken from one of his wife's most prophetic writings, and thus especially moving for him: "When you too have become a disciple of Jesus Christ and a living member of the Church, consecrate your life, transformed by grace, to prayer and to the gift of yourself in charity, and be an apostle."[2]

These precise instructions from Élisabeth would be those of his ministry.

What more beautiful testimony could he have given of a couple sanctified by the sacrament of Matrimony, in spite of himself, and of a priest guided and supported by the prayers of his wife before God?

[2] *Mon testament pour Félix*, 246.

34

Taking Flight

For Father Marie-Albert, life at Le Saulchoir was going to end. It was wrenching. Although the beginning had been difficult, he was now accustomed to this minutely regulated life. Those who had surrounded him for several years had become his family, his brothers. Everyone more or less knew that he had been married and that he had had a big position in one of the most prominent insurance firms in the capital; everyone had perceived his love for Élisabeth and the spiritual radiance of this wife who had led him to become a priest. Everyone admired his spirit of adaptation. Despite the generational differences, a genuinely fraternal atmosphere united them all.

On the eve of his departure, everyone took the traditional walk at Le Saulchoir together. The young brothers had organized a little party for him. One of them composed a song to the tune of *Lilas*, a popular song, and everyone together sang for Félix, who was on the verge of tears:

> We always called him "Father"!
> He called us his children,
> And toward our light-headedness
> He was always lenient!
> He pardoned our mischief,
> He often made his own.
> He had the soul of a twenty-year-old novice
> Yes, twenty years old,
> A true twenty-year-old novice.

More seriously, one of them, in the spirit of the "fraternal correction" customary at the time of departure, made him a kind of speech on behalf of everyone:

I am happy to be able to say a grateful thank you to Brother Leseur for the example he has never ceased to give us, during these four years of novitiate, of a perfect religious life led in silence and recollection with the generosity and impetus of a soul that seems utterly possessed by God.

I know little about the brother's past: I know enough, however, to guess how much this change of life must have cost him, all the sacrifices that an austere life like ours could impose on him. The brother joined us very simply; he made himself young because it was necessary to be young, shared our life, enlivening our recreation with his conversations, as kind as they were instructive, endlessly expressing profound charity to everyone.

I have only one word to add, and it is to tell Brother Leseur that I wholeheartedly ask the good God to accomplish his work in him, to give him even more of the spirit of prayer and recollection, the spirit of sacrifice, and thus to prepare him to rejoin, at the hour appointed by him, the one in whom the spirit that makes true saints was so perfectly abundant.[1]

---

[1] Unpublished letter from Marie-Louise Herking, *Le Pére Leseur* (Paris: Éd. J. de Gigord, 1952), 156–57.

35

"Go into All the World and Preach the Gospel . . ." (Mk 16:15)

Father Leseur was sixty-two years old when he left Le Saulchoir and a new life was going to begin for him.

His superiors gave him a first mission right away: editor of a Dominican journal.

At the end of the war, Father Janvier had founded a literature review: *Les Nouvelles Religieuses* (Religious short stories). He needed an experienced person in charge who would work at the Paris monastery, 222 rue du Faubourg-Saint-Honoré, where he would live.

For the former journalist of the *République Française* and the *Siècle*, used to writing articles of quality, it was continuity and a joy—and, what is more, in Paris where he met his friends again. However, the spirit of the Christian journals for which he was going to work was so much the opposite of that of the periodicals for which he had written articles that it was hardly credible. After having worked for so many years for the materialization of his readers, he was now going to supply them with arguments for spiritualization inspired by Élisabeth's writings. He could raise spirits by revealing to them the actions of God in this world through the hands, the actions, and the hearts of his faithful.

He would do this work as editor for ten years.

When he returned to Paris, once his address became known, a voluminous amount of mail arrived every day. Some of Élisabeth's readers requested prayers or advice; others expressed their gratitude to him for having published works that strengthened their faith; others asked him to implore his wife to obtain graces or healings. And most of all, from all over they asked him to come speak about her, he who had known her in everyday life and who had had, thanks to her, such an unimaginable journey.

His superiors encouraged him in this mission; he would from now on be the propagator of Élisabeth's thought, the person responsible for spreading her influence.

But was it only Élisabeth's influence for which he was going to be responsible?

For his listeners, to see him thus, in the Dominican habit, humbly recalling his wife's thoughts after so many years of hostility toward her faith was already a very strong testimony, the testimony of a couple chosen by God in a very special way to make his Kingdom grow. It was a call to which he joyfully responded.

Élisabeth, the wife he had so tenderly loved, had been an awakener of souls. He, in his turn, was going to take her place, and, thanks to her, he, too, would be an awakener of souls.

His first talk on Élisabeth took place in Belgium at Liège on November 14, 1924, in front of an assembly of women, undoubtedly attracted by Élisabeth Leseur's spiritual elevation, but also—they did not hide it from him—out of curiosity to see a Dominican convert speak of the wife he still loved. They wondered how he would talk about it, what he would call it, how he would describe it. Their curiosity was at least as great as their desire for spirituality.

He chose as his subject "The Life of Prayer", a subject that had been completely incomprehensible to him for many years. A subject that had now become essential in his life since he had, thanks to Élisabeth's writings, discovered the depth and power of that heart-to-heart with the Lord. Very simply, in everyday language, he laid out before these women the richness of such an intimate relationship with God, of this exchange full of love.

His listeners were immediately struck by his humility, by the sensitivity of his speech, which he read slowly, and by the practical guidance accessible to all who came away from it. They felt that he offered them a very simple, authentic approach, without big words, filled with Élisabeth's prayer. A testimony of love.

As soon as he returned to Paris, he was assailed by requests for lectures from very diverse groups. Word of mouth had certainly been very effective because a large public was soon aware of the simplicity and the spiritual impact of Father Leseur's talks.

He was busy full-time, almost overwhelmed, despite his ever meticulous and logical personal organization, carefully noted in his appointment book.

At that same time, printings of Élisabeth's works reached an unexpected number. His publisher informed him that they had reached one hundred thousand and that they had spread abroad thanks to unexpected translations. Even in Chinese.

Faced with the increase of requests for talks in every region of France, a question arose in his mind: "Why did I enter the Dominicans? Is this really the mission that my superiors expect of me? Did I take Holy Orders to speak almost exclusively about my wife? Are my talks about Élisabeth's spirituality really in the spirit of the order?"

It was essential for him to keep in line with what his superiors expected of him. He spoke openly to them about it with much frankness and simplicity. With the same frankness and the same simplicity, they responded to him:

—Do it.

Contemplari et contemplata aliis tradere. This is the motto of the Dominicans. What Father Leseur had "contemplated" without understanding it for almost twenty years beside Élisabeth, what she had given him through her writings, he was now going to sow in the hearts of thousands of strangers, like good seeds that in their turn would give birth to others and would lift up to God all these souls for which Élisabeth had prayed and offered her sufferings. This would be a very special vocation, but it would be his, the vocation of priest and husband.

He increased the travel, and he never gave the same talk; he always discussed the different aspects of Élisabeth's spirituality in practical terms.

A few titles:

"The Intellectual Radiance of Élisabeth Leseur".

"The Conquest of Souls".

"Élisabeth and the Duty of One's State in Life".

"Élisabeth and Suffering".

"Élisabeth, the Blessed Virgin, and Lourdes".

Over the years he gave lectures in Paris, but also in a great number of cities in France. They also led him abroad. He was requested

in Belgium, Switzerland, Portugal, Copenhagen, The Hague. He
gave more than one hundred conferences a year. He carried out his
mission with profound joy because he knew he was completing the
work and the apostolate of his wife in his own way. His faith led
him to believe that now, before God in heaven, she continued to
pray for him and to support him in this mission.

In 1925, when the priest of Jougne asked him to come speak
about the spirituality of Élisabeth, a local celebrity, he joyfully accepted and began his talk in this way:

> It is not without deep emotion that I go up to this pulpit. Who would
> have told me in 1895, the year of my first visit to Jougne, that I would
> one day find myself dressed in the white habit of Saint Dominic?
> That would have seemed outrageous to me then, and yet it has hap-
> pened. I did not come alone to Jougne; with me is my sweet Élisa-
> beth, who loved Jougne and loved you. Her active concern covered
> everyone. She was all goodness, all devotion because she was all for
> God and because the best way to love one's neighbor is to love God.
> And, in this regard, my very dear brothers, I must ask your pardon,
> and I do so very sincerely, very humbly. For too many years, alas! I
> gave you the bad example, the detestable example of irreligion. How
> I would now like to make amends! Fortunately, God has been merci-
> ful, indeed, as always. He has answered the constant prayers that Élis-
> abeth addressed to him for my conversion, which she never doubted.
> He accepted the sacrifices, the sufferings, the gift of her life that she
> offered him for souls, including my own. He allowed me to be the
> first conquest of this posthumous apostolate that for ten years has
> providentially spread throughout the entire world and whose influ-
> ence and outreach are so extraordinary that they cannot be humanly
> explained.[1]

The numerous talks he gave in all the cities of France put him in
contact with an entire world of important people in the Christian
world of whom he had not previously known or whose existence
he had despised: priests, nuns, or laity. He met doctors, journalists,
bishops, administrators. In Berne, after his talk, he had the joy of

---

[1] Unpublished letter from Marie-Louise Herking, *Le Père Leseur* (Paris: Éd. J. de Gigord, 1952), 166.

attending the creation of the Élisabeth Leseur Circle, of which they had of course asked him to be the patron.

His tours required him to travel a lot; he had always loved to travel; despite his preoccupations, he had time to visit or revisit the cities where he was expected and to admire in them architectural or natural beauties.

He also wrote a great deal. His publisher asked him for a biography of Élisabeth Leseur. He was happy because he had so much to say about her. But would he manage to find the time to write it? He had so many new occupations that had been added to his talks. He had to look for texts, letters, reread the notebooks. He set himself to the task with joy. He relived events experienced when they were together, their travels, their conversations, their meetings with good friends, and he went deeper still into the spirituality of the one who had shared his life for so many years, when he knew almost nothing of her inner life.

He wrote:

> My book progresses. *La Vie d'Élisabeth* (The Life of Élisabeth) will be bigger than I would have wanted. And yet I have packed in as much as I could, sacrificing a number of very interesting documents; but it is necessary to limit oneself and not make a little encyclopedia. Let us hope that, despite its size, it will not discourage the reader and will be favorably welcomed. I am convinced that the quotations from Élisabeth must do much good.[2]

At the same time, he had a wealth of new responsibilities: he became the chaplain of the nuns on the rue de Clichy. These nuns accommodated young student girls and worked hard to create in their home a familial and joyful atmosphere where trust, generosity, and joy reigned: the house of the good Lord. Father Leseur was also the confessor for two religious congregations in Neuilly and Asnières. He celebrated marriages, Baptisms, funerals.

For all that, he did not neglect family gatherings, since Élisabeth's entire family lived in Paris. Additionally, he liked to share a meal with them when he was not too busy otherwise. He offered great support to his old friend Louis Barthou, distraught since the death

---

[2] Ibid., 175.

of his wife, who had been comforted in her final illness by Élisabeth's writings.

Élisabeth's books had been translated into Portuguese and enjoyed an unprecedented popularity especially in Lisbon and Porto. So he was invited to Portugal for a series of talks.

On June 11, 1930, Father Leseur gave his first talk in Lisbon on "Élisabeth and Lourdes". The very elegant public was touched by the modesty and humility of the speaker. So many people had been turned away at the door that they asked him to give a second talk a few hours later. The cardinal received him at his home.

At Coimbra, in the oldest and most celebrated university of Portugal, he had a shock on entering the *Aula Magna*, where students and professors dressed in black with the traditional cape were awaiting him. A huge portrait of Élisabeth covered a wall.

Texeira Lopès, a renowned sculptor in the region, presented him with a statue that he had carved in stone depicting Élisabeth's face.

In Porto, he stayed with the bishop. He said his Mass in the private chapel and, in the evening, gave his talk from the day before on "The Conquest of Souls".

A letter addressed to Marie-Louise Herking better expresses his impressions and enthusiasm. Preoccupation with his talks and his meetings did not prevent him from admiring the beauty of the country:

> My trip was very consoling. I did not imagine that Élisabeth was so known and venerated in this country. I made the trip like a big celebrity there with delegations at the train stations, photographers, the front page of the newspapers crowded with articles about Élisabeth, me, my talks, etc. But this corresponded to deep feeling, and that is what is important. I was also surprised to see how familiar the French language was to the people of the Society. Think of it, at every gathering, I had at least eight hundred listeners! And in Lisbon, where I was to give two talks, they asked for three, the same thing in Porto. It was a touching enthusiasm.
>
> And what a remarkable country! From the point of view of nature, it is a splendor. Luxurious vegetation, European and tropical, everywhere an orgy of flowers, a mountainous country with splendid vistas. . . . With that, I missed seeing one of the most beautiful places in the world; in fact, a letter arrived for me in Porto from His

Excellency the bishop of Funchal asking me insistently to come to his diocese, which is none other than the Island of Madeira; alas! It was impossible for me. It was another fifteen days. I absolutely could not; I deeply regretted it.[3]

The *Journal* having been translated into Swedish and Danish, the Jesuit Fathers of Copenhagen and Stockholm in their turn invited Father Leseur. The day after his arrival, when photographers and journalists thronged to welcome him, the press multiplied the number of its articles on this French Dominican who, after having been a free-thinker, anticlerical, and married, came dressed in his white robe to speak about his wife's piety. Such sincerity, such a testimony was unheard of.

His very attentive audience was primarily Protestant. So, of course, there was no need to discuss questions of dogma in his talk.

Therefore, he chose a title with very concrete applications: "Élisabeth and the Duty of One's State in Life".

For an hour, he developed the very simple place of the duty of state in the life of an ordinary, loving young Frenchwoman, confined by illness but conscious of her responsibilities as a wife until the end. And he showed how that duty as she conceived it had been for her the source of his happiness and of a love that lasted twenty-five years. Some Protestant women were especially appreciative of Élisabeth's strong culture and did not hide their emotion in listening to the account of her heroism in suffering and her posthumous apostolate, not only to her husband but to the crowds that pressed around the Dominican.

The welcome that he received in Oslo touched him all the more because he stayed in a monastery where he was reunited with brothers he had known at Le Saulchoir; they took him to visit the Viking museum, to see the landscape of the fjord overlooked by the mountain.

Two days later, he was in Paris in his cell, and he wrote in his diary: "A beautiful and good trip. *Deo gratias*."

Summer 1931 was the Paris Colonial Exhibition at the Porte Dorée near the Bois de Vincennes. It had been organized by Marshall Lyautey, with whom the young Félix would have so much

---

[3] Ibid., 182.

liked to work. To the former colonialist that he had been, it was fascinating, especially since the exhibition's goal was to show the colonies' beneficial contributions to France, which he had always advocated. New technologies at the service of the public conveyed by rail on a network created for the occasion reinforced the prestige of French industry, which was in full expansion mode at the time.

Father Leseur, whom conventual life did not limit to his talks and who continued to be interested in everything happening in the world, came away enthusiastic. At seventy years of age, he redis-covered the gaze of wonderment he had had as a young student destined for a colonialist career in order to write:

> It is a truly remarkable achievement; we see that Lyautey's mind or-ganized all of this. It is splendid for the eyes, and it is interesting and instructive in the highest degree. I spent hours there that seemed very short to me. When we can compare, as I do, the evolution of a country like Equatorial Africa and, especially, the French East in forty years, we cannot but deeply and proudly admire the work that has been accomplished. It is something prodigious. What a wonder-ful example of genius, intelligence, and French labor.[4]

---

[4] Ibid., 179.

36

When Trials and Old Age Succeed One Another

This beautifully hectic life was abruptly interrupted one morning at five o'clock by a fall in his cell while he was preparing to go, as he did every day, to say Mass for the sisters on the rue de Clichy. After a few moments of collapse on the ground, he made superhuman efforts to get up, despite a severe pain in his right calf, which he hoped would ease with walking. Regardless, he decided to take a taxi. Suffering greatly, he celebrated his Mass and even prayed the rosary with the sisters as usual. But when he returned to the monastery, it was clear that he had a deep muscular tear with a ruptured vein and that he had to stay immobile for many weeks.

He was taken to the hospital of Perpétuel-Secours at Levallois-Perret run by "perfect" Dominican Sisters, he wrote to a correspondent. But he was chafing at the bit. He had to cancel both a speaking tour in Lille and throughout the Nord department and a meeting with the master general in Rome in December that was very important to him.

His difficult acceptance and his recourse to the example Élisabeth had given him are visible in his correspondence:

January 8, 1932

I began the year 1932 poorly. The Good God wants to try me, ask him to grant me the graces of acceptance and abandonment to his Divine Will, which I greatly need and which I am also asking Élisabeth to obtain for me; I try to rise to her example.[1]

Just when he thought he was leaving the hospital, he came down with double pneumonia at the same time as phlebitis. Again, he had

---

[1] Unpublished letter from Marie-Louise Herking, *Le Pére Leseur* (Paris: Éd. J. de Gigord, 1952), 182.

to remain in bed for weeks: they brought him the photo of Élisabeth's portrait in his room as well as the diary that would be his daily nourishment until the end of his life; his kindness made him loved by all the hospital staff as the interns brought a gramophone to his room so he could listen to Wagner's music, which he and Élisabeth loved so much.

In his bed, his greatest occupation consisted in responding, as much as he could, to the numerous letters that were addressed to him on the subject of Élisabeth's influence and her apostolate beyond death. He made it a duty to write each letter carefully in a personal way, recalling how much Élisabeth took care to respect and give due importance to each person, familiar or unknown, on her path. In one of his letters, Father Leseur revealed that he had sixty-nine of them on his bedroom table awaiting a response!

Little by little, he understood that his stay in the hospital would be longer than expected. It was a great hardship for him. He had wonderful plans, among others, that of going to Buenos Aires in Latin America, then to Rio and São Paulo, where twelve conferences had been planned for several months. Every day he began to doubt his being able to go there. His doctors were also skeptical: this long trip would jeopardize his recovery. He had to give it up!

> Five months in the hospital feels like ages! And it requires much patience and abandonment to the will of God, all easy virtues on the whole to practice broadly speaking, but in practical detail it is another matter. This becomes very difficult, and I do not have the beautiful serenity that you imagine. I am very cowardly and very self-centered, and I take little advantage of the graces of suffering that are offered to me.[2]

After three more weeks of treatment at Bagnoles de l'Orne, he at last returned to his cell and his office on the rue du Faubourg-Saint-Honoré. He also resumed life at a hectic pace: every morning, he took the metro at six-thirty to go say Mass for the sisters of Clichy at seven. These sisters were truly a family for him.

He also heard Confessions in four different religious communities. When he could, he allowed himself a few moments of relaxation; he saw his old friends; he returned to the booksellers he had

---

[2] Ibid.

once frequented; he went to lunch with his family, or even, more rarely, he went to see some exhibitions.

He was now seventy-two years old, and he had a little white beard and white hair; slightly stouter, he stooped on his cane when he walked for a long time so as not to lose his muscles.

He felt very tired by the evening. The sisters of Clichy sometimes saw him so tired when taking the metro that they offered him a taxi to take him back to the rue du Faubourg-Saint-Honoré. They were also often thoughtful enough to prepare him a gourmet picnic to his liking when he could not go home at noon. He called them "my daughters" and happily teased them; they were very attentive and affectionate toward him.

The letters and requests for conferences continued to pour in to his desk: organizations, sponsorships, youth groups, journalists, women's movements kept asking him to come speak about Élisabeth's spirituality. At times, he felt overwhelmed. He wrote in his notebook: "I am under great pressure. . . . I have been unusually immersed. . . . I am literally overworked, which does not go without a certain fatigue; I no longer manage to do what I have to do."[3]

In 1934, his old friend Louis Barthou, now minister of foreign affairs in Doumergue's cabinet, was mortally wounded in Marseille during the attack against Alexander I of Yugoslavia. It was a big shock for Félix, who had been very close to him since the death of his wife and had greatly supported him. Two widowers who understood each other without speaking.

So many deaths already among his family and friends whom he had known and been surrounded by with Élisabeth!

His friend Émile Bourgeois, history professor at the Sorbonne, had died a few weeks before, as well as Maurice Ordinaire, their old friend from Jougne and Paris. These three deaths, within a few weeks of each other, among his dearest friends, were very painful for him.

After the assassination of Louis Barthou, Father Leseur wrote:

Yes, blows follow one after another with a very harsh brutality. It was this morning that I learned of this catastrophe on the radio; at the moment I was stunned, not wanting to believe the reality of this

---

[3] Ibid., 184.

news. However, I had to resign myself to it, and I am sad, as you can imagine. I had such difficulty recovering from the shock I received by the death of Maurice Ordinaire, and then there was that of Barthou, which knocked me down all over again. It is terrible! When I return to Paris, I will no longer find any of my closest friends. May God's will be done! I offer all this suffering for these dear souls, especially for the latter. . . . Barthou's death not only assails me in my affection, it also strikes me in my love for France, which is suffering an irreparable loss. He was a great minister, and it is unclear who will have the stature to replace him and continue his work.[4]

The same day, he was telephoned and notified that Louis Barthou had expressed, several times, the wish that it would be his old friend Félix who would preside over the celebration of his funeral.

The final act of this long and beautiful friendship: Father Leseur sang the Absolution for him during a solemn celebration in the presence of the whole government in the church of Saint-Louis-des-Invalides. For him, it was no small event!

He then accompanied the body of his friend to his grave in Père Lachaise Cemetery, where he had difficulty mastering his emotion while giving a short homily full of hope and faith.

In front of his friend's coffin, one of Élisabeth's thoughts came to mind again and comforted him: he remembered that she had told him several times—at a time when it had made him shrug his shoulders—that the teaching of the communion of saints brought incomparable comfort to every Christian because it affirmed that bereavement, suffering, hardship, tears, and prayers were paramount aspects of life.

Furthermore, she was so convinced that the communion of saints keeps us in close contact with those who are no more that she had drawn from this belief the strength to overcome all her family bereavements. And this thought gave him courage.

The loss of that very close friend culminated with an unexpected twist: in his will, Louis Barthou had bequeathed his wardrobe to his valet, Gustave, whom Félix knew well. In that wardrobe was the minister's academician robe. His valet, who venerated Félix, had the idea of transforming this robe into a chasuble in order to give

---

[4] Ibid., 197.

it to Father Leseur. He had the golden embroideries cut off and applied to silk fabric, had a magnificent chasuble made, and had it taken to the sisters on the rue de Clichy. On July 7, 1935, Father Leseur inaugurated the use of this exceptional chasuble, so laden with symbols, during a morning Mass. Some old friends, whom he had met during the time of evening gatherings at Louis Barthou's, and some members of his family were disturbed by this very peculiar little celebration. What a symbol: the embroideries from the robe of an academician that take on a new life on the chasuble of his priest friend: "What we give flowers, what we keep rots!"

37

Vie d'Élisabeth Leseur
(Life of Élisabeth Leseur)

On August 12, 1930, before leaving for a few days of vacation at the home of one of his nephews in Anglet, near Biarritz, Father Leseur took his manuscript to his publisher, who had become his friend, on the rue Cassette. The book would be entitled simply *Vie d'Élisabeth Leseur.*

He had been carrying this project within himself for a long time. The previous books in which he had published Élisabeth's writings needed a unifying structure, a support. In this book, it was necessary to explain that Élisabeth had not been only a soul. She had had a body; she had been beautiful and elegant; she had loved traveling, children, and books; she had loved to fill her house with laughter and happy people. And above all, she had been loving, very loving, of a husband who had mocked her for years because of her faith and had done everything to turn her away from it. Despite those differences, she had been fortunate enough to live in a very united relationship. With her husband, she had experienced powerful moments such as few women could have experienced in her time, thanks to her love, her dynamism, her culture, and her intellectual life. And also her discretion.

She had never seen her husband's conversion in her lifetime. All this had to be said; he wanted to make it known so that Élisabeth's readers would fully understand that she had been a woman who, in an ordinary life as a wife, had been able to make the torches of faith and love shine. It was his duty as a husband, his fidelity to a marriage that was now spiritual, and, henceforth, his mission as a priest. In writing it, he was also thinking of so many couples who were living through a journey somewhat similar to theirs and who could be helped by his testimony.

Evangelization is done, not with words, but with deeds: what more beautiful testimony of the radiance of God's love on a human being than that of Élisabeth accepting, until her final day, her sufferings and early death for the sake of her husband.

Thinking of her, one cannot but recall that wonderful image, passed down through the ages and sung in Psalm 1: "Blessed is the man . . . [whose] delight is in the law of the LORD, and on his law he meditates day and night. He is like a tree planted by streams of water, that yields its fruit in its season and its leaf does not wither" (Ps 1:2-3).

The account of Élisabeth's life was a long and difficult task because it was a matter of conveying, above all, her thoughts, her faith, and, in particular, her reactions to the events of a life marked by renunciations and suffering. For the one who had shared a large part of her life, it was also simultaneously a return to the past and the actualization of a spirituality closely linked with everyday life and, therefore, accessible to everyone. It was Élisabeth's message for anyone who genuinely wanted to receive it.

But it was also the history of his relationship, a story that others could have lived by tearing each other apart or by leaving each other, a magnificent story because it ended in a love stronger than death, a love in and for God, everything given.

Élisabeth's attitudes toward life's events would often be able to inspire in her readers concrete human responses taken from the teaching of the Gospels. Our psychologists today could use them to prescribe a fruitful rule of life for human relationships.

> There is one way of living and thinking that I will call negative; another that I will call active. The first consists in always seeing what is flawed in people and institutions, not so much in order to fix them as to have an opportunity to prevail over them; to keep looking back and to prefer to look for what separates and what disunites. The second consists in facing life, and the duties that it imposes, joyfully, seeking what is good in every person in order to develop and cultivate it, never despairing of the future, the fruit of our will; feeling for human faults and misery that valiant compassion which produces action and no longer allows us a useless life.[1]

---

[1] Élisabeth Leseur, *Journal et Pensées de chaque jour* (Paris: Éd. du Cerf, 2005), 213.

Élisabeth's writings do not only propose approaches toward human relationships. They also intelligently anticipate the future of the materialism she saw emerging in the world. With realism, common sense, and truth, she traced the moral crisis that seemed to be taking shape for the years to come.

She sensed that the societies of the next century would be dominated by the easy life, by the money that would become the driving force of human relationships, and by the absence of any moral rule. Fundamental values such as the notion of family and homeland and the sense of duty would be rejected; contempt for sacrifice and the anarchy of thought about feelings and life would one day become the way of life for future societies. These predictions were great sufferings for her.

It was necessary to write all this and many other thoughts; it was necessary for future generations to know them. It was his mission to publish them.

Father Leseur wrote on August 15:

> This is a great relief! My book will be worth what it is worth. Not much. I am afraid of being very mediocre and very unworthy of the subject. A work like this would have benefited from being written in peace and continuity. This was not possible, so it is up to God's grace. But there will be at least one excellent thing in this book, this is Rev. Fr. Gillet's preface. It is a letter, but perfect. I could not have desired better. *Deo Gratias!*[2]

In fact, the preface by Father Gillet, master general of the Order of Preachers, was not exactly what he had been expecting, but a letter addressed to him from Rome:

> My reverend and dear Father,
>
> Your *Vie d'Élisabeth Leseur* does not need a preface. Written by you, of itself it commands the attention of the public who knows you and who will read it, like all your other works, avidly. . . . All the women reading it will learn how a woman of high culture, who was interested in everything, art, literature, science, philosophy, who maintained relationships with philosophers, scholars, men of letters,

---

[2] Unpublished letter from Marie-Louise Herking, *Le Pére Leseur* (Paris: Éd. J. de Gigord, 1952), 175.

artists, was able to unite all of this with a boundless love of God and neighbor, commanding even the respect of unbelievers by the surety of her judgment and the influence of her charity.[3]

And he cited some long lines, taken from the text itself, in which Father Leseur justified the motivation for his work. He sought to show that Élisabeth had not been a supernatural creature or an ethereal woman impossible to imitate. She had had both feet on the ground; she had been a woman like any other, but seized by the love of God and others, which had illuminated her life until the end.

Élisabeth is an example taken from life in our times, a kind of object lesson. She proves that it is possible for a woman, sharing in the worldly life of our twentieth century, married to an unbeliever, to have an informed and active religion, strengthened by prayer, inspiring all her actions and raising her to the heights of Christian perfection. In this way, she becomes a reliable guide and solid support for every woman of the world, and her example is, from this perspective, an apologetic argument of the highest order. . . . Her life unfolded very simply in the love of God and neighbor, in the trustful unity of family and home, in the accomplishment of the duties of her state in life, of all duties, sometimes in the acceptance of physical or moral suffering.[4]

---

[3] R. P. Marie-Albert Leseur, preface by Gillet, *Vie d'Élisabeth Leseur* (Paris: Éd. J. de Gigord, 1931), I.

[4] Ibid.

38

The Cause for Élisabeth's Beatification

Félix had been thinking about it for a long time. In the final pages of his *Vie d'Élisabeth Leseur*, he spoke about Élisabeth's "posthumous apostolate", which he witnessed every day, thanks to the large volume of mail he received or during his conference tours. In five years, he had made more than four hundred of them in all the major French, Belgian, and Swiss cities. For him and for his superiors, it was now without any doubt both his mission as a husband and his ministry as a priest.

With wonder, he frequently learned in this way of new graces obtained by means of Élisabeth, spiritual graces, but also temporal graces and surprising conversions. He wrote down every account. He was moved by all the veneration that her person inspired. Wherever someone prayed to Élisabeth or asked her to obtain graces, unexpected responses were received. The witnesses multiplied:

> I owe a debt of gratitude to Madame Élisabeth Leseur. Having great confidence in her, I had recourse to her intercession to obtain a grace. That favor was granted to me. Father, I am fulfilling my promise by allowing myself to inform you of it, and I give you my offering so that the Holy Sacrifice of the Mass may be offered for her intention.
>
> Her book *Journal et Pensées de chaque jour* (Journal and thoughts for every day) is a great comfort to me, and I frequently draw from it the strength necessary to sustain the fight.[1]

Another letter gave more details:

> Devotion to Madame Leseur is tending to grow in our home, and we have obtained special favors through her intercession. A parishioner, suffering from colon cancer, was in a hopeless condition, so much

---

[1] R. P. Marie-Albert Leseur, *Vie d'Élisabeth Leseur* (Paris: Éd. J. de Gigord, 1931), 365.

so that the surgeon had at first refused an operation, declaring it impossible. The sick person, ignorant of the seriousness of his condition, absolutely wanted to be operated on. The surgeon and the nuns declared that there was no hope of recovery: the patient would die during the operation.

With my wife and my cousin, the parish priest, I began a novena to Madame Leseur, whom we have never ceased to invoke since. Not only did the sick person not die during the operation that took place on October 12, but he has also been home for ten days.[2]

While numerous letters attested to physical healings, others mentioned spiritual healings: "Father, in informing you of my Baptism, I am paying a debt of gratitude. I had promised Élisabeth Leseur to tell you that the reading of her *Journal* was the origin of my conversion."[3]

Several letters informed him that young parents had named their little daughters Élisabeth in memory of Élisabeth Leseur, which deeply moved him. He learned that study groups or student houses bore the name Élisabeth Leseur in Berne, Nîmes, Arras. In Paris, secondary schools and, especially, the home for young girls on the rue de Saxe were placed under her protection. "The intellectual apostolate" that had been so dear to Élisabeth continued well beyond her time on earth.

At that time, Father Leseur was receiving around three thousand letters a year, which corresponded to the growing number of editions of Élisabeth's works and in particular of the *Journal*, now translated into the main European languages, Chinese, and Japanese.

Many correspondents asked him to undertake steps for her beatification. They tried to convince him with an irrefutable argument: our era, so minimally Christian, has need, more than ever, of contemporary lay saints who experienced ordinary life, who went through trials like everyone else and lived through them in prayer and faith.

He was swiftly convinced that it was to him that this task fell. His superiors fully shared this new vision of his mission and encouraged him to consult the competent authorities.

---

[2] Ibid.
[3] Ibid., 362.

He then launched alone into a lengthy process.

First, he put together an important dossier from the testimonies he had received. He divided it into three parts: physical healings, spiritual healings, conversions.

He met with Cardinal Verdier, archbishop of Paris, to keep him informed about his project and to ask him what steps to take for its completion. The cardinal, completely supportive, presented him with the first discussions to consider the preliminary steps.

The considerable task that he presented to him somewhat worried the elderly man that he now was. It would take him several years to go through all these steps one by one. And yet, he knew that only he could undertake the construction of the required files and that no one would take over them after him if, because of his health or likely death, he were not able to finish his projects.

For him, it was a real anxiety that tormented him, an obvious race against the clock that he was not sure of winning; but for him, it was also the least possible acknowledgment and repayment of his debt to Élisabeth. More than ever, he was resolved to dedicate all his strength and all his energy to it. Everything was in the hands of the Lord. "There is much work and effort in sight; this truly frightens me a little. But with God's grace. And if it pleases him to glorify his servant, it would be such an important event and such a great outcome! Women living in the world would at last have a patroness for themselves, like themselves, and from our times! Let us pray and encourage others to pray."[4]

Thus began, for the already septuagenarian priest, a heavy task in addition to his ministry: visits, requests for letters and to influential people, speaking tours where he gathered testimonies, lists of signatures.

He wrote to a nun:

> The start of the cause depends only on me. In fact, I must write the articles that are the legal basis for the process. It is a volume of seventy to one hundred printed pages, containing, in a canonical framework, a short biography, the way in which Élisabeth practiced the theological, cardinal, and moral virtues, responded to the gifts of the

---

[4] Unpublished letter from Marie-Louise Herking, *Le Père Leseur* (Paris: Éd. J. de Gigord, 1952), 203.

Holy Spirit, and indicating the graces obtained through her. It is on the basis of the articles that the tribunal questions the witnesses. So, I am going to shut myself in all of November for this difficult work (we must not put forward anything that cannot be proved) in order for my manuscript to be finished by the end of November, approved by the postulators, and printed in December. . . . Pray that I do this work as well as possible.[5]

That book of *Articles*, written in a conventional and impersonal style, contains 165 sections of biography or testimonies, all beginning with the same sentence structure: "It is the truth." Here are two examples:

—*Article 19*
It is the truth that the husband of the servant of God, though born into a very Catholic family and a former student of the Oratorians of Juilly, had lost faith during his training at the Faculty of Medicine in Paris, becoming a complete materialist. He even became antireligious. The friends he received in his home were, for the most part, indifferent, dilettante, sometimes hostile to Christian ideas. In marrying, he undoubtedly committed himself in good faith to respect his wife's beliefs and to allow her complete freedom of religious practice. But by the end of several years, he came to have difficulty tolerating her beliefs that he did not share, and he took the servant of God as the object of his reverse proselytism. Attacks against her belief, against priests, criticisms and arguments, books of rationalist and modernist inspiration, all these were used. So well that, with their social and traveling life-style contributing to it, he managed to detach her from religious fervor and disrupt her faith.[6]

—*Article 161*
It is the truth that Mademoiselle Marie Hours, servant in the house of Monsieur Meuse at Alès (Gard), had greatly suffered from kidney troubles for a long time. One night when she had a more painful attack, she addressed the servant of God: "Madame Leseur, come take care of me, as you would have cared for me if I had been your servant: Heal me!" Immediately, she felt well, and since then she has

---

[5] Ibid., 204.
[6] Articles from the informative process for the beatification and canonization of the Servant of God Élisabeth Leseur, 14.

had no more of these attacks that were so painful they made her suffer greatly in doing her work as a domestic.[7]

It was at this moment in his work, during which he remembered with emotion all the important moments of their married life, that Father Leseur met the postulator general of the Dominican Order passing through Paris, Father Lenzetti, from the convent of Fiesole near Florence. He was a specialist in causes of beatification and the writing of *Articles*. Therefore, his advice would be invaluable.

As a first step, Father Lenzetti asked to go to Élisabeth's grave in the cemetery of Montmartre. Father Leseur accompanied him, and there, in front of that grave where Félix had shed so many tears for so many years, he promised him he would use all his power to advance Élisabeth's cause, the significance and urgency of which he completely appreciated.

Father Lenzetti was impressed to see to what extent Élisabeth's grave had become a pilgrimage site. Unknown hands regularly left not only fresh bouquets of flowers, but also calling cards, engraved marble plaques, votive offerings, and even letters were placed on the slab to thank "the saint" for her intercession. The cemetery guards confirmed that every day visitors came to kneel on Élisabeth's grave. She had written in her *Pensées de chaque jour* that the influence exercised by a person was something subtle and penetrating, the power of which no one could measure. Simple contact with a soul in everyday speech was sometimes richer than scholarly preaching.

Father Leseur now had to copy by hand "legibly and with care" the four hundred pages of his deposition.

On November 30, 1936, the sessions began in front of the tribunal assembled in the great Albert-Le-Grand hall in the monastery on the rue Saint-Honoré. Every Monday, from morning till evening, for five weeks, he had to go plead the cause of his much beloved wife whose life he had shared for almost twenty-five years. Among the witnesses who appeared at the hearing was the very old Mademoiselle Mas, Élisabeth's teacher, practically a centenarian but in complete possession of her thoughts and memories!

---

[7] Ibid., 39.

The priest had not, however, foreseen that during that session, a major health issue—flu followed by superficial venous thrombosis —would lead to an emergency hospitalization that would last for six weeks and, thus, to a temporary halt in the sessions. Distraught by this setback, he considered how much of a disaster this delay was for him as he believed his future was now shorter than ever.

Even more determined, he asked his doctors at the hospital of Perpétuel-Secours for authorization to go to the rue du Faubourg-Saint-Honoré in an ambulance on Mondays. This permission was granted to him, as long as he stayed lying down during the sessions. And he agreed to it for Élisabeth. These assemblies were therefore very peculiar, with an old postulator with a keen mind who was pleading his wife's cause lying on a stretcher.

He still remained very concerned. For after that first "informative" process, an "apostolic" process still had to take place for which he again had to gather all sorts of documents written by Élisabeth.

Then it would be necessary to renew contact with all her correspondents, to find their names and their addresses, to visit or write to them, to insist that they give away often personal letters that they had kept.

He estimated that this represented at least another two years' work. At what age and in what condition would he arrive at the hearing in Rome in front of the Sacred Congregation of Rites? In two years at least and undoubtedly more, would he have the strength to go to Rome? He knew that this very heavy task rested on him alone, and he doubted his strength.

While he was obsessed with the future of this case, a new obstacle intervened: Father Lenzetti informed him that the transfer of Élisabeth's body was essential. She had been buried in the Arrighi family plot, but if even a single family member was opposed to her canonical recognition, he would have to give up advancing her cause. It would be an impediment without recourse.

Father Leseur, shaken by this prospect, however, did not hesitate. The cause had to advance, but at what a price! He organized all the administrative and material steps for this funeral ceremony and prepared himself for the trial of the transfer, more traumatizing for him than all the others combined.

On March 3, 1938, thirty-four years after the burial, accompanied by his Arrighi nephew, he attended the exhumation of his wife's body, a ceremony during which no cruel or painful detail was spared him.

Then he followed the coffin to the Parisian cemetery of Bagneux to the plot of the Dominican sisters of the rue des Plantes. And there, in front of that new grave, in his role as priest, and no longer as husband, he had the courage to intone the prayers of the liturgy of the dead and to sing alone the *Requiem aeternam dona ei Domine et lux perpetua luceat ei*.

When he left the cemetery with his nephew, such peace, such light, such beauty extended almost joyfully over all those graves that he understood that this was truly the duty he had to fulfill.

39

An Old Priest

"Élisabeth should have a little pity on the old man that I am!"

This was the phrase he liked to repeat with a smile when his legs betrayed him or when he felt a slight decline in his capacity for work. But right away he pulled himself together and responded with humor: "Just as there are volcanoes under the glaciers in Iceland, despite the years, the heart stays young", he wrote on March 22, 1938, on his seventy-seventh birthday.

This youthful enthusiasm encouraged him to accept a speaking tour in Holland where he had been invited by the "Élisabeth Leseur Circle" of Utrecht. He took the train at the Gare du Nord, still as happy to travel as in his youth. After Utrecht, he would go to Rotterdam, The Hague, Nijmegen, and Tilburg.

He wrote to Marie-Louise Herking: "The Hague was the high point. I was presided over by His Excellency the Papal Nuncio of Holland, very amiable and very simple. The minister of France, being absent, was replaced by a secretary from the embassy. You see from here. I was puzzled."[1]

The organizers of the Utrecht conference drove him by car to Amsterdam, where he had taken one of his last trips with Élisabeth. For him, that city full of charm and poetry, where the leaves of the willow trees were reflected in the water of the canals, was still completely inhabited by his memories.

He expressed a desire to revisit the Rijksmuseum. He stopped at great length in front of *The Night Watch* and the *Syndics of the Drapers' Guild*, those two great works of Rembrandt that they had

---

[1] Unpublished letter from Marie-Louise Herking, *Le Pére Leseur* (Paris: Éd. J. de Gigord, 1952), 209.

admired together; then he was taken to Doorn, the residence of Wilhelm II.

At his request, since for some years he had been very interested in the development of the polders contained in the vast dike, they took him to visit the Zuiderzee, then the castle of Princess Juliana, and then they drove him to the monastery of the Dominicans of Nijmegen.

He may well have been very busy and old, but he still had as much happiness traveling and discovering new landscapes. He gloated like a young man during his return to Paris on the train, delighted by this speaking tour about his dear Élisabeth. Thanks to her, he had been able to see Holland again in the company of young women totally filled with the spirituality of "his saint". And what joy to see the canals of his memories again!

Many tasks awaited him upon his return. The interviewing of witnesses for the informative process continued.

The dossier of Élisabeth's writings had to be finished as quickly as possible, conferences were calling him to Brittany, letters were piling up, telephone calls were constantly disrupting him, and too often he was requested in the visiting room.

He was tired, and this fatigue was reflected in the recurrent desire to sleep. He applied his principle: "We must go as far as we can because as soon as we stop, we are lost." But for him "to go as far as he could" every day became an increasingly onerous effort.

In 1939, war seemed to be looming. The French worried about Hitler. The priest, who regularly followed the news and who had always been interested in France's political situation, was not shy about repeating that every day the dominant neopaganism was seen preaching the worship of power and that, consequently, anything could happen.

It was with this anxiety of heart that he departed in the spring for a speaking tour in the South of France. Even in his old age, he would never hesitate to cross France to speak to young women of the one he now called "his saint", of the one who had shared a part of his life and who had given him so much. The sunlight that Élisabeth had made come alive in his life had to shine on the young generations.

Then he took the train, with all the connections it involved, to go from Cannes to Brittany, to his friends the Saucourts, where he thought to rest. It was there that he learned of the declaration of war, his second war since Élisabeth's death!

Despite the war, at that moment, everything seemed ready to go for Élisabeth's writings. All he had left was an approach to the archbishop of Besançon, who had to hear the witnesses from Jougne, and the dossier could be sealed, ready to go to Rome; this would be his first task when he returned to Paris, a simple matter of two or three days.

In agreement with his superiors, he went to rest in Cannes with the Dominican Sisters, whom he had known for a long time, having been their confessor when their convent was located at Bellevue, near Meudon. He knew them all and called them "my daughters". Indeed, they cared for him with all the attention the daughters he had never had would have shown. He was very touched.

Every day, he continued to receive abundant mail regarding the writings of Élisabeth, nearly three hundred letters a month.

Most asked his advice for leading their lives in the light of Élisabeth's spirituality. As the spiritual advisor responsible for the message of "his saint", he responded to each one without considering his time or his fatigue.

To the Dominican nuns who advised him to spare himself, he replied that Élisabeth had been committed to considering each person as unique, and not for anything in the world would he rush a response, even if to a stranger. For him, a letter must never be cold or impersonal. He always first addressed that which was most important to his correspondent. And based on that experience, he gave loving, almost fatherly, advice. The fatherhood that his married relationship had never allowed him to live, he now lived for all these young men and women who trustingly addressed him.

He spent the cold winter of 1940 in Cannes, where, from his window in the Villa Saint-Benoît, he could contemplate with youthful admiration "the snow on the palm trees". Every day, supported by his cane, he went walking along La Croisette, made his little tour of the bookshops, leafed through new works, followed very closely the progress of the war. And above all, he read. The old geographer and colonialist that he remained was intoxicated to read about expeditions that he could no longer undertake. History, biographies of heads of state or military leaders, biographies of Napoleon, Lyautey, Pétain, all fascinated him.

When he learned of France's collapse in June 1940, he believed more than ever in the power of prayer and in the power of the intercession of the saints, which he had drawn from the writings of Élisabeth.

> I am, and you understand without my needing to elaborate on it, in great sorrow. It is awful to see our dear France in the lamentable situation she is in. . . . It is shocking! We wonder how this debacle could see the light of day. . . . What a fall compared to 1914! We no longer have either Joffre or Marne, alas! So, let us pray and begin with the bodies and souls lost in service of the country. And despite everything, I keep all my trust in him. The France of Saint Genevieve, of Joan of Arc, of Valmy and of the Marne is the country of rebounds that always surprise and amaze the world. And this is accounted for by the spiritual values that watch over it. No other nation possesses a legion of saints that is anywhere near comparable to its. Let us pray then with fervor and confidence.[2]

Despite his great age, on July 31, as in all other years, he celebrated his wedding anniversary and gave thanks to God for all the graces he had received through his wife. He confided in a letter to a correspondent: "Élisabeth and I, in fact, were married at Saint-Germain-des-Prés, the old and magnificent Parisian church, on July 31, 1889, fifty-one years ago. How long ago it was! And how much has happened since then! I could never have suspected what the apostolate would be of the one to whom God united me, and of whom I was so unworthy! I can never thank him enough!"[3]

He would have liked to return to Paris. At that time, it was clear that France was cut in two by the German occupation; he would be prohibited from returning to Paris. He was furious: the formalities for Élisabeth's beatification were not finished, far from it! He still needed to complete a few dossiers and especially what he had long planned: to go to the archbishop of Besançon, where the interviewing of the witnesses from Jougne was to be done by the jurisdiction, that is to say, before the bishop.

---

[2] Ibid., 235.
[3] Ibid.

Stuck in Cannes, he felt powerless and idle because letters no longer passed through the demarcation line and thereby diminished.

Despite his age, he was so determined that nothing would stop him when it came to the cause of the beatification of his dear wife.

So, he undertook an astounding journey for a man of seventy-six: from Cannes, he went to Marseille, where he ran into complete chaos. All the hotels were packed. He spent the night on a bench in the waiting room at the train station. The next day, he reached Lyon, where he was able to rest a few days with the Dominicans of the rue Bugeaud.

He then took another train. In the compartment, he recounted his adventure to a Dijonnais who seemed trustworthy to him. This person told him the name of a certain butcher who could help him cross the demarcation line in the middle of the night and gave him precise instructions. He went to her house, he found her, but would still have to walk five and a half miles carrying his suitcase.

After still more adventures, he finally arrived in Paris on November 11 and returned to his monastery, his brothers, and his cell, which he had left two years before!

When the winter was over, he undertook a trip to Besançon, in whose archdiocese the town of Jougne was located. The testimony of the bishop of the place was indispensable for completing the dossier of Élisabeth's cause. But there, a very big disappointment awaited him. The archbishop received him for a few moments and quickly told him that in those years of German occupation, he had more urgent concerns than sending a delegate to Jougne to preside over the interviewing of witnesses in the Élisabeth Leseur process! He was crushed because it was the first time he had received such a welcome. And without this dossier, the cause was stalled.

40

The Wreck of Extreme Old Age

After his disappointment at Besançon, which he accepted as the will of God, he knew very well that his health would not permit him to live much longer. He also understood that he would no longer be able to go to Rome in due course and that he would not see the results of this enormous task begun years ago with so much love.

He realized that his intellectual faculties were beginning to decline, that his memory often failed, that his hearing was getting worse and worse. Little by little he had to give up saying Mass, which affected him greatly.

Perpétual-Secours Hospital of Levallois, where he had been hospitalized for several months, could no longer keep him, for lack of room. When he heard this news, he was distraught because he felt at home there. To reassure him, they told him this departure was temporary, that he would return shortly, as soon as they found him a place in the Saint Thomas Aquinas wing, reserved for Dominicans.

So they transferred him to Saint-Joseph de Chaudron-en-Mauges, near Cholet, to a small hospice in the countryside reserved for the very old. This establishment, light-filled and spacious, with high windows and slate-covered roofs, was run by devoted and attentive Dominican nuns of the Etrepagny congregation. But for him, it was complete deprivation, in an unfamiliar place with new faces, absolute poverty. For a few weeks he was disoriented, a bit lost; he understood that he would end his life within these walls, far from everything. He accepted it. The mother prioress said of him: "Those who approach him are surprised to find him so courteous. He never complains, makes no demands; he is a model religious, humble, obedient."[1]

---

[1] Unpublished letter from Marie-Louise Herking, *Le Pére Leseur* (Paris: Éd. J. de Gigord, 1952), 246.

A few months after his arrival, another fall in his room caused a fracture of the femoral neck. At the time, there was no surgery. He had to stay in bed. For him, this would be the fatal ordeal.

Little by little, his mind darkened. He still experienced moments of lucidity, but gradually they became less frequent.

When the sisters deemed the time had come, they had Extreme Unction administered to him.

Whereas he had always said "It is going very well" up until then, now, in his lucid moments, he said: "It is not going well."

One of the last things he said, while the mother prioress was taking his pulse, was: "The good God will finish by coming to get me! When he arrives, I will say to him: Here I am."[2]

And a few minutes later: "Eternity, what a great mystery!"[3]

Deep in a kind of half-sleep, ever so gently his heart finally stopped beating on February 25, 1950.

The work that the Lord had wanted to accomplish through him was finished. He had been a widower for thirty-six years, a priest for thirty.

Accompanied by the Office of the Dead, sung in its entirety by the community of nuns, who wanted to pay him this final tribute of affection, he was buried in the sisters' cemetery, far from his wife's grave, in the presence of his Leseur nephew and his wife.

---

[2] Ibid.
[3] Ibid., 244.

Epilogue

God's Gift for a Couple

Élisabeth and Félix Leseur regretted not being able to have children and to have had no descendants.

Their contribution was immensely rich. And God's gift for each of them was a miracle that can only inspire a Magnificat in the hearts of those who become aware of it.

One thinks of the parable of Jesus recorded by Mark: "The kingdom of God . . . is like a grain of mustard seed, which, when sown upon the ground, is the smallest of all the seeds on earth; yet when it is sown it grows up and becomes the greatest of all shrubs, and puts forth large branches, so that the birds of the air can make nests in its shade" (Mk 4:31–32).

Of course, during her life, Élisabeth did not see the "large branches" of her spirituality that, nevertheless, have extended into nearly every continent, thanks to her husband's unceasing work. And, on earth, she did not see her husband become Father Leseur, which was her deepest wish. We can hope, however, that, near the Lord, she saw him and that her intercession contributed to tracing that magnificent itinerary over the course of many years.

God's plans rarely correspond to human plans, but looking back we can always marvel at the path of grace: "If you knew the gift of God", Jesus said to the Samaritan woman! And what a gift of God in that home!

After studying this spiritual itinerary, we can reflect on the substance of that magnificent gift from God that was their love for each other and about the richness of the fruits that it produced. This love was rich and fruitful because it was given to the other, built to the measure of the events experienced by each person in his own way, on different paths.

"Everything is grace", and everything can be transformed into grace, even what does not seem to be so.

If Élisabeth's spirituality had not been opposed but, indeed, encouraged by her husband's atheism and hostility, would she have had the idea and the courage to deepen her faith to the point of developing such richness in her writings? No doubt she would have remained the "practicing" Catholic that she was at the time of her marriage who very quietly went to Mass on Sundays and said her morning and evening prayers, but who would never have known such a rich and radiant spiritual life.

Although it might seem paradoxical, in hindsight, we can think of her husband's atheism as God's gift for her, the point of departure for an entire intellectual and spiritual journey that produced the fruits of which we are aware.

If all during her life, her husband had not introduced her to atheists, agnostics, and harsh critics of religion, would she have had the same respect for the beliefs of others, the same approach to them, guided by an almost incomprehensible love drawn from the words of the Gospels? Yes, a gift from God, all those atheists to whom she gave the best of herself, if not the faith, and who were touched simply by what she was, by her smile, her goodness, her attentiveness, and by the love she showed to her husband. Against all odds, Élisabeth made flowers bloom on the anticlerical and atheistic terrain of her social environment.

In the spheres of politics and finance, where marital fidelity, endlessly scorned, was more a subject of laughter in vaudeville than of admiration, was it not a gift from God that this couple tacitly witnessed to their happiness in being together, their fidelity, their joy in sharing intellectual tastes, traveling together, having in common such a great love of hospitality and sharing?

It was God's gift that their unwavering love allowed Élisabeth to be surrounded and loved until her last day by the man she loved. And conversely, it was God's gift for Félix to be able to find the words and actions capable of softening his wife's illness for years. It was in the realization of this magnificent gift from God that Félix found the strength he later needed to change his life. Without Élisabeth's love, would he have become a priest? Would he have had such influence?

God's magnificent gift for Félix: those long and insistent calls to the priesthood after so much reluctance, calls that could never have existed without Élisabeth's death and without the reading of her diary, which was the triggering factor: "If the seed does not die . . ."

God's immense gift for Félix: the discovery of his wife's writings, which not only led him to the faith but which also subsequently enabled him to lead so many people to the sources of the Gospel.

God's gift: that courage which was given to Félix to consider and accept the immense material and human renunciations necessary to enter the Dominicans.

God's gift for Father Leseur: the intelligence of his superiors, who understood that his very special vocation would be to spread his wife's spirituality, which only his love could make known, and germinate it in the hearts of so many listeners and unknown readers.

God's gift for Father Leseur: the spiritual isolation of his wife, which one day he came to understand and which made him feel very guilty: without this painful discovery, he would undoubtedly never have devoted a part of his life to responding to letters from strangers who felt isolated, in search of God.

The list could be infinitely long; we could end it by saying:

God's gift for both of them: what each had been for the other; a gift of God, that love which united them so profoundly all their lives because it had its source in the love of the Lord, which knows no human limits.

God's gift: their sacrament of Matrimony followed by that of Holy Orders, profoundly complementary.

God's gift: that radiant family now reunited in the love of God to sing his praise in eternity.